Charm Offensive

Charm Offensive

How China's Soft Power Is Transforming the World

JOSHUA KURLANTZICK

A New Republic Book

Yale University Press New Haven and London

For Miriam. Nothing is possible without you.

A Caravan book. For more information, visit
www.caravanbooks.org

Set in Minion type by Integrated Publishing Solutions,
Grand Rapids, Michigan.
Printed in the United States of America by Vail-Ballou Press,
Binghamton, New York.

Library of Congress Cataloging-in-Publication Data
Kurlantzick, Joshua, 1976–
Charm offensive : how China's soft power is transforming the world / Joshua Kurlantzick.
p. cm.
Includes bibliographical references and index.
ISBN 978-0-300-11703-5 (cloth : alk. paper)
1. China—Relations—Foreign countries. I. Title.
DS779.47.K87 2007
303.48′251—dc22 2006038454

A catalogue record for this book is available
from the British Library.

The paper in this book meets the guidelines for permanence and durability of the Committee on Production Guidelines for Book Longevity of the Council on Library Resources.

10 9 8 7 6 5 4 3 2 1

Contents

Preface

When I arrived in Bangkok in 1998, to work first at a local newspaper and later for international publications, I had not thought much about China's influence in Thailand—or in the world. In fact, I was shocked by how Americanized Bangkok seemed, and worried that I would find the city not enough of an exotic experience: as it had been for five decades, the United States was the primary foreign influence on culture, business, and politics in Bangkok. Parts of the Thai capital, with their flashy malls and hip cafés, seemed little different from Chelsea in New York or Dupont Circle in Washington. Bangkok billboards advertised endless rows of fast food chains, like Swensen's, that had vanished from most of the United States and been revived in Thailand.

Overall, America's popular image was strong—in Thailand and nearly everywhere else I traveled in Asia. If I told a Thai taxi driver I hailed from the United States, he'd praise Bill Clinton, beloved in Bangkok for both his success with women and his foreign policies. American politicians and diplomats received a level of treatment and access in Bangkok offered no one else, except perhaps Japanese prime ministers. Wealthy Thai friends constantly asked how to get their children into

American universities, and societies of Thai alumni of the Johns Hopkins School of Advanced International Studies met monthly at a Thai-Chinese diner near my house. Thai friends knew more about American rap and *Seinfeld* episodes than I did, and American films and music dominated Bangkok malls.

But while I was living in Bangkok, America's image began to suffer, and I noticed China entering the picture. For decades, China had enjoyed a limited relationship with Thailand—and almost no relationship with much of the world. But after Thailand's economy melted down in the late 1990s, triggering the Asian financial crisis, the United States initially did not help bail Thailand out, causing intense resentment among average Thais and Thai leaders, and forcing people to look to other powers. By 1999, when I told cab drivers I came from America, they would complain that the United States had ignored the Thais or would refuse even to speak with me. Thai protesters had started smashing up 7–Elevens and other signs of American business; after September 11 and the beginning of the war in Iraq, America's public image in Thailand would bottom out. Polls in other parts of Asia would suggest that the United States had become more unpopular than crazed North Korea, that Osama bin Laden was more popular than George W. Bush.

By early 2001 I had started noticing busloads of Chinese tourists pulling up to Bangkok hotels and delegations of hundreds of Chinese businesspeople decamping in town to sign deals. China's diplomats suddenly were everywhere, fluent in Thai, opening new consulates and centers for Chinese studies across the country. Many of my Thai friends now wanted to learn Chinese, language teachers were opening Chinese schools throughout the Bangkok business district, and it seemed like every prominent Thai businessperson wanted to appear on television with Chinese officials. China was becoming Thailand's most important trading partner.

Yet when I asked Thai officials how China had so quickly become popular in Thailand, how China was building its relations to Thailand, few seemed to know anything concrete about China's strategy or goals. I could find almost no statistics, reporting, or academic papers about what appeared to be China's new charm offensive, or about how average Thais perceived their giant neighbor.

Over the following years, I watched as China repeated its successes in Thailand in first its near neighbors in Asia and then in countries far from China's borders, like Zambia and Argentina. Emerging from a shell of defensive diplomacy dating back decades, China suddenly was engaging with the world, wooing friends with a subtle, softer approach, and using its popularity to make gains, even as America's popularity around the world was plummeting. In Africa, newly popular China was winning oil and gas deals; in Latin America, China was signing strategic partnerships; in the Philippines, Chinese films were making inroads against American movies.

Three years ago, I started quizzing policy makers in Washington about China's new global influence, its soft power. I got mostly blank stares in return. Some asked me to brief *them* about the topic, and I realized that many policy makers had missed China's growing soft power. Used to dealing with the stiff, unsophisticated Chinese diplomats and officials of the past, few had anticipated this more nuanced and effective Chinese diplomacy. No one had any idea about the size of China's aid programs, or how China trained its diplomats, or how people in other countries responded to Chinese cultural exports—or whether China could use soft power to achieve any concrete goals.

Even the conservative American policy makers most skeptical of China, I found, had spent little time examining soft power. At a major 2005 conference held in Singapore, Donald Rumsfeld warned that China's military modernization threatened countries across Asia, and questioned why China needed to upgrade its military if not to dominate the region. Yet though Beijing is rapidly modernizing its armed forces, China's army and nascent navy cannot yet match the mighty American armed forces: the People's Liberation Army still relies too heavily on conscripts, wastes time studying useless political doctrine, and spends less than $80 billion per year on its military, in contrast to America's more than $400 billion annual budget. Still, I found few American defense officials who had considered how China's softer forms of influence might change countries' views of China—and thus might reshape US-Chinese competition.

Too often, I found, official Washington, whether focused on China's military or stuck remembering China's old blunt, gray diplomacy, simply had disregarded the gravity of China's growing soft power, or America's soft power deficit. During a luncheon I attended in Washington three years ago for the American ambassador to Thailand, attendees sat through questions about US software manufacturing in Bangkok, piracy protection for American firms, and other business issues. Finally, one person asked about recent unrest in southern Thailand, where America closed its consulate years ago—and where a resurgence of sectarian violence had made the area a hotbed of extremism. The ambassador mentioned that the United States was still trying to exert influence in the south and had opened a small "American corner" in southern Thailand, where Thais could come learn about the United States. "What happened to the US consulate in Songkhla?" a southern Thai city, asked someone else in the audience. The ambassador paused. "It's the Chinese consulate now," he said.

This book represents an effort to fill that gap in knowledge about China's soft power and increasingly sophisticated diplomacy, which will transform international relations. I have spent the past two years in Asia, Africa, and Latin America, trying on the ground to figure out exactly how China wields its soft power today—and why it matters, for the United States and other nations, that China is amassing this influence.

The stakes are high. No one has experience with today's China as a global player, or a model for how Beijing will perform on the international stage. In a short period of time, China appears to have created a systematic, coherent soft power strategy, and a set of soft power tools to implement that strategy. Through those tools—particularly its public diplomacy and its growing aid and trade—it has developed significant influence, though it is still in a honeymoon period in which many nations have not recognized the downsides of Beijing's new power.

As China has become a global presence, it has taken steps to wield its soft influence responsibly, joining multilateral institutions, supporting peacekeeping, powering economic growth in Latin America and Africa, and fighting drug and human trafficking. China even has begun to mediate other nations' conflicts and apply pressure on dangerous countries, a step from the recent past, when China avoided any involvement in other states' domestic politics.

Yet as China has become more powerful it has begun exporting its own domestic problems. Chinese companies' poor labor and environmental records and opaque business practices now are arriving in Zambia and Peru along with Chinese investment. China's lack of political openness and its state-centered model of development are strengthening unstable authoritarian regimes from Sudan to Burma to Uzbekistan. Its aid policies are undermining efforts to support better governance for nations from Angola to Cambodia.

Perhaps most important, China's soft power could have a significant impact on American interests. When China discovers that its own interests—in obtaining resources, or in building ties to certain countries—do not overlap with America's, it now has the tools to win friends to its side. And as the United States remains unpopular in many parts of the world, China finds willing partners. In the worst-case scenario, China eventually will use soft power to push countries to choose between closer ties to Washington and closer ties to Beijing.

Acknowledgments

This book could not have been written without the generous assistance and wise advice of many people. Support for the book came principally from the Smith Richardson Foundation, where Allan Song helped shape the idea for the project. The Carnegie Endowment for International Peace, and especially Carnegie's Minxin Pei, Paul Balaran, Doris Grage, Kathleen Higgs, and George Perkovich, provided vital research support, oversight, and guidance. The Long-Term Strategy Project also offered assistance, thanks to the great Samantha Ravich. At the *New Republic,* Peter Beinart helped shape the initial draft of the idea. Readers Josh Glazeroff, Michael Montesano, Jackie Newmyer, Minxin Pei, and Jason Zengerle provided thorough comments on later drafts of the manuscript and related articles. The Henry Luce Foundation first sent me out to Southeast Asia, where this all began. At Yale, Keith Condon and Dan Heaton shepherded the book and provided important insights.

In researching the book, I benefited from assistance across Southeast Asia, China, Africa, and many other regions. Research assistants George Caparas, Fanny Lioe, Baradan Kuppusamy, Soyoung Ho, and Am Kumpera, among others, helped arrange interviews, fact-checked, and basically made the research happen.

Many scholars shared their insights about China's diplomacy, its impact on developing nations, and US public diplomacy. Paul Marks provided essential translations of Cambodian newspapers and competed a research project for me about Chinese investment in Vietnam. Henry Yep, Michael Glosny, and Philip Saunders provided information on China's aid policies. Joshua Eisenman helped guide my knowledge of China's Africa policies, and Joshua Gordon led me on a fascinating tour of Mandalay, Burma. Brad Adams, Dan Blumenthal, John Brandon, Guo Changlin, Richard Cronin, Catharin Dalpino, Elizabeth Economy, Roland Eng, Roy Godson, Masao Imamura, Surapong Jayanama, Songpol Kaoputumtip, Walter Lohman, Joshua Marks, Bronson Percival, Kim Beng Phar, Andy Rothman, Eric Teo, Bill Tuffin, and Ruan Zongze all helped expand my knowledge, as did many, many others.

The support of my family and friends has been critical: my mother, father, and sister, who have always been my biggest fans; and the extended Laufer family, my newest fans. And of course, I cannot do anything without Miriam.

I
Courting the World

In October 2003 President George W. Bush arrived in Australia for his first visit Down Under, part of a presidential tour of the Pacific. Bush, who enjoyed a warm relationship with Australian Prime Minister John Howard and planned to scarf down some Australian-style barbecue, seemed excited to be there. For many American presidents, after all, Australia had served as friendly territory; for more than five decades, Australia had counted itself among the United States' closest friends, and Canberra and Washington had signed a formal treaty alliance. Australian grunts fought and died alongside American troops in the jungles of World War II's Pacific theater. During the Cold War, Washington viewed Australia as one of the outposts of freedom in a region threatened by communism, and in Korea and Vietnam, Australian soldiers once again fought alongside American troops. In the Iraq War, Australian troops were serving with the US military, and Howard repeatedly had refused any opportunities to remove the Australian forces from Iraq.

Bush would find the country familiar. In previous decades, as Australia had abandoned some of its traditional ties to Britain, it had developed closer cultural links to the United States. Australian entertainers like Nicole Kidman and Heath Ledger increasingly migrated to the United States for work, while American film, music, and books came to dominate Australian theaters, radio stations, and reading lists. Students from elite American universities chose Australia as a study-abroad destination, in part because Australia seemed so familiar.

When Bush landed in Australia, though, his enthusiasm must have quickly melted. Even before Bush arrived, thousands of demonstrators planned to greet him with protests in Sydney, Canberra, and other Australian cities against the White House's supposedly unilateral foreign policies, including its decision to invade Iraq. When Bush touched down, the demonstrations began, including marches on the American embassy, where protesters scuffled with police, and mock trials of the American president for his supposed human rights abuses. Some of the protesters crossed over from anger toward the American president to broader anti-Americanism, condemning US culture and values, and even average Americans as arrogant and disdainful of the world.[1]

Protected by an enormous security cocoon, Bush planned to address the Australian Parliament. But Bush could barely get rolling on his speech—in which he planned to tell the story of how American and Australian World War II troops together saved Australia from Japanese invasion—before Australian senators began heckling him. Two senators from Australia's Green Party yelled at Bush, screaming that America should follow international law and stop human rights abuses like those at the US prison compound at Guantánamo Bay. "Respect Australia. . . . If you respect the world's laws, the world will respect you," one senator shouted, forcing Bush to halt his speech and gamely quip, "I love free speech" as police pushed the senator-hecklers out of the chamber. Bush completed his speech and left the chamber—where protesters greeted him with a chorus of boos.[2]

Only days later, Australia offered Chinese president Hu Jintao a vastly different welcome, as the Chinese head of state became the first Asian leader to address Australia's Parliament. While Bush had visited Canberra for less than a day, Hu toured Australia like a hero. Though China's human rights abuses, like its religious repression and arbitrary trials, dwarf America's supposed crimes, like Guantánamo detentions, fewer Australians than expected protested against Hu. Even Australian Tibet campaigners, normally angry about China's treatment of Tibetans, went out of their way to be polite to Hu. One Tibet group purchased a full-page advertisement in a leading Australian newspaper telling Hu, "We welcome you to Australia and wish you a successful and pleasant visit."[3]

Few members of Parliament disturbed Hu as he unleashed a windy paean to the future of Australian-Chinese ties. Australia's business community feted the Chinese president at one lavish meal after another, where Australian politicians like Foreign Minister Alexander Downer lauded China, telling audiences, "China's rise is creating new opportunities. . . . China's industrial rise is clearly a major boon for the region."[4] Downer continued with his fulsome praise, saying, "Australian businesses need to understand . . . the very great goodwill there is in China towards Australia." Before Hu left, the two nations signed a framework for a future free trade deal.

Australia's responses to the Bush and Hu visits reflected shifts in Australian public opinion. Only twenty years ago, Australia viewed China as coldly as it greeted American warmly.

Australia itself had only begun to allow in waves of Asian immigrants, after trying to maintain its European character under the White Australia policy of immigration. Though China in the mid-1980s was opening its economy, many Australian opinion leaders and average citizens still viewed Cold War–era Beijing as a communist threat, a nation that had sponsored leftist movements in nations around Australia. Australian politicians won domestic support by claiming that Australia should ignore Asia, and Australia traded little with China, still an extremely poor country.

Precisely because Australia has been such a close US ally and so suspicious of China, the Hu visit and the results of a poll taken in early 2005 by the Lowy Institute, a respected Australian research organization, shocked Washington. In the Lowy survey, barely more than half the Australians polled had positive feelings about the United States, though 84 percent viewed Japan positively and 86 percent viewed the United Kingdom positively. Worse, 57 percent of Australians thought that America's foreign policies were a potential threat—equivalent to the percentage of Australians worried about the rise of Islamic fundamentalism. This despite the fact that in 2002 a massive bomb in Bali, Indonesia, allegedly planted by radical Islamists killed more than two hundred people, most of them Australians.[5] In the same Lowy Institute poll, nearly 70 percent of Australians viewed China positively. Lest anyone think that was an aberration, another study showed that more than 50 percent of Australians supported a proposed free trade agreement with China, while only 34 percent supported such a pact with the United States.

The transformation of China's image in Australia, from pariah as recently as the 1980s to close friend today, seemed remarkable. Yet the transformation is hardly unique. Since the middle of the 1990s, China has started to become an international power, a nation with global foreign policy ambitions. In fact, China may become the first nation since the fall of the Soviet Union that could seriously challenge the United States for control of the international system.

As Beijing has looked outside its borders, it has altered its image across much of the globe, from threat to opportunity, from danger to benefactor. This transformation has allowed China to suggest to the world that it can be a great power. The sea change has been most dramatic among developing countries, the group of nations with lower standards of living than the United States, Europe, Canada, Japan, and other major industrial powers, though it is noticeable even in some developed nations like South Korea and Australia. But it is in the developing nations where China, itself a developing country, has made major inroads in transforming its image.

This transformation is due to a range of factors, including some beyond Beijing's control. But it is due largely to China's growing soft power, which has emerged as the most potent weapon in Beijing's foreign policy arsenal. More than a decade ago, the Harvard academic Joseph Nye invented a concept he called soft power—a concept that then entered foreign policy discourse. As Nye explained, "soft power rests on the ability to shape the preferences of others. . . . It is leading by example and attracting others to do what you want." "If I can get you to do what I want, then I do not have to use carrots or sticks to make you do it," Nye wrote.[6] This attractiveness could be called a nation's "brand," and it can be conveyed through various means, including a country's popular and elite culture, its public diplomacy (government-funded programs intended to influence public opinion abroad), its businesses' actions abroad, international perception of its government's policies, and the gravitational pull of a nation's economic strength, among other factors.

When Nye coined the term *soft power,* he excluded elements like investment and trade and formal diplomacy and aid—elements he considered more concrete carrots and sticks. "Soft power is not merely the same as influence," Nye wrote. "After all, influence can also rest on the hard power of threats or payments." Nye focused purely on the attractiveness of a nation's brand, of its values and ideals and norms.[7]

But soft power has changed. In the context of China, both the Chinese government and many nations influenced by China enunciate a broader idea of soft power than did Nye. For the Chinese, soft power means anything outside of the military and security realm, including not only popular culture and public diplomacy but also more coercive economic and diplomatic levers like aid and investment and participation in multilateral organizations—Nye's carrots and sticks. Indeed, Beijing offers the charm of a lion, not of a mouse: it can threaten other nations with these sticks if they do not help China achieve its goals, but it can offer sizable carrots if they do.

Soft power can be "high," directed at elites in a country, or "low," aimed at the general public. It can stem from governments and nongovernmental actors—businesspeople and Peace Corps volunteers and pop music stars, as well as politicians and leaders. Nongovernmental actors do not necessarily operate in concert with the state, and no state can be said to have a completely coherent foreign policy. In addition, it can sometimes be difficult to separate elements of soft power and elements of hard, military or security power. In China's case, as we will see, Beijing sometimes uses its soft power to assist in harder goals.

Still, a government's broad strategies can boost its soft power, and it is possible that an authoritarian government may be better able to direct coordinated strategies than a democratic one. Think about how American policies were perceived abroad and how they made Washington popular across the world after the Second World War, smoothing the way for American soft actors to wield unrivaled influence. In the 1940s, the United States rebuilt Europe through the Marshall Plan while simultaneously creating a web of international institutions, like the United Nations, to help create a global order that could solve conflicts without resorting to world war. These policies proved highly popular in Europe, and the popularity of the United States helped American companies, from Coca-Cola to McDonald's, colonize the Continent.

Or look at the reverse—American soft power assisted in the promotion of US policies during the Cold War, when America's popular appeal made it easier for leaders in democratic Western Europe to follow Washington's lead. In 1953 the US government created the United States Information Agency to oversee American public diplomacy, and USIA oversaw a radio broadcasting effort, Voice of America, which helped sway foreign opinion, building support for American policies. During the early years of the Cold War, the US government, along with private foundations and American universities, also created programs for Soviet writers, scientists, artists, and other elites to visit the United States.[8] Many of these visitors, awed by America's cultural freedom, returned to the USSR and became advocates of reform and liberalism efforts promoted by the United States, efforts that eventually helped bring down the Soviet Union.

American soft power helped win the Cold War in other Eastern Bloc states. As Nye writes, the Czech film director Milos

Forman says that when Czechoslovakia's communist government allowed screenings of the US film *Twelve Angry Men,* which portrays a negative view of the American judiciary, Czech intellectuals thought, "If that country can make this kind of thing . . . that country must have a pride and must have an inner strength, and must be strong enough and must be free."[9] Enthralled by the film, and convinced of America's moral strength, many Czechs went on to tacitly support America's Eastern Bloc policies during the Cold War and then become a leading US ally after the fall of the Berlin Wall.

China now can wield this kind of soft power, and may use it to remake the world. China's policies could make it easier for Chinese actors, from language schools to businesspeople to Chinese pop stars, to have an impact on the ground. And China's new benign image, in places from Australia to Argentina, will help Beijing execute its foreign policy more successfully.

Since the mid-1990s, the response to Beijing's soft power has been overwhelming. In Thailand, formally a US ally, former Prime Minister Thaksin Shinawatra announced that China is one of the two "most important countries for Thailand's diplomacy," and Thailand is negotiating a partnership with China that could approximate its long alliance with the United States. Local opinion polls show that more than 70 percent of Thais now consider China Thailand's closest friend.[10]

Across Southeast Asia, in fact, elites and populaces in most nations see China as a constructive actor—and, potentially, as the preeminent regional power. Most scholars define Southeast Asia, a region of some 600 million people, as Burma, Thailand, Laos, Cambodia, Vietnam, Malaysia, Indonesia, Brunei, Singapore, the Philippines, Indonesia, and the new nation of East Timor. These countries were not part of British India, which today comprises modern South Asia. Nor, with the exception of parts of Vietnam, were they part of imperial China, as Mongolia and parts of modern-day Korea were at times.[11]

Still, many Southeast Asian nations share common borders with China, and nearly all have enjoyed long histories of trade and diplomatic interaction with China. During the height of imperial China, the Chinese court sent fifty vessels per year to trade with Southeast Asia. In some Southeast Asian states, like modern-day Singapore, this interaction and Chinese migration left an ethnic Chinese majority. In other Southeast Asian states like Malaysia and the Philippines and Indonesia, where the majority of people come from an ethnic Malay background, the Chinese migrants still constitute a sizable minority of the population.

But the response to China's soft power extends beyond Southeast Asia. Outside of the United States and Japan, far fewer world leaders than ten years ago question China's rise. Polls show that people in Africa and Latin America now have more positive feelings toward China than toward the United States, while ten thousand African professionals will head to China each year for postgraduate training. A 2005 British Broadcasting Corporation poll of average people in twenty-two nations across several continents found nearly all believed that China plays a more positive role in the world than does the United States.[12]

China also has been able to use soft power to get what it wants. Nations from Venezuela to Uzbekistan have proven increasingly willing to work with China, whether that means Venezuelan president Hugo Chávez vowing to reorient his massive oil industry toward Beijing and away from America, or Uzbek leader Islam Karimov tossing US forces out of bases in his country. Countries in Asia, Africa, and Latin America have increasingly cut off even their informal ties to Taiwan, which Beijing claims is a province of China.

This rise coincides with a sharp decline in America's soft power: in a recent poll of twenty-one nations commissioned by the British Broadcasting Corporation, only one-third of people polled wanted American values to spread in their nation, a sign of the world's disdain for the United States. This decline began in the Clinton 1990s and has spiraled further downward in the Bush 2000s, as cuts in American public diplomacy, scandals in American corporations, new restrictions on entering the United States, misguided trade policies, a retreat from multilateral institutions, and human rights abuses in Iraq, Guantánamo Bay, and other places have combined to undermine the allure of America's ideas, values, and models. As Andrew Moravcsik, a scholar specializing in European-US relations, admits, "Not only do others not share America's self-regard, they no longer aspire to emulate the country's social and economic achievements."[13] In other words, while once it seemed like everyone dreamed of being an American, from Eastern European anticommunists to students in Burma to liberals in China itself, today that dream may be dying.

It is in Southeast Asia where one can most easily notice Beijing's new soft power. Beijing first concentrated its charm on the region, before broadening its efforts to Africa and Latin America and the Middle East. Such a strategy makes sense. China's nearest neighborhood, Southeast Asia boasts nearly twenty million ethnic Chinese and has long historical, economic, and cultural ties to China. For a China still flexing its strength as an international power, Southeast Asia presents an opportunity. Perhaps, as a young United States once did in the

Western Hemisphere, China could make the region its own—a Chinese Monroe Doctrine for Southeast Asia would make Beijing the major influence over regional affairs and reduce US alliances in the region.[14]

Because Southeast Asia is the first region where China has unleashed its soft power, it also offers a vital window into how China will act as its influence grows. In some respects, China's new assertiveness is only natural. Between AD 500 and 1500 China often was the most powerful state in the world; at the beginning of the seventeenth century, China had a bigger population than all of Europe. Today Beijing is in many respects regaining the central position in foreign affairs it enjoyed for centuries, and inevitably great powers, whether China or America or the Soviet Union, exert soft power.

In this book I will trace how China has built its global soft power, analyze how China uses that power, and consider how nations are responding to Beijing. I will focus primarily on China's wooing of developing nations in Southeast Asia, Africa, Latin America, and Central Asia, but will occasionally address how China woos other key nations in Asia, like Australia, South Korea, or Russia. I will not, however, directly analyze the US-Chinese relationship, or China's relationship with wealthy nations in Europe or the Middle East. I will first analyze why China has engaged with the world, how changes within China itself led to a more proactive Chinese foreign policy, and what China hopes to gain from this engagement. Then I will examine how China actually achieves its goals, observing China's soft power strategies and tools of influence. Finally, having observed how China sets goals, creates strategies, and utilizes its soft power, I will measure the extent of Beijing's success—and failure—in order to learn what it may mean for the globe.

II
Changes on the Home Front

Back in 1949 Beijing also believed it might wield power in the world, but not soft power. Triumphing over both the Japanese invaders and Chiang Kai-shek's seemingly superior Nationalist forces, Mao Tse-tung's communists thought themselves invincible when they established the People's Republic of China on October 1, 1949. After all, the communists had ended the "century of humiliation" for China that started with the Opium Wars in the 1840s and 1860s, when Britain and other European powers had crushed China's military and begun a process of national disintegration that precipitated the end of the Chinese empire.

Mao decided not only to create a revolutionary society at home but also to foment armed revolution around the world, helping nations rid themselves of colonial masters and capitalist systems. "We must give active support to the national independence and liberation movements in countries in Asia, Africa, and Latin America," the Chairman announced.[1] China took part in the Bandung Conference, a meeting of newly independent African and Asian nations in 1955, and promoted itself as a leader of the developing world, a strategy Beijing is reasserting today.

Mao quickly put his ideas into practice. He pushed through one of the most radical revolutions in history, trying to create a totally communitarian economy and remake a whole society. The government took control of agriculture, creating collectives out of small plots and large landholdings; it banned supposedly feudal traditions, including religious ceremonies; it restricted travel within China; it created Party cells to monitor minute details of people's lives.

With the Great Leap Forward, a late 1950s plan to industrialize the country, Mao tried to make agrarian, rural China a manufacturing power in just one generation. He encouraged average citizens to produce steel in backyard factories, embarked on massive capital construction projects, and increased the mass mobilization of peasant groups, supposedly to improve grain production and increase harvests, but also to boost the Communist Party's control over the populace.[2]

When the Great Leap Forward failed, resulting in massive famine and damaging Mao's image, the Chairman responded with the Cultural Revolution, unleashing Red Guards against his enemies. This campaign resulted in chaos, with Red Guards destroying any traditional pillars of society left in China, from monasteries to schoolhouses to artists' studios.

Across the world, meanwhile, China tried to support what Mao called "righteous struggles"—like-minded communist revolutions that wound up alienating some leaders in developing nations, who feared being targeted by these leftist insurgents. In Burma, China bankrolled a communist insurgency, offering arms and military instructors to the Burmese fighters. In Cambodia, China cultivated the Khmer Rouge, which envisioned an even more radical remaking of their society than Mao had considered. In Latin America, China supported revolutionary movements; in African states, China trained antigovernment guerillas; in the Middle East, Beijing funded communist insurgents in Yemen and Oman.[3]

These insurgencies created disdain for China and for ethnic Chinese abroad, and developing nations fought back against groups supported by Mao. Thailand and Burma, for example, battled guerrillas who had taken to the jungles of northern Indochina. By the middle of the 1970s, most of these communist insurgencies had either fizzled or, as in Cambodia, succeeded in toppling former regimes. But China's support for revolutionary movements had poisoned relations with a generation of policy makers in the developing world. In response, many leaders from Asia and Africa and Latin America cut off relations with China, established alliances with the United States, created regional organizations that excluded China, like the Association of Southeast Asian Nations, and tightly monitored and circumscribed the lives of their own ethnic Chinese minorities. In Indonesia, the government essentially banned ethnic Chinese from politics, outlawed Chinese literature, and questioned many ethnic Chinese's devotion to Indonesia. Even in Vietnam, a fellow communist nation, China's backing of the Cambodian Khmer Rouge, which eventually went to war with Vietnam, alienated Hanoi from Beijing, leading to a brief border war between the two in 1979.[4]

Apart from trying to export revolution, China's other tools of influence remained weak. Mao's economic mismanagement kept China impoverished; as an example of economic success, China seemed a model few countries would want to follow. Mao himself knew little about real-world economics, and he refused to listen to confidants who counseled restraint, like Deng Xiaoping, a pragmatist who wanted to launch economic reforms. (For his ideas, Deng was purged as a "capitalist roader" during the Cultural Revolution, sent to a tractor factory in rural Jiangxi Province to perform manual labor.) The public face Beijing presented to the world was blunt and gray, just monotone statements from official spokesmen who understood nothing about the modern media. Older officials, who'd grown up in the Maoist period—when any deviation from Party principles could still land you in jail—still dominated the diplomatic corps, and could barely communicate China's message, except to selected socialist audiences. "They had these diplomats who were so stiff they'd just read statements to you," says one Western diplomat. "If you questioned anything, they would just repeat what they read, like a robot."[5]

After Mao's death, Deng returned to power. A savvy political infighter, Deng carefully cultivated top members of the Communist Party, then used his backers within the regime to outmaneuver the Chairman's appointed heir, Hua Guofeng. By the early 1980s, Hua conceded that he had lost the support of the Party, and Deng essentially took control of China, appointing his reform-minded protégés to top positions. And since Deng's restoration, twenty-five years of unparalleled economic growth has changed China enormously. The drastic changes in China itself have set the stage for China to exert soft power around the world. Within China, the country has witnessed growing economic dynamism, a surge in nationalism, a new Chinese middle class knowledgeable about the globe, and a vastly more sophisticated leadership that recognizes the need for public diplomacy to protect its domestic and international interests. Combined, all these factors have created pressure for China's new international engagement, as more sophisticated and proud Chinese citizens desire a state that plays a large role on the world stage.

Deng Xiaoping could claim much of the credit for China's changes. A leader within the Communist Party of China since the 1920s, the pragmatic Deng had seen the excesses and chaos of the Chairman's policies firsthand. After Mao's death, Deng understood how Maoism had alienated China's neighbors, created instability on China's borders, and impoverished China itself. China would need decades to recover, and would require a peaceful external environment and massive inflows of foreign investment and technology to become strong. Deng counseled his proud countrymen, heirs to a Chinese kingdom that once called itself the center of the world, to bide their time. China should "keep a low profile and never take the lead" on global issues, Deng warned—Beijing wasn't strong enough to expose itself to a world leadership role.[6]

At home Deng launched the Chinese economy on pragmatic reforms. At the landmark Communist Party plenum in 1978, Chinese leaders decided to stop focusing on "revolutionary" class warfare, the major task of Mao's governments, and instead to try to modernize the economy. Deng opened China to foreign joint ventures, tasked the government to court foreign investment, and created special economic zones like Shenzhen, in southern China, designed to lure foreign firms by offering them massive tax concessions. Deng allowed farmers to again grow crops for profits, and ultimately pushed China toward dismantling its massive state enterprises. Most important, he changed the mindset in China, exhorting his countrymen that "to get rich is glorious," thereby telling individuals that entrepreneurship, discouraged for decades, was once again acceptable, even laudable.[7]

As the China scholar David Lampton shows in his landmark edited study of post-Mao policy making, in foreign affairs China under Deng played defense, reacting when threatened but generally avoiding most global issues. Deng ended China's ties to communist insurgencies abroad, which had drained China's treasury, and established closer relations with developing countries like Malaysia that had been targets of left-wing insurgencies. (Malaysia and China had established formal diplomatic relations in 1974.) He strengthened China's growing ties to the United States, now its most important source of technology. He praised America's power and acted the role of a humble student even toward small nations, ordering Chinese leaders to "learn from Singapore" about how to build a modern economy, and sending provincial and national officials to universities in that tiny city-state. He shunned multilateral organizations and treaties, and Chinese diplomats at the United Nations seemed almost invisible, barely commenting on important issues.[8]

Deng's pragmatism resonated with a society recovering from Mao. The chaos of the Cultural Revolution, when hundreds of thousands of people were purged to the countryside or killed, and teachers and other intellectuals were terrorized by waves of ideological Red Guards, had shocked the Chinese population.[9] Average Chinese had seen power and ideology wielded by the state bring nothing but misery to average people; now they remained weary from decades of this internal turmoil.

Meanwhile, many Chinese intellectuals greatly admired the United States, which had formed an alliance with Beijing during the latter half of the Cold War, as China and the Soviet Union split. To these Chinese intellectuals, no country could possibly challenge the United States' influence. A poll taken by the research organization Horizon Group in 1995 asked Chinese citizens their views of the "most prominent countries in the world"; one-third ranked the United States most prominent, with only 13 percent choosing China. Earlier, in the liberal 1980s, many Chinese academics and students idolized the US political system and tuned to Voice of America for their news. One study found that in the 1980s some 70 percent of Chinese university students trusted Voice of America but 75 percent distrusted the Chinese media—numbers that would shift in the 1990s.[10]

In fact, throughout the 1980s China's economic opening seemed to signal the creation of a cosmopolitan, inquisitive intellectual class committed to China's eventual democratization. Inside the government, officials created a task force comprising primarily liberal intellectuals and designed to examine and push for political reforms. Even senior Party leaders appeared committed to opening up China's political system. Zhao Ziyang, one of Deng's top lieutenants, advocated for elections in China. As Zhao reportedly told acquaintances, "Give people more freedom. . . . The people's demand for democracy is a trend. We must meet their demand to the fullest extent."[11]

Zhao was not yet in charge, though. The man in charge, Deng Xiaoping, though he advocated economic reform, did not share Zhao's liberal political sentiments. Deng was known for bluntness, and he made his feelings clear—China could pursue gradual economic reform without having to rapidly open the political system. "We cannot abandon our dictatorship. We must not accommodate the sentiments of democratization," Deng told officials.[12]

In the climax of that decade, on June 4, 1989, this pro-American bias appeared again, broadcast to the world. Days of protests against the Beijing regime had culminated in demonstrations attended by hundreds of thousands of Chinese in Tiananmen Square, the central plaza in Beijing located in front of the Forbidden City, where generations of Chinese emperors had ruled over China's empire. In 1989 young protesters from the Central Academy of Fine Arts carved a "Goddess of Democracy"—a giant statue resembling the Statue of Liberty—to symbolize their desire for democracy in China. The protesters stayed until troops and tanks, on the orders of Deng Xiaoping himself, cleared the historic square by firing automatic weapons into the crowd, killing perhaps two thousand people.[13]

Following June 4 those warm feelings toward America cooled. After the crackdown in Tiananmen, the Chinese regime purged Zhao Ziyang from power and placed him under house arrest for the rest of his life. It tossed other liberals within the Party into jail. After the crackdown in Tiananmen, memories of the event were buried under an avalanche of nationalism and growing pragmatism by the Chinese population, which essentially seemed to accept their authoritarian government, at least for the time being. Beijing tightened its controls over society, alternatively cowing and co-opting elites to keep them in line, and forcing dissidents into exile. And after the crackdown in Tiananmen, the appeal of the United States to average Chinese faded. In 2003 the Horizon Group polled randomly chosen Chinese citizens again. This time, nearly 40 percent picked China as "the most prominent country in the world." The United States placed a distant second.[14]

In the years after Tiananmen, both the Chinese public and the Chinese leadership gained vital confidence—confidence that China had a right to become a global power. More than two decades of post-1979 breakneck economic growth, during which

China's trade with other nations grew some eight times faster than overall world trade, allowed China to build trade surpluses with the world of more than $100 billion annually. China amassed the largest currency reserves on earth and lifted 200 million people out of poverty, one of the greatest economic accomplishments in history. China became Asia's largest recipient of foreign direct investment, receiving more than $60 billion in investment in 2005. By 2025 China should become the world's second-largest economy; measured by purchasing power parity, it already is.[15]

China's growth has defied regional shocks like the Asian financial crisis of the late 1990s, internal financial problems like Chinese banks' morass of nonperforming loans, and endless predictions by experts (including myself) of an imminent downturn in the Chinese economy. In places like vibrant Wenzhou, a city in eastern China's Zhejiang Province packed with companies that specialize in cigarette lighters, the Chinese private sector has created highly skilled and efficient firms, a far cry from China's state-owned industrial giants.[16]

The impact of this growth can be seen even in the most remote parts of the country. On a hundred-degree day in August of 2002, vendors and buyers crowded into the open-air plaza in front of Idh Kah Mosque, a central structure in Kashgar, the westernmost city in China, closer to Afghanistan than to Beijing. Kashgar sits near the border with Muslim Central Asia, and it is populated by many Uighurs, a Muslim, Turkic ethnic minority in China. In a Kashgar side alley, an old man with a thick beard and a white Muslim skullcap sat in front of a shop, banging an insistent, Arab-sounding rhythm on a hand drum. Next to him, a younger man with thin stubble kept up a keening wail, like a snake charmer, on a tiny flute and mouth pipes. In front of the mosque, olive-skinned men wearing large cotton mitts pulled naan bread out of a stone oven; kebab sellers molded fresh lamb onto small skewers. Merchants greeted each other with "salaam alaikum," and then crowded in close—prodding and cajoling potential customers.[17]

Only two years later, Kashgar looked far different. As China's economy boomed, the Chinese government in the late 1990s developed a plan it called "Develop the West" or "Western Development." Under this plan, the central government would build new infrastructure in the western part of the country and provide financial incentives, like tax exemptions, to encourage entrepreneurs and investors to migrate to that poorer region. Between 2002 and 2004 Develop the West had landed in Kashgar. The Chinese government had cleared the central plaza of merchants, replacing them with new luxury condo-type buildings, metastasizing construction sites, and a modern stone plaza. Smooth new highways now connected Kashgar with the rest of the country, traversing the long, ocher deserts and deep purple-and-red canyons of Xinjiang. The highways, and the financial incentives, had attracted new businesspeople to the city, though Develop the West had not addressed the overall wealth gap between western and eastern China. Thousands of these businesspeople had decamped on Kashgar, where they bunked, three or four to a room, in shabby long-term hotels.[18]

Even the carpet merchants sensed they had to take advantage of rapid change. Walking around Kashgar one day in 2004, I stumbled into an indoor market. Behind individual counters, merchants competed for customers, grabbing people as they walked by and hollering out deals. The old vendors huddled around a few counters, comparing prices, their arms around each other's shoulders. As my eyes focused, I realized where I was. It was the cell phone market, where the carpet sellers haggled over mobile phones as aggressively as they'd once touted thread counts.

Economic growth transformed Chinese society. It transformed even remote backwater cities like Kashgar and allowed urban Chinese to amass the kind of luxuries they'd once only heard about. It built up the Chinese academic system, and it stoked a growing demand for energy to fuel the Chinese economy, so much so that China, self-sufficient in oil as recently as 1997, may have to increase its energy consumption 150 percent by 2020 to maintain its rate of growth. (Current Chinese Prime Minister Wen Jiabao recently admitted that shortages of oil and gas have limited China's development.) Economic growth pushed urban Chinese to learn about the world, through the influx of Chinese Internet news portals. On the Web, they could watch foreign businesses flocking to China like modern-day vassals, making any concessions necessary to enter the Chinese market—even, like Google, tailoring the content of their sites to please Beijing.[19] They could learn about Chinese who'd studied and worked in America choosing to come back to China to work, since the country now offered greater economic opportunity.

This powerful growth, technological change, and academic progress, incessantly highlighted in the state-dominated Chinese media, fostered a new sense of confidence in China, particularly among young people who had come of age after the chaos and disorder of the 1989 Tiananmen crisis. In recent years, several academics have studied this rebirth of confidence. As Peter Hays Gries, an expert on domestic Chinese politics, chronicles in a recent study of Chinese nationalism, the idea that China had become a rising power swept through the domestic and foreign media, partly replacing images of China as a weak state preyed upon before 1949 by foreign powers and then decimated by Mao's changes.[20] And like the United States in the nineteenth century, as a rising power China began to reconsider the world system it had accepted when it was weaker.

Young Chinese also began to travel abroad, with the number of outbound tourists rising from 4.5 million in 1995 to more than 30 million in 2005. As they traveled, urban Chinese may have lost some of their awe for America and Europe—one recent group of editors compiling a Chinese-language collection of people's views toward the world noted that other nations were no longer mysterious to average Chinese. The travelers saw that the United States was far from perfect, that it, too, suffered from poverty and crime and grime that might weaken the American social fabric. They realized that their own big cities, like Shanghai, now could match any world capital for nightlife and culture and technology and economic dynamism. In one recent poll only 40 percent of Chinese had a favorable impression of the US.[21]

Recognizing that communism held little appeal in a nation urging its citizens to get rich as quickly as possible, the post-Tiananmen leadership, eventually headed by President Jiang Zemin, needed to offer a substitute ideology to keep the population united. What they came up with, as the China expert Jasper Becker describes, was a kind of updated nationalism. This drew upon China's history of patriotism—nationalism had played a role in the early-twentieth-century revolutions that eventually brought Chiang Kai-shek to power.

But the new nationalism did not only look back. It played on anger about foreign powers' domination of China in the nineteenth and twentieth centuries, but it also emphasized China's growing strength and its past grievances. Beijing built enormous new projects, like the Chinese space program, designed to rally public opinion around the state. It launched mass rallies and rewrote school textbooks to emphasize that China was gaining strength again; at the same time, the textbooks reminded average Chinese of how foreign powers had preyed upon China. Beijing's leaders began stressing that China must become stronger, to face down external enemies, even as some top officials worried that the nationalism could backfire, leading to protests against the government. As Becker notes, "Jiang and his successors see their country in the midst of a Darwinian struggle between nations. . . . Jiang has warned the party faithful, 'Competition in overall national strength is becoming increasingly fierce.'"[22]

Newspapers like the state-controlled Beijing *People's Daily* and best-selling books touting China's strength and questioning the "cultural colonialism" of Western products in China only reinforced the nationalist mindset. The *People's Daily* sparked nationalism in a sophisticated manner, sometimes featuring Chinese successes abroad and running supposedly neutral commentaries, taken from Middle Eastern papers and other anti-US news sources, on America's "failing" foreign policies around the world. At the same time, the Beijing regime successfully co-opted forces that foreign scholars had predicted would pry open Chinese society—building firewalls, for example, to control the Internet even as some 150 million Chinese logged onto the Web.[23]

By the end of the 1990s some young Chinese urbanites no longer resembled the idealistic, liberal men and women who had hopped trains from across China to get to Tiananmen Square in 1989. Most were too young to remember the Cultural

Revolution, and so were less distrustful than their elders of the state's wielding of power and ideology. Unlike their elders, who'd come to Tiananmen in 1989 furious that they were earning meager salaries in academia and business even as Party officials seemed to be rolling in cash, these younger elites were more comfortable, and often had shunned political science or history at university in favor of business and computer technology.

The Party had reached out to these urbanites, essentially buying them off. As Minxin Pei of the Carnegie Endowment for International Peace writes in a new study of China's political system, "The Party showers the urban intelligentsia, professionals, and private entrepreneurs with economic perks, professional honors, and political access. . . . Nationwide, 145,000 designated experts, or about 8 percent of senior professionals, received 'special government stipends,' or monthly salary supplements in 2004."[24] What's more, Pei notes, tens of thousands of former college professors have been recruited into the Chinese Communist Party, where leaders have promoted them to senior, and well-paying, government positions. Party committees in Chinese universities offered house allowances, stipends, and other benefits to promising young students who agreed to become Party members.

In essence, young intellectuals, who throughout China's history had led reform efforts, had made a pragmatic deal with their government. The state would deliver growth, and they would focus on making money. In one study of Chinese students, 83 percent ranked the following value statement as most important: "A modern person should be able to make money." In a May 2005 poll of average Chinese citizens taken by the Pew Global Attitudes Project, more than 70 percent of Chinese said they were satisfied with current conditions in their nation. By comparison, even in normally patriotic America, fewer than 40 percent of people said they were satisfied with national conditions. As one scholar writes, Chinese intellectuals' "writings today in academic journals and high-brow magazines are imbued with a sense of satisfaction. There are exceptions, of course, but most intellectuals tend to accept and approve of the status quo."[25]

In the 1990s several prominent intellectuals even revolted against the ethos of China's liberal late 1980s, calling for a stronger role for the Chinese state; many other liberal intellectuals had fled the country, leaving them incapable of influencing China's youth. Young Chinese now wrote nationalistic books and dominated the chat rooms of China's most popular Web bulletin boards, like the Strong Nation forum, where they competed to attack the government from the right, as soft on the United States. In the 1980s the Chinese intelligentsia was opposed to the Chinese Communist Party's rule, notes Ying Ma, a specialist on Chinese domestic attitudes. Now, Ma says, though many Chinese have become "Americanized" by working for multinational companies, traveling abroad, and accessing American culture through the Internet, "Chinese increasingly view America today as a bully who . . . attempts to thwart the rise of their country's international influence."[26]

This rising nationalism might not have peaked, except for two disastrous events. In 1999, relying on an outdated CIA map, NATO forces accidentally bombed the Chinese embassy in Belgrade. (The United States apologized for the mistake and paid restitution.) The bombing killed three Chinese and injured at least fifteen others. To Chinese convinced that their nation was rising, skeptical of American motives, and stoked by the Chinese media suggesting that the bombing was deliberate, this was a sign. The more nationalist in the population called for military retaliation against America, and thousands of young Chinese led boycotts of American products and besieged the US mission in Beijing, trapping the US ambassador in the compound for four days, and battering the embassy with rocks and bottles.[27]

The Belgrade bombing was followed by the EP-3 incident in early 2001, when a Chinese F-8 fighter collided with a US Navy reconnaissance plane finishing a routine mission off the coast of China. The Chinese plane had been tailing the American craft, and some American officials suggested that the Chinese pilot had flown recklessly close to his US counterpart. In any event, the collision killed the Chinese pilot, and the Chinese government briefly seized and imprisoned the crew from the American plane on the island of Hainan. Beijing demanded that the United States apologize for the collision, but America refused to do so.[28] Eventually, Washington and Beijing agreed on a compromise letter of regret that admitted no guilt, but most Chinese I have met remained convinced that the Americans were responsible for the Chinese pilot's death.

The EP-3 incident further soured young Chinese on the United States, no longer the shining model of 1989 but rather a competitor and potential enemy. Only a tough police response, probably mandated by Beijing, kept young Chinese from demonstrating against the US embassy, as they had done in 1999. In one recent major poll of Chinese, twice as many people in their twenties had a negative view of the United States as had a positive view.[29]

Even Chinese who had previously paid little attention to foreign affairs suddenly became interested. The Belgrade bombing and the EP-3 incident sparked their interest in foreign policy, and made them rethink whether the United States and China could indeed be "strategic partners," as President

Clinton once had promised. Constant criticism of China by US human rights advocates and other pressure groups only stiffened Chinese views; as Ma notes, no one, whether Americans or Chinese, likes to have his country criticized by outsiders. And so the Belgrade bombing and the EP-3 incident fostered the most significant domestic discussion of China's global role in years. Across China's eastern cities, businesspeople, academics, students, and other intellectuals began to consider whether China should abandon playing defense with the rest of the world—a debate captured by growing coverage in the Chinese press suggesting that China should develop a more aggressive foreign policy.

The September 11 attacks further exposed China's nationalist sentiment. "When the planes crashed into the World Trade Center, I really felt very delighted," one Chinese student told Chinese pollsters. "They expected that more places in the United States would be bombed," said another Chinese student, talking about how he and his friends gathered in a dorm room after September 11 to celebrate as Americans leaped from the burning towers to their death. "The more severely the United States was bombed, the more excited they would be." Though shocking, these feelings were widespread. In a broader study of post–September 11 opinion, researchers found that "most Chinese college students . . . were immediately excited because the United States, an abhorrent, overbearing, and arbitrary country in their minds, suffered an unprecedented heavy strike."[30]

Older Chinese liberals, who remembered how a strong central government fomented the Cultural Revolution, could hardly understand their nationalist progeny. "Today, my students don't care about political science," complained one politics professor at Fudan University in Shanghai, a man who had been a young academic during Tiananmen. "They want to take business, or computer science, or something else that will get them a good job. . . . They think [the Chinese leadership] is too weak, and should be harder on the US." He paused, looking befuddled. "I don't know how to talk to them."[31]

Just as the Chinese public started to consider a more proactive foreign policy, China's leadership, too, was becoming more confident and more knowledgeable about the world.

Until the mid-1990s, the generation that had grown up around Mao—including Deng Xiaoping himself—still dominated China's inner circle. But this generation passed away in the 1980s, or was forcibly retired to make way for younger officials.

This provided an opportunity for Chinese and foreign scholars of the Beijing regime to assess their replacements. H. Lyman Miller and Liu Xiaohong produced one of the most comprehensive assessments. As they found, of the twenty-four officials who became full or alternate members of the Politburo at the Fifteenth National Congress in September 1997, only six had served in the Party leadership before 1992, and most were at least ten years younger than the men they'd replaced. Many of these new leaders hailed from China's urbane eastern provinces, which had benefited the most from economic reforms and which were most open to external influence. In contrast to older leaders, they had completed undergraduate and even graduate studies. They had studied outside China, often in Western nations. But these leaders also had seen Western nations shun China after the Tiananmen crackdown. As Chinese officials told me, they recognized that Beijing could not rely on the United States but must develop its relations with its neighbors, with Africa, and with Latin America; it was Argentina's president, Carlos Menem, who became the first leader from the Western Hemisphere to visit China after the Tiananmen crackdown.[32] What's more, Chinese leaders recognized that, with the end of the Cold War, Russia no longer threatened China, freeing Beijing to use some of the resources it had spent protecting its northern border on other efforts, like increasing pressure on Taiwan and building up its forces across the Taiwan Strait.

From their time in the West, these younger men and women also had seen how think tanks, career diplomats, academics, and public opinion helped American officials process world events and make policy. They began to follow more closely Chinese public opinion, as the number of voices trying to make an impact on Chinese policy making was expanding rapidly. Compared with the past, when scholars and officials had kept any criticism of foreign policy silent, a growing number of prominent Chinese intellectuals began to publicly air policy debates, such as an argument in the 1990s by left-leaning scholars that the breakup of Chinese state-controlled enterprises would damage China's national security. As a result, leaders like former Premier Zhu Rongji increasingly read academic papers, watched television shows like *Focus* that reported on Chinese opinion, and even used the Internet to gauge public sentiment.[33]

These leaders increasingly supported a network of Chinese think tanks like the Chinese Academy of Social Sciences in Beijing, the China Reform Forum, and the Central Party School. At these think tanks, Chinese scholars would learn from Western think tanks and then be called upon to provide sophisticated analysis to the government, upgrading China's strategic thinking. As the scholars Evan S. Medeiros and M. Taylor Fravel note, the Chinese foreign ministry even created an internal agency focused on long-range thinking, like the State Department's Bureau of Policy Planning.[34]

The impact of China's economic growth trickled down to midlevel officials as well. Two decades of development has sharply raised the education level of China's leaders. As the former *Time* foreign editor Joshua Cooper Ramo notes in an essay called *The Beijing Consensus,* "There has been a head-snapping rise in the education level of China's regional leaders. . . . In 1982 only 20 percent of China's provincial leaders had attended college. In 2002, this number was 98 percent. . . . Among younger leaders, those 'fourth generation' leaders under 54, two-thirds hold Masters or PhD degrees."[35]

As a result, today even midlevel Chinese leaders have become vastly more knowledgeable about the outside world and enjoy far better access to current events. Former State Department Deputy Assistant Secretary of State Susan Shirk remembers that in 1993 it was "easier to persuade the North Koreans to come [to an informal diplomatic meeting] than it was the Chinese," since the Chinese were so isolated and distrustful. Ten years later, one former US diplomat marveled at the Chinese diplomats' knowledge, telling me, "Chinese officials now can describe to me in detail the splits within the American neoconservative movement."[36]

With a more sophisticated knowledge of the world, these leaders recognized that China must become a greater international player. China had pressing great-power needs—needs for oil, allies, markets, and security, among others. Yet the United States had built alliances around the world that could constrain China one day if Washington chose to contain Beijing the way it had tried to contain Moscow and if nations agreed to join in that effort. America's relationships in Asia also could prevent China from eventually regaining control of

Taiwan. In a study of articles from Chinese-language journals on international relations, which often reflect government thinking, the China scholar Biwu Zhang found that many pieces focused on how America had wooed friends and now was "capable of establishing regional defense headquarters in various corners of the world." To break through this American containment, and to potentially increase pressure on Taiwan, Beijing would have to rely on developing nations, which were more willing to overlook China's human rights abuses. As Zhang Xizhen, a professor of international relations at Beijing University, said, "Threatened and actual economic sanctions and international political isolation [after Tiananmen] jeopardized our opening up and reform process. [We had] to strengthen relations with our neighbors and break out of the Western blockade."[37]

The Chinese leaders also increasingly understood that as China continued to grow and opened its borders, it could not avoid the world's problems, like HIV and drugs seeping from Southeast Asia into southwest China. Fighting HIV, said Jiang's successor, Hu Jintao, would be "a major issue that has a bearing on the nation's quality and destiny," and would require global cooperation.[38]

Chinese officials could not help noticing another important change. Foreign leaders were beginning to marvel at China's economic miracle—as one Afghan vice president recently put it, "China has made significant [economic] achievements . . . so we Afghans are looking forward to learn[ing]"—and Beijing began to realize that China has an image it can sell to the world. At the same time, America's international image was slipping. In Chinese publications, Wang Jisi, one of China's elite intellectuals, noted that America's weakness was its soft power, not its hard power. And after the Iraq War began in 2003, the scholar Biwu Zhang found, Chinese authors agreed that America had suffered "a serious setback in terms of soft power."[39]

Wang was right. After the end of the Cold War, America had retreated from the world, consumed with its own economic boom, with the Internet, and with American culture wars. Significant pluralities of Americans opposed US interventions abroad and called for Washington to cut foreign aid, and the White House listened. Washington slashed aid and public diplomacy, long a linchpin of American popularity, and merged the United States Information Agency, the main public diplomacy outfit, into the State Department. The Clinton administration neglected many of the multilateral institutions that America had built after the Second World War, creating perceptions of the United States as a unilateral actor, while the White House also refused to intervene in important crises in the developing world, from the genocide in Rwanda to the financial meltdown in Thailand. By the end of the 1990s the appeal of American-style economics, political systems, and even popular culture had begun to wane.

America's unpopularity provided an opportunity. When Thailand devalued its currency in 1997, after speculators had attacked the currency because they believed that Thailand's strong growth hid major economic weaknesses, the devaluation spiraled into a full-blown financial crisis. As the Thai economy cratered, Bangkok lurched into a panic. Investors pulled out of the stock market, and depositors lined up at banks, causing a run on cash at many branches. When I visited one branch, employees had locked themselves inside to avoid being gang-rushed by Thais desperate to withdraw money.

Construction halted on flashy condominiums launched in Bangkok's go-go early 1990s, leaving cranes scattered everywhere like a life-sized Erector Set. Nearly every day it seemed as if another Thai financial company declared bankruptcy and the government released another report on unemployment. Bangkok airport remained crowded: foreign companies flocked to town to buy Thai assets on the cheap before jetting off to resorts for a round of cheap golf. Bangkok newspapers kept busy too, reporting stories of former tycoons brought low. One real estate magnate, Sirivat Voravetvuthikun, had amassed enormous debts. Sirivat lost at least $10 million in assets, and he could no longer pay his creditors. Desperate, he started selling sandwiches on Bangkok's steamy streets to survive.[40]

When I drove one day to the prime minister's official residence in Bangkok, I found the road blocked by a tent city. Entire villages from Thailand's impoverished rural Northeast, hit not only by the financial downturn but also by a withering drought, had moved themselves to the streets of Bangkok, where they rebuilt their thatched huts by the prime minister's house. They camped there for months—sinewy, malnourished-looking farmers with creased faces protected from the sun by straw hats, monks distributing Buddhist amulets and blessings for sick children. As the villagers protested, one Thai government collapsed and another stepped in. Handed the keys to the treasury, the newly appointed Thai finance minister went ashen. "He realized that, basically, there was nothing there," remembers one foreign diplomat in close contact with Thai leaders at the time.[41]

The Thais had hope, though. Many believed that, as a formal US ally, Thailand would soon receive help from America. After all, Washington had bailed out Mexico when the Mexican economy imploded. Now, inside the National Security Council, Southeast Asia experts pushed for a bailout package for Thailand.[42] But, at least at first, the NSC advisers couldn't get the ear of their bosses. American officials refused to take the lead and organize a bailout of the Thai finance system. The United States even killed the idea of a regional fund to bail out Asia, anteing up money only as the crisis spread to South Korea, a larger economy, and threatened the entire global economy.

When the Thais realized that help wasn't on the way, the mood in Bangkok toward America turned sour. Thai officials blasted American counterparts for their sloth. At the tent city, I started seeing signs damning the United States, a symbol of the free-market economics that had brought Thailand low, and effigies of Bill Clinton, his red, bulbous nose turning brown as the demonstrators set his cardboard double on fire.

As the United States flubbed its initial crisis response, China made a symbolic move, publicly refusing to devalue its currency; if Beijing had devalued, it could have forced further devaluations of other Asian countries' currencies. It was a minor remedy compared with the massive financial bailout eventually offered by Japan, the United States, and the international financial institutions like the International Monetary Fund, which gave Thailand a credit line. But Beijing smartly advertised its decision as standing up for other Asian nations. "The Chinese Government, with a high sense of responsibility, decided not to devaluate its renminbi in the overall interest of maintaining stability and development in the region," said the Chinese foreign ministry. "It did so under huge pressure and at a big price. But it contributed considerably to the financial and economic stability and to the development in Asia."[43]

China's move seemed to work. "The US response or failure to respond to the Asian financial crisis in 1997 strengthened China's standing in the region," Singaporean ambassador to Washington Chan Heng Chee said later. Indeed, after the crisis, Rodolfo Severino, head of the Association of Southeast Asian Nations, the leading regional political bloc, announced, "China is really emerging from this smelling good." Nearly ten years later, Thai officials still seethed at America's initial inaction, and even Thai friends snapped at me if I reminded them that eventually the United States did help Bangkok rebuild its economy. But when I asked one Thai leader who had come to Thailand's rescue during the crisis, he responded immediately. "China," he said. "Only China."[44]

Nineteen ninety-seven marked a turning point. For the first time in decades, China had taken a stance on a major international issue and had banked credit as a benign force in global affairs. In the following years, as the Chinese leadership became richer, worldlier, and more confident, and as it came to be supported by an increasingly nationalist public, China's mandarins reassessed their place in the world. Rather than playing defense, rather than just reacting to international affairs, they were ready to take the offensive, building a more sophisticated and powerful foreign policy.

Chinese leaders and scholars started referring to the country, in Chinese publications and to Chinese audiences, as a *daguo*—a great power—and to suggest that China should adopt the mentality of a daguo.[45] And by the time Deng's successor, Jiang Zemin, stepped down in 2002, giving way to the next generation of leaders, that daguo had created a global strategy.

III
A Charm Strategy

By the early 2000s China's charm offensive had begun. From the top, the Beijing leadership set out its goals. As Chinese leaders constantly emphasized, China desires stability and peace with all countries, and especially those on its borders—frontiers with fourteen nations, ranging from dynamic Vietnam to tiny Laos to colossal Russia to backward North Korea. "Safeguarding peace, promoting development and enhancing cooperation, which is the common desire of all peoples, represents the irresistible historical trend," China's Foreign Ministry announced in a white paper.[1]

Chinese scholars and officials eventually developed the term *heping jueqi*, or Peaceful Rise. First used by Zheng Bijian, a powerful senior adviser to the Chinese leadership, the term soon became a part of Chinese leaders' speeches and central to academic studies of China's future, though some Chinese scholars thought *rise* sounded menacing, and Chinese leaders now often use the phrase "Peaceful Development" instead. At its core, explained Zheng, a close associate of Chinese President Hu Jintao, Peaceful Rise meant that, unlike past emerging powers whose new might had caused shock waves across the world, China would threaten no nation, even as it becomes a global power. China's rise "will not come at the cost of any other country, will not stand in the way of any other country, nor pose a threat to any other country," said Prime Minister Wen Jiabao in a 2004 speech that encapsulated the Peaceful Rise idea.[2]

The Chinese leadership created Peaceful Rise as it realized that its hard power remained relatively weak. In the mid-1990s, China had tried to use military strength to intimidate other countries in Asia, by aggressive moves like sending ships to unoccupied, disputed reefs in the South China Sea. At the same time, Beijing called on other nations in the region to abandon their alliances, mostly with the United States, arguing that these had been made obsolete by the Cold War. This strategy backfired. Countries across the region condemned Beijing's aggressive behavior and solidified their military links with the United States, drawing the US armed forces closer into the region, and closer to China—exactly what Beijing did not want. Nations like the Philippines, located right in the South China Sea, started convening National Security Council meetings just to deal with the possibility of Chinese military activity. China would then criticize nations like the Philippines for their response, only engendering more mistrust of Beijing. Overall, as the regional specialist Denny Roy found in the late 1990s, China seemed to have no coherent, effective foreign policy in Asia.[3]

Beijing eventually recognized its mistakes: seizing reefs had turned countries against China, but offering assistance during the Asian financial crisis had won friends. As Chinese officials told me, after internal debate, the leadership in Beijing decided to tone down the military action and instead focus on building China's global soft power. In his landmark study of China's new engagement of Asia, the scholar David Shambaugh, too, suggests that after an internal policy discussion in Beijing, Chinese leaders decided "to have a peaceful environment conducive to domestic development" and that "China needed to be more proactive in shaping its regional environment." Furthermore, by focusing on soft power, the former intelligence officer Robert G. Sutter notes in his recent book *China's Rise in Asia: Promises and Perils*, Beijing could avoid directly confronting the United States, the unrivaled global hard power, while possibly weakening America's soft power in the longer term.[4]

Wooing, not intimidating, would now be the order of business. "We should . . . establish a publicity capacity to exert an influence on world opinion that is as strong as China's international standing," announced Jiang Zemin. Promoting peace would serve several functions for Beijing. It would allow China's economy to continue growing, holding up the regime's end of the bargain with the Chinese intelligentsia, and therefore forestalling any major national protests. Peace would foster prosperity, providing opportunities for Chinese companies looking overseas for outlets for their goods, allowing resources like oil to flow in and out of China unimpeded, and paving the way for China to build its own national science and technology capabilities, which still relied heavily on imports of foreign research and technology. "China aims to be one of the front-runners [in technology] among developing countries around 2010 . . . and [to be in] the medium level among world giants in science and technology eleven years later," noted Bai Chunli, vice president of the Chinese Academy of Sciences.[5]

Peace also would help China portray itself as a benign, peaceful, and constructive actor in the world. In the West and in many developing nations, China's military actions in the 1990s, and its powerhouse economy, had created a "China threat" school of thought among many scholars—the idea that, indeed, a rising China, like rising Japan and Germany in the early twentieth century, would threaten the world. As the China scholar David Lampton outlines, policy makers in many countries responded to this idea of a Beijing threat and adopted what he calls a strong China paradigm. In Lampton's strong China paradigm, policy makers take for granted that China will increasingly use its strength to wield power abroad, and they consider how other countries should prepare for potential power rivalry with Beijing.[6]

Changing China's image and undermining the scenario of a China threat, then, were vital to Beijing—and crucial to the future of its foreign policy. With this change, Beijing would diminish fears of China's future military power, or concerns that China's massive economic growth would divert trade and foreign investment from other nations. Chinese leaders drove this point home in speech after speech. "It is only through the road of peaceful development that the progress of the human race . . . can be achieved," Hu Jintao said in one such speech. "History tells us that any attempt by a country to realize its interests through the use or threat of force, or to place its interests above those of other nations, will get nowhere. Such attempts are against the tide of history of human development and against the fundamental interests of people all over the world."[7]

Peace also would allow Beijing to pursue its second goal: obtaining enough resources to feed its economy. Soon to become the world's largest consumer of oil, already the major market for copper, iron ore, aluminum, and platinum, and desperate for timber, China needs access to critical commodities. More than 300 million people may migrate from rural areas of China to cities and towns by 2020, only adding to demand. In his major address of 2006, Wen Jiabao mentioned energy a whopping twenty-eight times. China faces a "growing dependence on imports of some important minerals from foreign countries," Wen told his countrymen in another briefing. As a measure of how important access to resources has become to Beijing, Prime Minister Wen also has formed an internal government task force focused on the nation's energy needs, and staffed the task force with China's highest officials.[8]

According to Erica Downs, an energy analyst at the Brookings Institution in Washington who closely follows debate within the Chinese leadership, Beijing believes that it cannot trust the world markets for long-term supplies of oil, gas, minerals, and other commodities, since the United States controls the global sea lanes and has long-standing relationships with key oil suppliers like Saudi Arabia. China has no real strategic petroleum reserve, and its own domestic oil and gas production continues to decline, so Chinese leaders, Downs says, fear that the United States could stop China from obtaining resources if there were a conflict between Washington and Beijing. To prevent this possibility, China must win the trust of foreign states that control stakes in oil, gas, and other resources. In the long run, most energy analysts believe, China wants to control the entire process of resource extraction, from taking commodities out of the ground to shipping them back to China. "If the world oil stocks were exceeded by growth, who would provide energy to China?" one informal adviser to the Chinese government mused to reporters, explaining China's desire for control. "America would protect its own energy supply."[9]

Smoother international relations would facilitate China's third goal: building a ring of allies who share Beijing's suspicion of nations intervening in other countries' affairs. In some developing nations, like Iran or Burma or Zimbabwe, China may also seek to help these countries to remain authoritarian states—states thus more likely to remain close to China.[10]

Not all of Beijing's goals follow from Peaceful Rise, though. Taiwan is a special case. The Chinese leadership wants to reduce the international influence of Taiwan, which it considers a province of China. Beijing first enunciated this strategy in 1994, when the Chinese leadership declared that it would "use all economic and diplomatic resources to reward countries that are willing to isolate Taiwan." In the 1990s, as Taiwan became a democracy, the Taiwanese leader Lee Teng-hui had tried to boost Taiwan's power through a "Go South" strategy of boosting Taiwanese investment in Southeast Asia and upgrading Taiwan's informal relations with developing nations around the world.[11]

But China wants to roll back any of Taiwan's gains. Since most of Taiwan's remaining formal allies are in Africa and Latin America, China hopes to persuade these nations to switch recognition, establishing formal diplomatic relations with Beijing and stating that Taiwan is an integral part of China. By winning friends away from Taiwan, China also could tighten Taiwan's room to maneuver in international organizations.

China also wants to demonstrate to the world that it can be a great power, a *daguo,* and perhaps ultimately an equal of the United States. As the scholars Evan S. Medeiros and M. Taylor Fravel have found, in Chinese journals Chinese strategists emphasize that China should conduct great-power relations with other leading nations, like the United States. Indeed, throughout Chinese-language journals, scholars argue that China must show the globe it has arrived as a great power. "By the middle of the 21st century China will be among the great powers in the world," noted Xia Liping, professor at the Shanghai Institute of International Studies, summing up the conventional wisdom among Chinese officials. "Although the United States wants to realize a single-polar world . . . the trend of multi-polarization"—the rise of other great powers—"will continue to develop."[12]

As a great power, China might even shift influence away from the United States, creating its own sphere of influence for places like Southeast Asia, where China's power is strongest. In this sphere, countries would subordinate their interests to China's and think twice about supporting the United States should there be any conflict in the region, and China would have a final say on important political, economic, and strategic issues.

By the early 2000s Beijing also had developed the subtle strategies needed to achieve these goals. These strategies were not entirely responsible for changing global views of China—international events, like the declining image of America, came into play, as did individual countries' strategic calculations of how best to respond to China's charm. But Beijing clearly has come to employ conscious strategies. In statements and speeches, Chinese leaders began to enunciate a doctrine of "win-win" relations, highlighting that Latin American and African and Asian and Arab nations might benefit from their relationships with China even as China benefits from its relationships with them. In one major address given in 2005, entitled "An Open Mind for Win-Win Cooperation," Chinese President Hu told Asian leaders, "Dialogue and consultation . . . is an important avenue to win-win cooperation. . . . [China] will only [promote] peace, stability, and prosperity." "The aim of Sino-African cooperation is mutual benefit. . . .

It is particularly conducive for the development of African countries," echoed assistant Foreign Minister He Yafei, in a speech marking Prime Minister Wen's 2006 tour of Africa.[13]

In other words, China would be everyone's friend; Beijing would listen to the needs and desires of other nations, supposedly without asking for anything in return; China would not interfere or meddle. Foreign nations could benefit because China would not make demands upon other nations' sovereignty, economic models, governance, or political culture. China also would not threaten or sanction anyone—it would reassure other countries that it had no aggressive desires. "To achieve peaceful development is a sincere hope and unremitting pursuit of the Chinese people," Beijing announced in a landmark policy statement entitled "China's Peaceful Development Road," playing into the broader concept of China's peaceful rising to power. China will "opt for dialogue in resolving disputes[,] step up cooperation in maintaining security, and bring about lasting peace and stability in Asia," Wen Jiabao told an audience of Asian leaders in 2003.[14]

This Chinese doctrine of noninterference, which would help build a string of allies like Iran and Venezuela, coincides with an era when, at least since the mid-1990s, American interventionists have become more influential in US foreign policy making—both liberal moralists who argue for humanitarian intervention and neoconservatives who support intervention to preemptively halt threats to American security. Consequently, American foreign policy elites increasingly have questioned the balance Washington should strike between respecting nations' sovereignty—a traditionally realist foreign policy position—and pushing for humanitarian action or democratization, whether in Iraq or Ukraine or anywhere else. Going along with this trend toward greater interventionism, in recent years the United States also has relied more on sanctions as a weapon, from comprehensive sanctions on new business in Burma to more targeted restrictions on the export of certain types of goods to countries like Syria. By comparison, Wen announced, in one speech, "We believe that people in different regions in countries . . . have their right and ability to handle their own issues."[15]

In supposedly trying to be nearly everyone's friend (Taiwan and Japan stand as notable exceptions), Beijing was displaying a type of pragmatism unthinkable to a previous generation of Chinese leaders. For past leaders, ideology defined relationships, trumping other factors. Now China would deal with any state it thought necessary to its aims. In the Philippines, China would ask to mediate between the government and communist insurgents, so alienating the communists that they started threatening Chinese businesspeople investing in the Philippines. In Nepal the Chinese government would offer support to the monarchy, even reportedly sending truckloads of arms and ammunition, despite the fact that the king was fighting—and eventually lost to—a *Maoist* rebel group pursuing the very military tactics that Chairman Mao himself had pioneered.[16]

In Cambodia, I discovered China's new pragmatism for myself. In the bowels of the Cambodian Parliament, a low-rise building crowded with tiny cubbyhole offices, I met Keo Remy, an outspoken member of the Sam Rainsy Party, a liberal Cambodian party known for its supporters in America and in Taiwan. Sitting on a small couch in an office packed with aging computers and unmatched tables and chairs, Keo Remy looked the part of a beleaguered opposition politician. A wispy goatee framed his narrow, sallow, worn face, and he rubbed the bags under his eyes and cracked his long, thin fingers.[17]

Keo Remy never had it easy. This was January 2006, and the head of his party, a mercurial former finance minister named Sam Rainsy, had fled Cambodia because the prime minister, the tough and ruthless Hun Sen, had charged him with defamation. (Rainsy eventually returned to Cambodia and reconciled with Hun Sen.) Another friend of Keo Remy's, an opposition activist, had been arrested for criticizing the government. Occasionally, Keo Remy stopped our interview to take calls from well-wishers worried he might be the next one heading to jail.

For years, Beijing had only complicated Keo Remy's troubles. Since 1997 China had become vastly more influential in Cambodia, as Beijing built close relations with the government in Phnom Penh, offered Cambodian sizable new aid flows, and promoted closer trade links with Cambodia. But none of this warmth filtered down to Keo Remy. The Chinese embassy in Phnom Penh had ignored the Sam Rainsy Party, perhaps because the party criticized China for its suppression of human rights, and because the shoestring party had little real power in Phnom Penh. Keo Remy received no invitations to Chinese embassy functions, and when he ran into Chinese officials in Phnom Penh, they never spoke to him. When Sam Rainsy had attended the inauguration of Taiwan's president, Chen Shui-bian, Beijing had demanded that Rainsy break off any future contacts with Chen's party. When he refused to do so, the Chinese government announced that it would aggressively monitor Rainsy's future behavior toward Taiwan.

But in 2003 a deadlocked national election—Hun Sen's party failed to get enough seats to form a government—left Cambodia without a Parliament for more than nine months. Suddenly, the Sam Rainsy Party seemed like a potential kingmaker, able to create a coalition with other opposition parties and maybe even form a government, which might put members of Parliament like Keo Remy into positions of serious power. "Then the Chinese ambassador started calling us," says Keo Remy with a laugh, even though his party's liberal members still had no love for Beijing. Keo Remy paid several visits to the Chinese embassy, where Chinese officials explained Beijing's growing trade with Cambodia and chalked up all the old friction with his party to misunderstandings. As Keo Remy left the embassy, he remembers, "They'd invite us to banquet with them [at the Chinese embassy], they'd drop hints about how they could aid us."

In July 2004 Cambodia ended nearly a year of political deadlock, as Hun Sen picked off some of the Sam Rainsy Party's allies, persuading them to form a government with him by offering them political pork by the truckload. The Sam Rainsy Party did not become part of the governing coalition. Calls from the Chinese embassy, Keo Remy says, immediately ceased.

China has backstopped this "win-win" rhetoric with real initiatives. Beginning in the late 1990s China enunciated what it called a "new security concept," in which it emphasized that Beijing and other nations could guarantee their security by working more closely with multilateral institutions and building mutual trust with their neighbors. (Elements of the "new security concept" were later incorporated into Peaceful Rise.) China soon began putting the new security concept into practice. These initiatives receive little coverage from a Washington press corps that focuses on summits, state visits, and other grand events of international relations, but they are vital to wooing developing nations. China has ended nearly all of its border disputes and has signed the Treaty of Amity and Cooperation, a document that commits the signers to mutual respect for the sovereignty and equality of the ten countries in the Association of Southeast Asian Nations. Beijing has committed to creating a code of conduct on the South China Sea; it has signed the Southeast Asian Nuclear Weapon Free Zone, which commits the signers to forgo using, developing, or testing nuclear weapons in Southeast Asia; it has enthusiastically signed bilateral cooperative agreements and strategic partnerships with several Asian states, on a range of economic and strategic issues. In 2005 China even agreed to work with Vietnam and the Philippines on a joint exploration of the disputed South China Sea. Some of the agreements and partnerships are no more than vague commitments; others, like China's strategic partnership with Thailand, are more substantial, and contain specific elements that could eventually lead to more formal alliances.[18]

In Latin America and Africa the Chinese government has used similar initiatives. It has signed as many cooperative agreements as possible, to boost China's image as a benign, nonthreatening actor. These cooperative agreements eventually could be used as building blocks for more substantial partnerships. During a trip to Mexico in January 2005, Vice President Zeng Qinghong signed seven cooperation accords on maritime transportation, judicial assistance, and other issues, then signed an agreement with the foreign ministers of the Andean states to deepen political links. Similarly, on a visit to Venezuela in 2005, Zeng signed nineteen such accords on technology transfer and other topics. In Africa, Beijing helped establish a Forum on China-Africa Cooperation in 2000, then used the forum to create a Program for China-Africa Cooperation in Economic and Social Development, which outlined plans for closer cooperation on economic, health, development, and diplomatic issues. It also signed more than forty bilateral cooperation agreements with African nations.[19]

Beijing seems willing to sign these agreements, leaving details to be hammered out later. "The Chinese just say, 'Here, let's deal, and we'll take care of the particulars . . . later,'" said one Southeast Asian diplomat. In the lawyerly—but democratic—American political system, this type of sign-first-talk-later diplomacy would be virtually impossible, anathema to Congress and American businesses used to scrutinizing every detail and every sector of a US agreement with a foreign nation. The United States has not signed Southeast Asia's Treaty of Amity and Cooperation, and as one congressional official says, "We need to participate in some of these events, the high-profile ones, even if we think they're stupid. The symbolism matters."[20]

In general, China's soothing language of nonintervention can provide a sharp contrast with the United States, which Chinese officials paint as a hegemon unwilling to listen to other nations' concerns and slapping sanctions on other countries, like Burma or North Korea and Cuba. By allying with China, Beijing suggests, countries can avoid the onerous economic and political changes demanded by Washington and its Western allies. "The Chinese government has always advocated full respect for sovereign equality [and] noninterference in the internal affairs of other countries," China's deputy permanent representative to the United Nations said at the UN General Assembly in 2001, during a debate about Cuba. "The international community as a whole has a strong desire for a certain country to forsake its outdated practice of economic embargo."[21]

This message can be compelling, and not only to leaders in the ring of authoritarian states China may want to cultivate.

Elites and populaces in many newly democratic nations, such as Mexico or Indonesia, often resent US criticism of their human rights records. When these countries were ruled by authoritarian regimes, US pressure on human rights often resonated with local democrats. But today even some committed Mexican or Indonesian democrats disdain US criticism of human rights records, which they see as demeaning and blind to their nations' progress. In Mexico the government, now led by a former opposition party, has expressed anger after American officials criticized Mexican police for corruption and use of torture.[22] Beijing has responded by engaging Mexican officials in discussion on human rights issues—a discussion probably designed to portray both China and Mexico as unfair targets of American criticism.

China's noninterventionist language also mirrors some of the ideas enunciated by many developing nations' own regional organizations, since smaller developing countries often fear being overpowered by larger states. To take one example, since its founding four decades ago, the Association of Southeast Asian Nations has always adhered to a code of noninterference in member states' affairs, a code that fits easily with China's message.[23]

Beijing also reversed its previous disdain for multilateral organizations, which older Chinese leaders had seen as constraints on China's power and venues for other nations to criticize China. "Over the past decade . . . China has become a born-again regional multilateralist," said Susan Shirk, the former deputy assistant secretary of state. In part, China may have realized that by avoiding multilateral organizations in the past, it had only stoked fears of Beijing, since other countries had less interaction with Chinese diplomats and few forums to discuss issues of concern with Chinese leaders. By engaging with multilateral organizations like the Association of Southeast Asian Nations and fostering more interactions between foreign and Chinese officials, China can reduce fears of Beijing, giving it time to gain more influence without troubling other countries about its rise.[24] By working with multilateral organizations, Beijing also can signal to other countries that it can play by international rules and be a responsible power. It cannot have hurt that as the United States became less interested in multilateralism, China's participation in multilateral organizations made Beijing look more cooperative by comparison.

Again, China backed up its changing strategy with real initiatives. In Latin America, it joined the Organization of American States, the most important regional group, as an observer; it observed at the Inter-American Development Bank, the major international financial institution in Latin America; and it signed an agreement on closer relations with the Andean Community. In Africa, China began to provide support to the African Union and to play a larger role in the African Development Bank. In Asia, China joined the Association of Southeast Asian Nations as a dialogue partner, played a growing role in the Asean Regional Forum, became a major force behind the first East Asia Summit, and created an Asia Cooperation Fund to help Chinese government agencies increase their cooperation with Asean. In fact, according to Asian diplomats, China has initiated far more joint projects with the Association of Southeast Asian Nations than other Asean partners, like Japan or the United States.[25]

While the Bush administration focused its foreign policy strategy before September 11 on US relations with major powers, and then after September 11 on fighting terrorism, China also began portraying itself as the natural guardian of developing countries—more natural than the United States. "In 2002, the Chinese government looked at its foreign policy and ranked relations with the US first, and then relations with neighboring countries second," says Ruan Zongze, vice president of the China Institute for International Studies, a prominent Beijing think tank. "By two years later, China changed the rankings and ranked relations with neighboring countries first"—reflecting its priority on the developing world. Indeed, in the Chinese Communist Party's 2002 work report, the most important record of CCP priorities, the leadership made "becoming friends and partners with neighbors"—that is, nearby developing nations—a top strategic priority.[26]

At times, Chinese officials hit the idea of solidarity with the developing world hard. In an address in Brazil in 2004, Hu Jintao announced that China would always "stay on the side of the developing countries," and the following year Hu met with the leaders of Brazil, India, Mexico, and South Africa in an attempt to build a broader partnership of leading developing countries, so that they could work together in international organizations. Lower-ranking officials echo the message. In an address to the China-Latin America Friendship Association, National People's Congress Vice Chairman Cheng Siwei said, "Both [China and Latin America] belong to the developing world and have identical or similar views on many issues." Cheng also frequently refers to China and Latin America's shared histories of imperialism, telling one audience of Latin Americans, "I think we have very good feelings toward each other because we both have a history of being invaded by colonialists."[27]

In Asia the story was similar. "It was very clear that at meetings of the Asia Pacific Economic Cooperation [a group that promotes trade on the Pacific Rim,] that China was looking to be the spokesperson of the Third World countries," Federico Macaranas, a Filipino scholar who helped run APEC for years, told me. "They know if they ally themselves with the Third World, they can portray themselves as on our side." Macaranas was impressed by China's solicitousness. "Japan asks talented Filipino scientists to come to Japan and learn, and the Chinese send their scientists here, to look at the Philippines, to learn from the Philippines," he says. "If you want to really have partnership with the Third World, you can go see [them] on the ground."[28]

China's strategy also includes focusing on developing nations whose bilateral relationships with other major powers are faltering. Often, these countries are either authoritarian states or nations whose leaders display some autocratic traits, and thus could be sympathetic to Chinese influence; many also have significant energy resources, though energy is not the only reason China cultivates them. Beijing has aggressively courted Hugo Chávez as the Venezuelan leader has stepped up his confrontation with Washington, repeatedly inviting him on state visits to China, upgrading trade ties, and supporting Venezuela's bid for a seat at the United Nations Security Council. Though Chinese officials tried to downplay the Venezuelan leader's anti-US rhetoric, Chávez called China's moves a "Great Wall" against US hegemony and touted the two nations' "strategic alliance," while proclaiming that Beijing and Caracas were united in standing up to America.[29]

Similarly, when the left-wing populist Evo Morales won the presidency in Bolivia in 2005 and the United States responded by quickly proposing cuts in aid to Bolivia, China invited Morales to Beijing for one of his first state visits. Morales proclaimed China an "ideological ally" and asked China to help Bolivia develop its reserves of natural gas. In Uzbekistan, after the Bush administration criticized Tashkent following a massacre of some four hundred Uzbeks in 2005, China quickly expressed "resolute support" for Tashkent, inviting the Uzbek dictator Islam Karimov for a state visit highlighted by a twenty-one-gun salute and a treaty on friendship and cooperation. In Sudan, as Western nations isolated the Khartoum government for its human rights abuses and supposed links to terrorism, China stepped up its support. While the United States slapped sanctions on Khartoum, top Chinese politicians cultivated the Sudanese dictatorship, reportedly speeding up Chinese megaprojects in Sudan in time for the tenth anniversary of the dictator Omar Bashir's coup, to bring him more prestige.[30]

Iran is probably the most obvious example of China's cultivation of isolated autocrats. Though clearly uncomfortable with Iranian President Mahmoud Ahmadinejad's strident anti-American and anti-Israeli rhetoric, the Chinese government invited him to address the Shanghai Cooperation Organization, a leading summit of Chinese, Russian, and Central Asian leaders, held in China in June 2006. There the Iranian president delivered a major address on Chinese state television and touted Tehran's and Beijing's "identical" views on world issues. Meanwhile, China has hosted senior advisers to Supreme Leader Ayatollah Khameini, instructing them in Chinese economic and political management, and has backed massive investment into Iranian infrastructure by Chinese firms.[31]

But China has not only wooed autocrats. As the United States threatened to cut off military assistance because Ecuador would not agree to exempt US soldiers from prosecution at the

International Criminal Court, China invited Ecuadorian officials to Beijing and later offered Ecuador pledges of new assistance. In South Korea, a vital US ally, relations between Seoul and Washington have faltered in recent years over how to handle North Korea: South Korea, on North Korea's doorstep, prefers engagement to the Bush administration's harder-line approach. Seeking other partners, Seoul has looked to warmer ties with Beijing. Although China has never called on Seoul to choose between Beijing and Washington, it has cultivated politicians close to President Roh Moo-Hyun and former President Kim Dae Jung, according to numerous South Korean officials. Beijing also has launched a comprehensive cooperative partnership with Seoul and has publicly supported South Korea's engagement policy toward the North. Seoul's engagement of Pyongyang is in China's interest, since Beijing does not want the rapid collapse of the North Korean regime.[32]

Even in the Philippines, a former American colony where cable channels screen American National Basketball Association games and US fast food outlets employ bouncers, like chic bars, to keep out the crowds—"Is T.G.I. Friday's fine dining in the US?" one Filipino journalist asked me—China has waded in as US-Filipino relations grow less steady. After President Gloria Macapagal-Arroyo pulled Filipino troops out of Iraq in 2004, part of a deal to win the freedom of a Philippine hostage, the United States cut assistance to Manila. Shortly after, China invited Macapagal-Arroyo for a state visit, then aggressively wooed Philippine policy makers, offering greater cooperation and aid. "My boss came to Los Angeles and he was personally offended when he was searched down at the airport," said one Filipino official charged with escorting a top cabinet member to the United States. "Then he came to Washington and for forty-eight hours he didn't get any answer from the [US government representatives]. That really angered him. . . . Then when you go to China, they roll out the red carpet."[33]

A major component of China's appeal to developing nations is that Beijing portrays China as a potential ideal. In their dealings with other developing nations, Chinese officials suggest that China has developed a model for social and economic success, and in speeches to developing-world audiences they increasingly sell the China model. The former *Time* foreign editor Joshua Cooper Ramo calls this model the "Beijing Consensus," in contrast to the "Washington Consensus" of the 1990s, which stressed rapid free-market reforms as a path to prosperity. In the Beijing Consensus, Ramo says, growth comes from the state directing development to some degree, avoiding the kind of chaos that comes from rapid economic opening, and thus allowing a nation to build its economic strength. Minxin Pei calls China's model gradualist reform dictated by authoritarian politics: the Communist Party introduced economic reforms and built economic institutions slowly, maintaining a large state sector in the economy, and simultaneously did whatever was necessary to ensure the Party's survival.[34]

Whether or not one calls it a Beijing Consensus, China clearly promotes its socioeconomic model through speeches overseas, a model of top-down control of development and poverty reduction in which political reform is sidelined for economic reform. (In Chinese publications, Chinese government-linked think tanks and media have embraced Ramo's phrase and have contrasted it with the Washington Consensus.) And this model stands in direct contrast to democratic liberalism, the economic and political model emphasizing individual rights and civil liberties that has underpinned the societies of the West, and of its democratic allies in Asia.[35]

On the road, Chinese officials do not shy away from advertising the benefits of China's socioeconomic model. As Drew Thompson, a China scholar who has studied Beijing's advances toward Africa, found, "The Chinese government has also actively promoted their own brand of economic development and reform model to African countries, encouraging . . . African governments to fashion their economic systems after [China's] own."[36]

China seems to have enjoyed striking success with its antiliberal model—decades of economic success and poverty reduction other developing nations can't help but notice. At the same time, the Washington Consensus has failed many developing nations. During the late 1980s and the 1990s, many African and Latin American nations opened their economies, slashed tariffs, and undertook other painful economic reforms, yet few nations in either Latin America or Africa saw their economies take off. Even when these poor regions boosted growth, it seemed to have no measurable impact on employment, leaving masses of unemployed people willing to try another economic model, and leaders groping for answers as well. In Africa, for example, the United Nations Commission on Africa reported that while "Africa's real Gross Domestic Product grew by 4.6 per cent in 2004 . . . the growth has so far not been translated to employment creation or poverty reduction."[37] This failure of the Washington Consensus opened the door for nations like Bolivia or Argentina to embrace state-driven economics once again, even though that state-led model also had failed in the developing world in the past.

China's model particularly appeals to rulers in authoritarian or semiauthoritarian nations Beijing is cultivating. This only makes sense. Rapid market reforms like the ones promoted in the Washington Consensus historically also have created pressure for political liberalization. With rapid economic reforms the ruling regime has less time to try to adapt to change and to figure out ways to co-opt the new businesspeople and other economic elites being created by reform. With the China model, the regime has time to co-opt the businesspeople and other elites it needs to keep on its side to remain in power. To someone like the head of the Communist Party in Vietnam or the president of Uzbekistan, the proof cannot be ignored: China has liberalized much of its economy, yet the Communist Party still rules the country.

In small countries, China's friendship can seem almost overwhelming in its generosity. China offers the smallest nations significant respect, in contrast to the supposed American preference for building bilateral ties with the most important actors. "Smaller countries like the fact that they are treated as heads of state when they come to China—so even if they come from St. Kitts and Nevis, they get great deference in Beijing, which they might not get in Washington," says Dan Erikson, head of a project on China–Latin America relations at the Inter-American Dialogue, a Washington think tank.[38]

China's focus on small nations receives little attention in the US policy community or media, a lack of attention Beijing may prefer. Without any spotlight, it is easy to apply pressure on smaller countries, getting them in the habit of surrendering to a larger country's will. Small gains add up: as anyone who plays the Chinese classic strategy game Go knows, one way to beat your enemy is to quietly build relations with small players until your rival is surrounded.

Countries don't get much smaller than Laos, a poor

country of six million people, most of whom survive by subsistence farming. In 1975, after the Vietnam War, which resulted in the Lao communists overrunning the country, Laos slipped into slumber, a landlocked backwater run. On my first visit in 1998, I noticed that several hundred yards from the airport in Vientiane, the capital, the "highway" turned into a narrow dirt road. Along the sides of the road, water buffalo threshed rice and barefoot children rode the backs of wooden oxcarts. Laos's small, secretive ruling elite also had been ignored by most of the world. For decades, the United States still did not grant Laos normal trading relations, though Laos's human rights record was no worse than the record of China, with whom America traded vigorously. American sanctions on Laos infuriated Lao officials, who didn't understand why such a big country like the United States would punish a minnow—especially since during the Vietnam War, America had dropped more bombs on Laos than it dropped on Germany and Japan together during World War II, leaving Laos riddled with unexploded ordnance.

In the late 1990s Laos suddenly found another potential patron—one that didn't bother with sanctions and, Lao officials said, seemed to understand what a poor country needed to survive.[39] Senior Chinese officials started showing up in Vientiane, dragging Chinese business delegations with them. Though China had long enjoyed relations with Laos, a supposedly brother communist country, now it was stepping up its courtship. And Laos's leadership welcomed the attention.

Around this time, in the fall of 2000, I was sent to Laos to cover a story. Knowing that I would be spending several days in somnolent Vientiane, I called a woman I knew who lived there and who I hoped might take a romantic interest in me. We met one night and she suggested an evening sipping cold beers at one of the quaint stands overlooking the broad Mekong River. But we couldn't find any Mekong stands. Jiang Zemin had arrived in town, the first state visit by a Chinese leader to Vientiane. For Jiang, the Lao government spared no expense, though Laos suffers from African levels of poverty. Laos was throwing endless banquets in honor of the Chinese delegation—and tearing down the beer stands to make room for the parties. A grateful Lao prime minister told Jiang that his trip was "a historical visit" and that China's economic growth "has set a good example for us in constructing and developing our country." Jiang responded, playing the developing-country solidarity card: "All countries in the world, small or large, have their own merits. Thus, each should learn from others' strong points." Just to make his point clear, Jiang announced, "The characteristics of our ties can be summed up as mutual trust, mutual support, equal treatment, non-interference of the other's affairs, and sincere cooperation."[40]

The story of Jiang's visit had a happy ending for my friend and me. Instead of beers, we migrated to an Italian restaurant in town and hit it off; three years later we were married. It had a happy ending for the Lao government too, if not always for average Lao people. Soon after, Laos, like other countries being wooed by China, was hit with China's whole toolbox of influence, from aid to trade to promotion of Chinese culture and language. When I returned to Vientiane five years later, a new delegation of top Chinese officials had arrived in town. This time, Laos did not need to move any stands or vendors to make way for the Chinese. The Chinese delegation could meet their hosts inside the giant new cultural hall in downtown Vientiane, paid for by Beijing.

IV
The Tools of Culture

As China has built a global strategy, it also has developed more sophisticated tools of influence, which it deploys across the world. These tools fall into two categories. First, China utilizes tools of culture and diplomacy—tools related to Chinese culture and arts and language and ethnicity. China's growing economic might allows Beijing to deploy these tools, since of course it costs money to hold cultural summits or send language teachers to other nations. But these tools are not dependent upon trade and investment.

China's cultural promotion is part of a broader effort at public diplomacy. Public diplomacy, according to one accepted definition, is the cultivation by governments of public opinion in other nations; by cultivating this public opinion abroad, states can more effectively pursue their national interests. Until recently, China either paid no attention to public diplomacy or, when it did, made clumsy attempts that bordered on pure propaganda, like China Radio International, an international broadcaster with programming that merely repeated

Chinese leaders' statements. According to a study by the scholar Rumi Aoyama, since the end of the Cold War, China has moved away from this pure propaganda toward more nuanced public relations, even changing the name of the Party's Propaganda Department to the Publicity Department. In the post–Cold War era, Aoyama found, Chinese public diplomacy has five main objectives: "Publicizing China's assertions to the outside world, forming a desirable image of the state, issuing rebuttals to distorted overseas reports about China, improving the international environment surrounding China, and exerting influence on the policy decisions of foreign countries."[1]

Since China announced the idea that peaceful development would be the core of its foreign policy, its public diplomacy has taken on another objective—selling the idea that China will not be a threat to other nations, a major undertaking for Beijing. China's public diplomacy efforts reinforce the concept of peaceful development, efforts like organizing an eleven-nation performance tour entitled "Voyage of Chinese Culture to Africa" and museum exhibits in Malaysia and Singapore to celebrate the six hundredth anniversary of the voyages of Zheng He, or Cheng Ho, a Chinese admiral who sailed across Asia, the Middle East, and Africa, encountering but never conquering other nations. "Zheng He treated other countries with friendship and respect instead of occupying a single piece of land, establishing a fortress, or seizing any treasure," Chinese Vice Minister of Communications Xu Zu-yuan announced, drawing an implicit contrast with Western colonists of that era. (Zheng He's voyages, scholars note, did sometimes include violent encounters with locals, and they may have facilitated a kind of Chinese economic colonialism of other regions of the world.)[2]

Part of this new public diplomacy has been an effort to increase cultural exchanges with the developing world. China has begun hosting overseas scholars, the kind of programming that the US State Department has long conducted. "China shows its understanding of Thailand by inviting people from every circle of Thai society to China—artists, academics," says one professor at Bangkok's Kasetsart University. "The Chinese inviting of Thai professors to study in China has really grown in the past four or five years." Beijing also has created a Chinese version of the Peace Corps, run by the China Association of Youth Volunteers, to send idealistic young Chinese on long-term volunteer service projects to developing nations like Laos, Ethiopia, and Burma, where fifteen Chinese volunteers arrived in early 2006 to work on Burmese agriculture and sports projects.[3]

China also has expanded the international reach of its media. It has upgraded the Chinese newswire Xinhua, created new overseas editions of the *People's Daily* newspaper, established a formal briefing system at the Ministry of Foreign Affairs so that journalists can hold modern press conferences, and expanded and professionalized the international broadcasting of CCTV, Chinese state television. This expansion included hiring Western anchors and making CCTV news look more polished. Satellite television subscribers in Asia now can receive a package of Chinese channels, just as Spanish-speaking viewers can watch CCTV's new Spanish service.[4]

Meanwhile, though Xinhua originally fed news back to Chinese publications—and to the Party—now it is picked up in newspapers across the developing world and even by American news sites like Google. Since newspapers run it, Xinhua also gets cited by scholars as a real news source, just like another newswire; when I pick up the paper in Indonesia or Argentina, I often see stories by Xinhua and wonder whether locals think the service is any different from Reuters.

Yet Xinhua is not Reuters or another private corporation: it remains run by China's State Council, essentially an organ of the government; the Xinhua office even served as the de facto Chinese embassy in Hong Kong before the handover in 1997. Xinhua takes orders from the Party's Publicity Department, exhibiting the kind of reverence for government spin that the White House could only dream about. It cannot produce evenhanded coverage of topics sensitive to Beijing, like Taiwan or Tibet. After the death in 2005 of Zhao Ziyang, the most reform-minded Chinese leader, who was purged after the Tiananmen riots of 1989, state media published only a brief obituary, though Zhao had been one of the most important leaders in modern Chinese history. Xinhua's reporters still receive training, or indoctrination, sessions heavy in seminars on the necessary role of the Communist Party. Its journalists also still provide a kind of intelligence information service for top Chinese leaders. According to the global watchdog Reporters Without Borders, "Hand-picked journalists, who are regularly indoctrinated, produce reports for the Chinese media that give the official point of view and others—classified 'internal reference' for the country's leaders. . . . Xinhua remains at the heart of the censorship and disinformation system established by the Chinese Communist Party."[5]

The new Chinese public diplomacy also includes setting up networks of informal summits, either in China or in the developing world, designed to bring together opinion leaders. These summits allow China to subtly emphasize its role as a potential partner for investment and trade and its position as a leader of the developing world. The larger informal summits include the China-Caribbean Economic and Trade Cooperation Forum, attended last year by nearly one thousand officials from China and the Caribbean; the Boao Forum for Asia, which brings together Asian businesspeople into a Davos-style World Economic Forum–like event; and the Asean-China Eminent Persons Group, which unites former statesmen and has produced a comprehensive roadmap for the future of Southeast Asia–China relations. The Chinese government also has promoted smaller summits, making Beijing a center for meetings of international Chinese-language media and of Chinese studies associations.[6]

As China has upgraded its public diplomacy, like broadcasting and visitor programs, it also has invested in improving its diplomatic corps. Over the past fifteen years, Chinese diplomats told me, the Ministry of Foreign Affairs has begun to retire older, more ideological diplomats, replacing them with a young generation of envoys who speak better English and local languages. One 2005 study suggested that one-half of the country's four thousand diplomats are less than thirty-five years old. According to another study of China's relations with Latin America, since the 1980s Beijing has actively tried to upgrade the quality of its diplomats in the Western Hemisphere. It has sent 110 young Chinese officials to a university in Mexico to learn Spanish and deepen their understanding of Latin America. It has improved the capacity of its own think tanks focusing on Latin America, ensuring that comprehensive research was available on the Western Hemisphere for Chinese officials. And China kept its Latin America specialists focused on Latin America, so that someone like Jiang Yuande, China's ambassador to Brazil in 2006, had already done thirty years of tours around the Portuguese-speaking world, in countries like Angola and Cape Verde, before he arrived in Brasilia.[7]

China can keep these diplomats in the region because, unlike the United States, which until recently allowed Foreign

Service officers significant leeway to choose postings, the Chinese Ministry of Foreign Affairs can mandate overseas assignments. Chinese diplomats say that the ministry has pushed envoys to focus on one country and repeatedly return there, rather than moving from, say, Uzbekistan to Mexico, as an American diplomat might. Top Chinese diplomats in nations like Cambodia or Thailand now often have done three or even four rotations in those countries before rising to the rank of ambassador, developing extensive contacts in the local business and political communities and building language skills to the point that locals sometimes think they are native speakers. "China sends the A team here," says one US diplomat in Thailand. "Their ambassador here is really plugged in, and speaks excellent Thai." "It used to be that the Chinese officials just stayed in the embassy, and you never saw them," says one Asian diplomat who served in the Philippines. "Now they are so skilled on the ground they know more than anyone else. If someone's wife is having an affair, they know it. If someone is having problems with their kid, they know it." By comparison, a Council on Foreign Relations analysis of Southeast Asia warned that a "critical shortfall in US regional policy is our lack of a skilled core of professionals familiar with the language, culture, and political-military climates."[8]

Beijing supports its diplomacy through constant visits by senior Chinese officials to developing nations, and through nonstop coverage in Xinhua. In a study of China's new global foreign policy, National Defense University's Philip Saunders found that in 2002 China's president and premier spent more than four times as many days abroad as they had in 1993. In Asia, a short hop from Beijing but a twenty-hour flight from Washington, the contrast in face time by senior officials can be stark. A Singaporean diplomat estimated that China sends nearly three hundred senior-level delegations annually to the city-state, far outstripping any American efforts; many visits include the signing of new agreements on trade or investment. As one US ambassador in Southeast Asia remembers, when Southeast Asian nations last year decided to create an early warning system to prevent future tsunamis, the United States sent a low-level official to the brainstorming group. The Chinese, by contrast, sent a senior cabinet-level official, who reaped plaudits for Beijing. "It was like God had appeared at a conference," the ambassador remembers.[9]

Across the developing world, in fact, diplomats constantly complain that they do not see enough of top American officials, who have focused intensely on the Middle East. Southeast Asian nations raged that Secretary of State Condoleezza Rice skipped a major annual regional meeting in 2005. One White House policy maker bemoaned that she could not persuade America's former trade representative, Rob Portman, to make even one extended visit to Southeast Asia. In fact, when I compared visits by top Chinese and American officials—cabinet rank in America or the Chinese equivalent—to Thailand and Cambodia in 2004 and 2005, I found that senior Chinese officials made at least twice as many visits to Bangkok and Phnom Penh.[10]

Promotion of Chinese-culture and Chinese-language studies is a major component of this public diplomacy. As Hu Youqing, a deputy to the National People's Congress, told the *China Daily*, promoting the use of the Chinese language will contribute to spreading Chinese culture and increasing China's global influence.[11] "It can help build up our national strength and should be taken as a way to develop our country's soft power," Hu said.

Around the world, the Chinese government has launched several measures to increase the teaching of Chinese. Beijing now funds at least the first year of what it calls Confucius Institutes, Chinese-language and -culture schools created at leading local universities in countries from Kenya to South Korea to Uzbekistan to Australia. China plans to open at least one hundred Confucius Institutes around the world within the next five years. These Confucius Institutes are reminiscent of the British Council or the Alliance Française, which have helped promote British and French cultural brands without being explicitly linked, in people's minds, to Whitehall or the Elysée Palace. (The name Confucius Institute betrays no links to communism or to the Communist Party, and actually repudiates Mao, since the Chairman had tried to wipe out the teaching of Confucian beliefs.) If local universities that desire China studies beyond the Confucius Institute curriculum suffer from a lack of resources, they can call upon the Chinese Ministry of Education to lead intensive short courses for local Chinese-language teachers, or even to send Chinese teachers for a period of time. In Cambodia, for instance, the Chinese government, working with provincial governments in China, sends hundreds of instructors to Phnom Penh's Chinese schools, sparking requests for still more instructors from China. Similarly, in countries like Indonesia, Argentina, Kenya, and Thailand, China's Ministry of Education has begun dispatching groups of language teachers for one- and two-year stints, which are normally at least partially funded by the ministry.[12]

Beijing also has tried to push instruction in Mandarin and in Chinese culture in overseas primary schools, partly by signing agreements with countries like Thailand to help integrate Chinese into public schools' curricula, and partly by helping students in poor nations like Cambodia attend private local Chinese-language primary schools. In Thailand the Chinese Ministry of Education has vowed to help train one thousand Mandarin teachers per year and offer other Chinese-language resources. Generally, these private schools receive some assistance from mainland Chinese governmental and private sources—the Chinese newspapers in Cambodia are full of reports of small grants given to Cambodian Chinese-language schools from mainland Chinese governments and language associations. Because the Chinese-language schools in Cambodia receive this outside funding, they can charge less than many public schools, where impoverished (and sometimes corrupt) Cambodian teachers demand excess payments, in addition to their salaries, just to teach classes. Cambodian parents thus view the Chinese-language schools as providing a finer, less corrupt education, and not surprisingly want to send their children there.[13]

While promoting Chinese studies in other nations, Beijing also has tried to lure more foreign students to China. The Ministry of Education has done so by advertising Chinese universities abroad, creating new scholarship programs for students from the developing world, loosening visa policies for foreign students, and increasing spending to lure elite foreign scholars from the West to teach in China, thereby upgrading China's university system. Beijing has focused intensely on Chinese-born scholars working in the West, creating national programs named *rencai qiang guo* (Strengthening the Country Through Human Talent), charging the Finance Ministry to make funds available to entice these Chinese-born scholars, or *haigui pai,* to return, and pushing select Chinese universities to use 20 percent of their government funding on hiring scholars from abroad.[14] Returnees have been welcomed from the very top: Hu Jintao himself announced that the returnees would be "irreplaceable" in China today.

The incentives may be working. In places like Cambodia, a kind of feeder system has been created. Students who do well in China-backed primary schools in Cambodia often can obtain assistance from China to continue studies in the People's Republic, in either middle school, high school, or university. (China has opened roughly five hundred of its primary and middle schools to foreign students.) The Overseas Chinese Affairs Office of the Chinese government has provided scholarships for poor Cambodians to study in China since 2000; in Laos, the Chinese government hands out some 230 scholarships per year for students to attend Chinese universities. One study found that the number of Chinese returning to the mainland from Hong Kong, to take one example, rose from seven thousand in 1999 to thirty-five thousand in 2005, though China is not yet attracting back the top echelon of Chinese scholars. Meanwhile, in 2006 China landed one of its university MBA programs in the top twenty-five on the *Financial Times'* ranking of the world's finest business schools, alongside such luminaries as Wharton and Insead in France.[15]

Taiwan and the United States, both of which historically trained many students from the developing world, unwittingly have helped China's efforts to woo foreign students. Between the 1960s and the 1990s Taipei provided funds for thousands of ethnic Chinese students from across the world to study Chinese language, culture, and other topics at Taiwanese universities—a traditional source of Taiwan's soft power. But the current government in Taipei, worried about tight budgets and Taiwan's weak economy, has cut subsidies for foreigners to study in Taiwan. So while generations of older Malaysian Chinese received their higher education in Taiwan, built links to Taiwanese elites, and developed sympathy for Taiwan, today Malaysian Chinese told me their sons and daughters study in Beijing University or Fudan University in Shanghai. As a result, these children know almost nothing about Taiwan.[16]

After September 11, meanwhile, the United States tightened student visa policies, making it far harder for students from most developing nations to attend school in America and for academics to come to the United States to lecture or learn. Even for foreign students already studying in the United States, life became harder: in 2003 Washington announced that men from Muslim countries like Bangladesh, Indonesia, and Jordan residing in the United States would have to register with American immigration by a specified deadline or face criminal prosecution. Many foreign students simply left, and no one replaced them. In 2003, for example, the number of Indonesians studying in America plummeted by more than 20 percent.[17]

Many of the students heading to China for higher degrees, or signing up for Chinese-language courses in Buenos Aires or Jakarta or Bangkok, already come from ethnic Chinese backgrounds. On a hazy Saturday in March 2006, with thick humidity that verged on actual raindrops, I walked through the major Chinese cemetery in the Philippine capital of Manila, set on a high point near the city's Chinatown, a narrow warren of stores and tiny alleys, where traditional medicine shops featuring personal feng shui advisers abut Filipino Chinese gold merchants and street vendors hiding pirated copies of *Brokeback Mountain* and other new Hollywood releases inside their shirts.

From the cemetery hills I could look out onto Manila's endless sprawl of poverty, tin-roofed shacks and "jeepneys," the main means of public transport for Filipinos—aging Japanese trucks painted with lurid murals of Christ and pictures of naked women, and carrying crowds of passengers sardined into their bays. Although many Southeast Asian nations have prospered over the past five decades, the Philippines has remained a Latin American–esque economy, with a tiny, wealthy elite and a vast underclass. Fifteen percent of Filipinos earn less than a dollar per day, and in Manila tens of thousands of poor people climb through garbage dumps, scavenging through the trash to survive. Manila residents have grown so desperate that thirty thousand of them recently stampeded the gate of a reality television show giving away cash prizes, crushing at least seventy-nine people to death.[18]

Inside the cemetery, though, it's easy to forget about the filth and stench and chaos outside. Filipino Chinese have constructed elaborate, gated, aboveground tombs of marble and granite and plaster, some as large as a small home. The tombs sit next to each other in long rows, with small roads leading through the tomb city. Inventive families have commissioned pagoda roofs or detailed metal grilles or gargoyles for their crypts, or constructed vaults that resemble stark modernist architecture, all glass and metal and sharp angles. The most elaborate structures contain full sets of modern appliances like televisions and microwaves, presumably so the dead can enjoy the latest DVD soap operas and prepackaged food in the next life. Every few minutes, I see a late model Mercedes or Lexus pull up to one of the tombs and disburse a large Chinese Filipino family, the boys in sharp suits, the girls carrying packages of offerings like fruit and fresh flowers for their dead relatives, the family drivers in sharp livery wear.

The cemetery reminds me that ethnic Chinese minorities, many originally from the coastal provinces of southeastern China, where arable land is scarce and population pressure intense, have long played an important role in the Philippines—and across the developing world. Even before the Spanish colonists arrived in the Philippines five hundred years ago, small-scale Chinese merchants were trading with indigenous villages across the Philippine archipelago. Some of these Chinese merchants stayed, building settlements or integrating themselves with the local population.[19]

For centuries, many nations viewed these ethnic Chinese arrivals as outsiders, even after they had lived in places like the Philippines for centuries. And after they left China, the imperial Chinese government shunned them, too. Before the nineteenth century, the Chinese imperial government branded Chinese émigrés as traitors to the nation—traitors to their homeland and ancestors. The Ming government issued orders prohibiting Chinese who emigrated from ever returning to the country. "I believe that the majority of those who go overseas are undesirable elements," the Ming emperor announced.[20]

In response, ethnic Chinese outside China often formed close-knit social and business communities, relying upon informal means of raising capital, sometimes agreeing not to compete with other ethnic Chinese companies, and often keeping company shareholdings limited to family members, even as their firms grew into giants. That states targeted Chinese communities during times of turmoil—as in Indonesia in 1965, when fears of communist influence from Maoist China resulted in massacres that targeted Indonesian Chinese and killed at least half a million people—only tightened the bonds among ethnic Chinese and led them to avoid ties to mainland China during the Maoist era.[21]

Like the Philippines, Thailand boasts a sizable ethnic Chinese community, comprising 10 to 15 percent of the total population—mostly emigrants from Fujian and Guangdong provinces in southeastern China. During much of the twentieth century, as China descended into economic backwardness and Mao's revolutions alienated the Chinese diaspora, the Chinese in Thailand intermarried with Thais, took Thai names, and became Thai citizens. They came to dominate Thailand's economy, with a small number of Thai-Chinese families controlling Thai manufacturing.[22]

The Thai Chinese built conglomerates like Charoen Pokphand (CP), which started from typically humble origins. A CP founder, Chia Eksaw, came to Bangkok from China in 1921 with little more than a signboard, a ledger, and some vegetable seeds. He put out his sign and established a small seed shop in the Thai capital. When his fourth son, Dhanin, took over the business in 1964, he expanded it into a larger feed shop, and then diversified into farm equipment and other agricultural products. CP built close relations with important Thai officials and constantly innovated to improve its feed and chickens and other products. CP grew and expanded across the region, eventually becoming the biggest agroindustrial company in Southeast Asia, headquartered in a high-rise overlooking Bangkok's central business district and decorated with landscape paintings of Chinese mountains and rivers. By the beginning of this millennium, Dhanin alone controlled personal assets worth more than $1 billion.[23]

The company also maintained deep links to China, even during the Maoist period. When other foreign investors pulled out of China after the Tiananmen crisis, CP stayed in; it smoothed its China business through unusual favors like finding Thai elephants to provide to a Chinese tourist site. Eventually, in the 1990s, CP became the largest foreign investor in

China, though it probably has since been passed by Western multinationals.[24]

As in Thailand and the Philippines, in Indonesia, Malaysia, Cuba, Peru, Singapore, and many other countries, Chinese diaspora businesspeople have enjoyed similar success. Magazines have estimated the total wealth of the Chinese diaspora at more than $1.5 trillion; in Indonesia the ethnic Chinese comprise roughly 3 percent of the population but reportedly have controlled as much as 80 percent of the nation's economy. The ethnic Chinese tycoon Robert Kuok of Malaysia (estimated net worth $5 billion) built the Shangri-La Hotels chain; the ethnic Chinese tycoon Li Ka-Shing of Hong Kong (estimated net worth $13 billion) amassed a property empire; the ethnic Chinese tycoon Lucio Tan of the Philippines (estimated net worth $1.9 billion) constructed brewing and banking giants; and the ethnic Chinese tycoon Thaksin Shinawatra (estimated net worth $1.3 billion), who later became prime minister of Thailand, used political connections to start a computer business that he then expanded into a telecommunications and satellite technology empire.[25]

Of course, few diaspora Chinese reached this level of success. Most arrived in their new countries poor and stuck to small business or hard labor; many failed. Chinese came to Panama more than a century ago as low-wage laborers and concentrated in small-scale retail shops, creating a tight-knit community that follows news about Asia in local Mandarin-language newspapers and Cantonese radio stations. Chinese businesspeople settled in tiny East Timor decades ago, and today working-class ethnic Chinese merchants traverse the country on the back of pickup trucks, peddling clothes and cheap electronics out of burlap bags. Nearly 100,000 Chinese were shipped to Peru to work as coolies during the nineteenth century; many stayed on as laborers or small businesspeople.[26]

When Deng Xiaoping opened China's economy in the late 1970s, he realized that the People's Republic could draw upon this Chinese diaspora for capital. Deng and other top officials called on overseas Chinese to invest in mainland China and set up Special Economic Zones in places like Shenzhen, near Hong Kong, and Xiamen, near Taiwan and Southeast Asia, which were easily accessible to overseas Chinese capital. (Charoen Pokphand received foreign investment certificate 0001 in the Shenzhen Special Economic Zone.) Beijing passed a range of laws giving diaspora Chinese preferential treatment over other foreign investors and created more than fifty industrial zones specifically for Chinese returning from abroad. Provincial governments in places like Fujian added to these incentives with their own offers of land, industrial parks, and tax breaks for diaspora returnees.[27]

These policies worked. Between 1990 and 2002 foreign investors—primarily overseas Chinese—invested nearly $30 billion in Fujian Province alone, almost 7 percent of all foreign direct investment in China during that time period. Overall, between 1990 and 2002 just five countries—Thailand, Malaysia, Singapore, Indonesia, and the Philippines—invested roughly $90 billion in China, with most of the capital coming from diaspora Chinese firms. One study estimates that diaspora Chinese, including Chinese from Taiwan and Hong Kong, account for 80 percent of all foreign investment in mainland China.[28]

In the past ten years, the Chinese government has begun to view ethnic Chinese as more than merely sources of investment and technology. Diaspora Chinese have become vital to

Beijing's global charm offensive. In recent years, Beijing has rebuilt relations with ethnic Chinese organizations around the globe—groups ranging from cultural associations to clan organizations to business chambers—and directly called on these diaspora Chinese to help boost relations between China and the developing world.[29]

Some rebuilding simply involves recognizing diaspora Chinese groups' importance, by hosting meetings like the World Chinese Entrepreneurs Convention or sending important PRC ministers to visit ethnic Chinese abroad. According to Hong Liu of the National University of Singapore, in 2001 top officials from Beijing's Overseas Chinese Affairs Office visited more than twenty countries to hold meetings with leaders of diaspora Chinese communities. These meetings inspired diaspora Chinese to return to China; the number of Thais visiting China, for example, rose by more than 60 percent between 1997 and 2003, with most of that visitor traffic coming from ethnic Chinese Thais. China assists with return trips through programs like government-run summer camps for diaspora Chinese children entitled "Travel to China to Find your Roots." It supports new Chinese history textbooks designed for diaspora schools, produced in Hong Kong and emphasizing China's history of *guochi,* or national humiliation, at the hands of external powers.[30]

Some rebuilding involves cultivating leading ethnic Chinese tycoons in each nation, wooing them to publicly support Beijing. The tycoons' influence then trickles down into the larger ethnic Chinese community; in many cases, they can push the boards of Chinese chambers of commerce to remove pro-Taiwan members and develop closer ties to Beijing. In the Philippines, for example, Chinese officials and business delegations have taken care to woo Lucio Tan, not only one of the country's wealthiest men but also a major political player who was close to former President Joseph Estrada. Tan has installed businessmen close to him at the head of the powerful Filipino-Chinese Chambers of Commerce, which has promoted better relations with China.[31]

China has utilized this strategy in other countries with sizable ethnic Chinese communities. In Panama, for example, a 200,000-strong ethnic Chinese population relies on Chinese-language schools, which begin the day with a common anthem and learn from a standard curriculum. Unlike in Chinese schools in much of the world, this curriculum has an unusual component—the Panamanian students learn that Taiwan is a sovereign nation, near-heresy in most countries. Panama remains one of the few states that maintain diplomatic relations with Taiwan; Taiwan has given some $200 million to Panamanian schools, which are plastered with posters of Taiwanese tourist attractions.[32]

But Panama may not recognize Taiwan much longer. As China has become wealthier, and more aggressive diplomatically, it has reached out to Panama's ethnic Chinese. Whereas Taiwan traditionally brought important Panamanian Chinese opinion leaders to Taiwan for higher education, now China does the same. Whereas Taiwan has long sent Panama cultural entertainment like troupes of Chinese acrobats, now China does the same. Whereas Taiwan historically holds lavish national day celebrations in one of the classiest hotels in Panama City, now Beijing holds lavish national day celebrations—in the same hotel.

On one trip to Thailand, I found myself in one of the square, squat new office buildings that make every area of Bangkok look the same. A secretary escorted my friend and me into the offices of Amorn Apithanakoon, chairman of Galaxy, one of Thailand's biggest entertainment companies, which sells arcade games, karaoke machines, and anything else you need for a flashy new nightclub in Asia. Amorn sat in one corner of his massive office, at a small table, next to a Buddhist monk. Amorn had plastered the walls of his office with photos of himself alongside Thailand's royal family and sculptures made from jade, a symbol of good fortune in Chinese culture. There was so much jade in his office that it resembled the lair of some archvillain gem runner from a B spy movie.[33]

I sat down next to the monk, dressed in the traditional saffron robes and sandals. Amorn had laid three cell phones on the table. The monk and Amorn took turns fondling a new digital camera. "This man is good," the monk said to me in English, pointing at Amorn, a short older man with sleepy eyes, wearing a finely tailored suit and dirty running shoes. "He's a good man." Just to make sure I understood, he said it again: "Good man." Amorn and the monk returned to speaking in Thai (which I speak), and I learned that the monk previously had worked as a policeman, until he decided to switch to the clergy. Amorn apparently had become one of the monk's personal patrons. After about twenty minutes of chatting with him, Amorn finally dispatched the monk, who offered a stream of blessings as Amorn lowered his head. The Galaxy chairman handed the monk a wad of cash, and the clergyman left the room.

Like many Thai-Chinese businesspeople, Amorn's family hailed from southern China. Galaxy had made Amorn rich, but he wasn't content with just the company. Amorn had founded an organization in Bangkok called Uniting Chinese, which he said was designed to foster interaction among ethnic

Chinese around the world. Despite chatting with Amorn for over an hour, I could never tell whether he started the organization himself or whether someone had pushed him to do it. I did learn that the organization helped promote trips by Thai Chinese back to China, as well as to conferences in Bangkok about diaspora Chinese culture.

But the group also had become a kind of proxy weapon for Beijing. Twenty years ago, a tycoon like Amorn, or a group like Uniting Chinese, would not have attracted much attention from the Chinese embassy in town. But now the Chinese embassy in Bangkok was one of the largest and savviest in the entire Chinese foreign service, and Amorn said diplomats at the embassy had reached out to his organization. They invited him to informal strategy sessions and had cultivated close links with Thai-Chinese business associations that tycoons like Amorn patronized. After our interview, Amorn rushed to a meeting at the Thai-Chinese Chamber of Commerce with the Chinese ambassador.

Whether the embassy in Bangkok had an influence on Amorn or he came to his views all by himself, Uniting Chinese proved a useful vehicle for Beijing to woo diaspora Chinese. When the United States and China got into disputes, like during the EP-3 incident, Amorn would criticize Washington and lead anti-US demonstrations in Bangkok. "I had to protest, I felt too strongly," he said. Amorn's organization later wrote articles in local papers stressing that Taiwan needed to return to mainland China, and it helped host conventions of diaspora Chinese in Bangkok. The conventions supposedly promoted the "peaceful reunification" of China but mostly served as an excuse to blast Taipei and demonstrate to diaspora Chinese that anyone who still supports Taiwan has few allies left among ethnic Chinese anywhere. At one conference, Amorn called the

Taiwanese leader "pathetic" and accused him of "wreaking chaos." At the end of the conference, which attracted more than one thousand people, participants issued a "Bangkok Declaration" that called on all diaspora Chinese to join to "strongly oppose any attempts by Taiwan authorities to bring Taiwan to the brink of 'independence.'"[34]

V
The Tools of Business

For a man who could be arrested at any moment, Harry Roque Jr. seemed remarkably placid when I met him in March 2006. Dressed in a white *barong tagalog,* the long, delicately embroidered shirt worn untucked by Filipino men, he welcomed me into his law office in downtown Manila, a small room crowded with stacks of books on Philippine constitutional law and photos of his family. "Three days ago, it was broadcast that I had been arrested," he said. "Everyone was calling me, but I was still here." A laugh boomed out of his jiggling stomach, and his wide, round face broke into a grin. Still, he said, though the initial report was wrong, "There's a short list of people who have been arrested and longer list—two hundred people—who could be arrested."[1]

Roque's offense? Just a few weeks earlier, Philippine president Gloria Macapagal-Arroyo had declared a state of national emergency, similar to martial law, citing an alleged coup plot against her. In coordination with the state of emergency, she had created lists of people, including many of her political enemies, supposedly involved in the plot; these targets could be arrested for rebellion and sedition at any time. The Philippine police had raided the offices of the *Tribune*, a newspaper critical of the government, and had attempted to arrest at least five opposition congresspeople. The congresspeople holed up in the Philippines' legislative building, a situation akin to Barack Obama and Nancy Pelosi barricading themselves in the Capitol while George Bush's Secret Service tried to starve them out.[2]

For several years, Roque, a longtime activist and human rights lawyer, had auditioned for the list, blasting Macapagal-Arroyo's administration for nearly every decision it made. Recently, Roque had embarked upon a crusade against a government-backed project called Northrail, an attempt to build a railway from Caloocan to Malolos on the central Philippine island of Luzon. The Philippines initially had signed a contract with a Spanish firm to build Northrail. But then, according to Roque and several Filipino politicians, the Philippine government junked that contract and agreed to use Chinese firms, without any public tender; at the same time, the Chinese government offered more than $400 million in assistance for the project, then an additional $500 million. "Northrail signified a shift in policy from China," which used to keep a low profile in the Philippines, Roque said. "It's aggressively pushing its aid and capital and goods. The Philippines already had a contract with the Spanish company . . . and just jettisoned this. The speaker of the [Philippines] legislature negotiated directly with China for the project, and the Department of Justice never even gave its clearance for the Northrail." Along with several other prominent lawyers, Roque had completed a study of the Northrail project that concluded that it was improperly managed and financed, and would not be contracted out for competitive bidding.[3]

Roque thinks that Beijing understood how to make

Northrail happen in one of the world's most contentious and corrupt democracies.[4] "The Chinese zeroed in on what local politicians wanted, which is why in the contract there was a 30 percent up-front payment in the financing," Roque says. "You have to wonder, why this up-front payment? Who was this to benefit?"

Worried that Northrail had been handled so opaquely, and concerned that a Chinese contractor hired without competitive bidding might have poor standards of transparency and corporate governance, Roque had filed a case to challenge the project as unconstitutional, further angering the Philippine government. He soon got his answer. The government "hired a Philippine public relations firm to neutralize me in the media," he said. Now, he feared arrest—for his Northrail opposition and for his criticism of the emergency law. And Roque had not succeeded in stopping the project, though he did stay out of jail. The Philippines' Supreme Court tossed out one of his petitions, and even as he and a group of plaintiffs filed another suit, the Northrail project marched forward.[5]

The size of Chinese aid to Northrail also instantly put Beijing in the same league as other traditional aid donors to the Philippines, like Japan and the United States.[6] In fact, Northrail provided a window into how quickly China has developed its other set of soft power tools, tools of business. In addition to cultural tools, these levers of power—trade, investment, aid, and the appeal of China's economic model—make up the second potential weapon in China's arsenal. Indeed, over the past decade, Beijing has begun to use aid, trade, investment, and the allure of China's economic model, which combines growth with state control, to charm other nations. China's tools of business, in fact, have become powerful enough that even when people like Harry Roque raise concerns about

Chinese aid and investment, their own governments sometimes shut them up.

As with tools of culture, not everything wrought by tools of business stems from one grand Chinese strategy. In business, even more than in culture, Chinese companies may make decisions based on corporate rather than national interests, while companies in other nations are not passive actors—they aggressively seek Chinese investment and aid. Still, the policies Beijing has designed have helped its tools of business flourish.

Since 1979 the world has witnessed what happens when you unleash the entrepreneurial activity of more than one billion people, most of whom will work for the monetary equivalent of a Starbucks latte per day, and then combine this with the insatiable desire of foreign firms to tap this labor and also to sell products to the world's biggest market. As the China business expert Joe Studwell chronicles in his study *The China Dream*, the idea of selling to the Middle Kingdom's vast population has been a fantasy of Western companies for centuries—in the nineteenth century, English tailors rhapsodized that if they "added an inch of material to every Chinaman's shirt tail," Manchester weavers would be flush forever. Today, this dream often results in multinationals committing to China investments without adequate due diligence. According to Studwell, the British brewing giant Bass tried to peddle high-end imported brews to Chinese consumers used to cheap local beer, and advertised Bass drafts with dancers dressed in kilts, which only confused most Chinese. Bass lost millions and shuttered its factories, so angering its local Chinese staff that managers at Bass facilities wound up needing bodyguards.[7]

Despite multinationals' misadventures in the People's Republic, every major company remains convinced that it must have a China strategy, and many years China attracts the biggest pool of foreign direct investment of any nation, more than $500 billion in total since 1979. The retailing giant Wal-Mart alone has an inventory of goods in China worth at least $18 billion, the size of Bolivia's gross domestic product. Since the early 1980s China has posted average annual growth rates of more than 8 percent—in a great year the United States would hit 5 percent—and in the near future probably will contribute more than 25 percent of the growth in the global economy. China runs record trade surpluses, and it is moving into value-added industries like automobile manufacturing. The Chinese automobile companies Chery and Geely have begun shipping cars abroad, probably a trial run for entering the US market. China boasts a national savings rate of more than 40 percent, compared with the American population's negative savings rate in 2005.[8]

This part of the China story is well known, the subject of bookshelves worth of business tomes and reams of studies by economists examining China's path to prosperity. Less understood is what happens now. For some nations, fear of China's military power has been replaced by fear of China's economic power—of markets being swamped by cheap Chinese goods, companies ruined by China absorbing investment that would have gone elsewhere, workers laid off by competition from China's massive labor force. Beijing apparently has realized that, like the United States and Japan before it, it also can utilize its economic heft to minimize these concerns, and even to boost its appeal in foreign nations, if it portrays its growth in a certain light, and if other countries can benefit from China's consumer power.

In pursuing this goal, China has first tried to demonstrate that as it grows, it also will become a much larger consumer of other nations' goods, creating "win-win" economics, central to the idea of China's rising peacefully. This comes from the top: though Beijing, like most governments, cannot coordinate all its policies, in 2004 the Chinese government organized an internal conference on "Economic Diplomacy Toward Developing Countries," at which officials planned to increase economic cooperation with developing nations.[9]

To be sure, China cannot yet match American or Japanese or European investment in the developing world, and some media accounts overhype Chinese outward investment. In Singapore, one of the most open and business-friendly economies on earth—and a state that has encouraged mainland Chinese companies to enter its market—American companies have invested more than $40 billion. According to the most recent official statistics available, Chinese investments in Singapore have not yet cracked the $1 billion barrier.[10] Instead, Beijing promotes the idea that China eventually will become a major source of outward investment: China's appeal to the developing world rests in part on portraying China's potential as an investor.

Chinese officials often do so by providing trade and investment and tourism targets. These targets, for five or ten years in the future, tend to be enormous and to obscure the fact that, at present, Chinese direct investment into regions like Southeast Asia and Latin America still lags far behind investment from the United States and other wealthy countries like Japan. "While China has not committed much money to Cambodia, recent high level visits . . . highlight . . . the promise of more trade and investment," notes one cable from the US embassy in Phnom Penh obtained through the Freedom of Information Act.[11]

Indeed, when Chinese President Hu Jintao visited Latin America in 2004, he pledged that China would invest $100 billion in Argentina and Brazil. Since overall net foreign investment in Latin America has dropped from $76 billion in 2000 to $68 billion in 2005 (partly because of investors going to China instead) this Chinese investment could be especially important to the region, and Hu's pledges dominated the local media. When Chinese officials visit Africa, they can highlight some nine hundred Chinese companies invested in the continent, and promise more of the same; China has created a fund worth $5 billion to encourage Chinese firms to invest in Africa. When Hu met Philippine President Gloria Macapagal-Arroyo in 2005, he promised more than $1.6 billion in new Chinese investment and aid to Manila; in 2005, when China hosted Indonesian Minister of Finance Jusuf Anwar, the Chinese announced that PRC investment in Indonesia could triple within five years, to as much as $20 billion.[12]

China's outward investment comes partly from a national policy, not just from Chinese companies seeking profits overseas. The Chinese government encourages firms to invest in strategic industries and select countries. In the late 1990s, and then again during China's economic Five Year Plan for 2001–2005, Beijing created a policy of pushing Chinese companies to invest abroad. Chinese leaders called this policy the "Go Out" or "Go Global" campaign. "To encourage capable Chinese companies to go out is an important policy of the Chinese Government," Vice Premier Wu Yi told the audience at an international trade fair in 2004.[13]

During the late 1990s and early 2000s, China's Ministry of Foreign Trade and Economic Cooperation selected some thirty to fifty top Chinese companies to take the lead in overseas investment. As they look to invest overseas, these national champions enjoy a range of benefits that will help them compete, including low-interest funding from Chinese banks—banks primarily controlled by the government. In 2004, for example, according to a report by the consulting group Accenture, one of these Chinese banks provided the Chinese telecommunications giant Huawei with a $10 billion low-cost loan to help Huawei internationally.[14]

Looking to invest abroad seemed natural: as Accenture noted, China recognized that it "needs to develop its relationship with the global economy beyond a simple export-driven model. . . . China's outward investment has a dual purpose of building China's political capital and influence around the world."[15] Furthermore, Accenture found, because many Chinese companies gained experience in China, a developing nation itself, "their better understanding of emerging markets provides a stronger guarantee of success in their initial overseas expansion plans." In other words, with their background in China's often lawless business climate, Chinese companies have the experience to invest in Liberia or Cambodia or many other countries with little rule of law.

As China's national outward investment strategy has developed, provincial governments have announced complementary programs to encourage Chinese companies to venture into neighboring countries. The national government sweetens the pot for Chinese companies with soft loans designed to encourage Chinese firms to invest in neighbors like Laos, with centers for trade promotion providing consultation to Chinese enterprises investing in Africa and Southeast Asia, with information programs for officials in countries like Pakistan on how to attract Chinese investment, and with assistance to business delegations that accompany Chinese officials' trips abroad.[16]

On these trips, Chinese leaders often bring along large mainland business delegations to meet with local businesspeople and politicians. Developing-world businesspeople thus can execute deals directly with Chinese political leaders and heads of Chinese companies without worrying about legislators back in China holding up completion of the deals, as might happen in the United States or any other democratic nation. "I went to Beijing with Thai officials and met [Vice Premier] Wu Yi," says Vikrom Kromadit, CEO of the Amata Corporation, one of the largest companies in Thailand, which manages industrial estates east of Bangkok. "She asked me what kind of companies I'd like in my industrial park, and I told her, and she sent over twenty companies on my list of [Chinese] companies I wanted to get."[17] No American or European politician could so easily direct a business.

Beijing particularly leans on Chinese companies in the energy industry to invest abroad. Even more than in other sectors, these energy companies, which do have some autonomy, remain dominated by the state or at least retain close links to the Chinese government. In interviews with CLSA Asia Pacific Markets, a leading research company in China, state-owned resources firms admitted that Beijing had been pushing them to invest abroad, though they insisted that their own management made the final decisions. Furthermore, as the energy analyst Erica Downs notes, Chinese companies making foreign investments worth more than $30 million require approval from the National Development and Reform Commission, the country's top planning agency. This suggests that the government has some significant degree of oversight, even if it is not planning each purchase by a Chinese company.[18]

In the past five years, Chinese firms indeed have embarked upon a frantic shopping spree for commodities, buying up $15 billion in oil and gas fields and companies worldwide, and often paying above market price. In Venezuela, China National Petroleum Corporation (CNPC) has established a joint venture with Petroleos de Venezuela, the state oil company of a nation whose leader prides himself on opposing US foreign policy; overall, China has invested roughly $2 billion in Venezuela. In Peru an arm of China National Petroleum Corporation has purchased a stake in Pluspetrol, which has oil fields along the Ecuadorian border. In Sudan, Chinese firms have become the biggest foreign investors in that nation's oil industry, plowing in some $4 billion. In Nigeria, the state-owned Chinese oil giant CNOOC purchased a $2.3 billion stake in a major oil and gas field in the Niger Delta. In Iran, China has signed a deal to develop one of the country's major gas fields, putting China in position to become the largest player in a nation with some of the world's largest gas reserves. In 2005 CNPC purchased PetroKazakhstan, one of the biggest oil companies in Central Asia. In Burma, PetroChina signed a deal in 2006 for 6.5 trillion cubic feet of Burmese natural gas.[19] The list could go on, well into several pages.

Just as it focuses on strategic industries, the Chinese government also pushes investment in strategic nations—countries on China's borders and in regions with resources. In the government's Five Year Plan for 2001–2005, Beijing focused on three strategic regions of the developing world: Latin America, North Africa, and Central Asia, all of which have extensive oil and gas. Prodded by Beijing and by provincial governments, Chinese firms have poured into Cambodia, Burma, Laos, Thailand, Central Asia, Pakistan, Vietnam, and Pacific Russia. China has become the largest source of investment in Cambodia and, anecdotally, in Burma, Laos, Pacific Russia, and Kazakhstan. According to official statistics, in 2005 China's outward investment rose nearly 1,000 percent, though many of these investments are merely unfulfilled commitments. Within a decade, China could become the biggest investor in all the developing nations on its borders, from Mongolia to Vietnam. "If the goal of Chinese investment has been not so much to make money as to win the charm offensive, then victory has already been delivered," wrote one US diplomat in Asia, in a cable obtained through the Freedom of Information Act.[20]

Western companies competing with these Chinese firms realize that they cannot match China's low labor costs or Chinese firms' willingness to invest in risky places like Sierra Leone or Burma. Instead, Western companies compete by advertising their sophisticated technology and their years of experience operating abroad, but these advantages may be diminishing. "In Indonesia, American companies will say, 'If you want US technology, you have to go with us,'" explains Walter Lohman of the US-Asean Business Council, a trade group in Washington. "But now, for example with telecommunications, the Chinese are competitive with the technology." "I was quite surprised with the Chinese knowledge of oil fields," agrees Lin Che Wei, head of PT Danareksa, an Indonesian state bank that coordinates investments. They seemed as advanced as Exxon-Mobil, Wei says.[21]

Even if China's technology lags behind that of American or Japanese or European competitors, some poorer nations think that Chinese companies will be more willing to share what they know, and that Chinese firms, with backgrounds in the developing world, might be better suited for Africa or Latin America or Southeast Asia. In Nigeria, where the government chose the Chinese aerospace giant China Great Wall Industry Corporation to launch a new Nigerian satellite, one foreign affairs official told the *Financial Times:* "Being a developing country, they understand us better. They are also prepared to put more on the table. For instance, the western world is never prepared to transfer technology—but the Chinese do."[22]

While China cannot yet challenge the United States, Europe, or Japan as a source of outward investment, it already can match other major powers as a consumer and as a trading partner. And China's consumption is focused on the developing world: while China imports little from the United States outside of high-technology products, its imports from the developing world are worth more than seven times its imports from the United States.[23] As a result, countries from Asia, Latin America, Africa, and other regions, hardly passive actors, are scrambling to take advantage of China's enormous appetites for resources, industrial components, and other products, to play China's growth for all its worth. Many of these nations, particularly in Africa, saw their economies blossom in the 1960s and 1970s, another time of high demand for commodities, demand that waned in the 1980s. Today China's demand offers these nations another shot.

By the end of 2006, in fact, Southeast Asia's total trade with China probably will eclipse its trade with the United States or Japan. In 2005, for the first time in decades, the economies of Asia outside Japan were larger than the economy of Japan, showing China's increasing importance to the region. Over time, as American and Japanese consumption of Asia's exports continues to decline, China's consumption will become even more important to the region's economies, giving them the potential to benefit enormously from Chinese growth. Eventually, China will become the center of trade and economic integration in Asia, providing Beijing with the goodwill that accrues from being the economic locomotive, the engine that lifts millions of people's incomes.[24]

South Korea, an industrialized economy with close links to the United States, provides a snapshot of the rapid growth in trade with China. For centuries, China and Korea disputed parts of Northeast Asia, and in the modern era South Korea normalized trade relations with China only in 1992. Yet within a decade China had passed the United States as South Korea's biggest export market, and hundreds of thousands of South Korean businesspeople were heading to China for trade. Booming trade was a major reason why Seoul developed what some Koreans called "China fever," an interest in all things Chinese, from Korean students flocking to Chinese universities to some eight thousand South Korean companies investing in China.[25] Those economic links soon had ramifications for Korea's political relationships, from Japan to the United States.

Outside Asia, trade with China is skyrocketing as well. In sub-Saharan Africa, Chinese-African trade grew by more than 250 percent between 2001 and 2005, and China has become the continent's third-largest trading partner, behind the United States and France. Chinese exports to Africa, meanwhile, appeal to a wide section of African consumers, because they tend to be far cheaper than European or American goods. In Latin America trade with China has grown from only $200 million in 1975 to more than $40 billion. Mines across Latin America report that they are working twenty-four hours per day just to keep up with Chinese demand for commodities; companies are melting down all the scrap metal they can find to ship to the People's Republic. China's trade with Iran has risen from virtually nothing fifteen years ago to $10 billion annually. In Central Asia the numbers are even more impressive. To take one example, Chinese trade with Uzbekistan, a nation with high barriers to trade, has grown by 1,000 percent in the past five years.[26]

Since most economists project that China's economy will continue to expand between 7 and 10 percent per year, Beijing can continue its rapid growth in trade. China's trade volume with Southeast Asia could reach $1.2 trillion within a decade. In Africa trade with China probably will top $100 billion within the decade, putting China within striking distance of the United States as the continent's leading trading partner. In Latin America, China could be the region's second-largest trading partner as soon as 2010.

Sensitive to fears of China's economic power, Chinese officials also try to reassure developing nations by signing free trade deals and making trade concessions—another economic tool of soft power. Until the past decade, Beijing actively shunned bilateral trade agreements, but today China has learned from its mistakes. In fall 2001, to the surprise of many Southeast Asian diplomats who had been unsuccessfully pressuring other countries to consider a trade deal with the region, Chinese officials suggested creating a free trade zone between China and ten Southeast Asian nations, which immediately leapfrogged China over Japan, traditionally the region's economic leader. This Chinese–Southeast Asian agreement, signed in 2002, will create the largest trade area in the world. "We were shocked that the Chinese would come up with a deal," says one Southeast Asian diplomat. "The Japanese thought they could just wait and wait to negotiate with us, and they were totally unprepared for the Chinese move." Pressing its charm, China then offered Southeast Asia an "Early Harvest Package," which even before the trade agreement comes into effect will reduce tariffs on some types of Southeast Asian goods—primarily agricultural products from poor Asian countries.[27]

In the wake of the Southeast Asian–Chinese free trade announcement, Chinese officials apparently recognized the kind of goodwill they were earning. Since then, China has started work on at least sixteen other trade agreements with countries from Chile to New Zealand. In all these deals, Beijing presents itself as committed to free trade without imposing any conditions on trade partners related to governance, environmental issues, or labor rights, a stance that plays well in many countries. Beijing also may duplicate the Early Harvest trade concessions in other developing nations. China has signed a deal similar to Early Harvest with Pakistan and has promised African nations easier market access and duty-free privileges for some categories of goods. In the longer run, Beijing promised in a recent white paper, China would attempt to negotiate a free trade deal with African regional groupings.[28]

The United States, Europe, and Japan, by contrast, have to deal with more powerful and vocal domestic business interests, and with legislatures that respond to these businesses. This is one reason why the United States has not launched a trade agreement with all of Southeast Asia, and why Japan has been unable to complete a bilateral agreement with any Asian nation except Singapore and the Philippines.

Western protectionism has complicated trade with even the poorest countries. As the United States and Vietnam established closer trade relations in the 1990s and early 2000s, twenty-five years after the end of the Vietnam War, Vietnamese catfish farmers in the Mekong River Delta, who previously had sold their catches to Vietnamese state firms for break-even prices, saw an opportunity. Hundreds of catfish farmers began exporting to the United States, and by 2001 Vietnamese catfish exports to America reached $38 million, a significant sum for the Vietnamese farmers but a small figure in the $11 billion US market for seafood imports. Still, American catfish farmers, who had seen the Vietnamese capture at least 20 percent of the US market, lodged a complaint with Washington, charging that the Vietnamese were selling fish below cost, or dumping. The Vietnamese argued that they could sell fish cheaply simply because of low labor costs, but the US Commerce Department disagreed, imposing steep tariffs on Vietnamese imports.[29] Vietnamese catfish exports to the United States plummeted.

Backing up its investment promises and its trade, China has developed a substantial aid program. From almost nothing in the mid-1990s, Chinese aid now can compete with American aid programs in parts of Southeast Asia, Latin America, and Africa. Chinese aid tends to be opaque; according to several sources, China determines its aid policies through informal meetings of its ambassadors in Beijing, where the envoys essentially bargain over the amounts of assistance.[30]

A true understanding of Chinese assistance necessitates looking beyond traditional definitions of aid, as assistance provided for economic development. A true understanding must include soft loans given by Chinese banks with the imprimatur of Beijing, assistance not explicitly targeted for economic development but rather for cultural promotion and language promotion, in-kind swaps like China's trade of armored personnel carriers for dried Thai fruits, or concessional loans given by China's state-controlled banks.[31] Already, in fact, China's Export-Import Bank has become the largest source of loans to Africa, surpassing the World Bank.

The Export-Import Bank, for instance, claims that it makes its own decisions on potential loan recipients without any interference from the central government. But loans made to state companies like Huawei are not the only indications of a connection. Ex-Im Bank officials often travel with Chinese state-linked companies on business delegations accompanying Chinese officials, and then offer loans for deals favored by Chinese officials. As the Export-Import Bank's own literature admits, it sees itself not just as a commercial institution. "The development of this business has not only proved effective in boosting the economic and social development of the recipient countries but has also improved the friendly economic and trade cooperation between China and other developing countries," the bank says in an annual report.[32]

In Asia, China's aid has exploded, rising from roughly $260 million in 1993 to more than $1.5 billion in 2004—even as the United States cut its aid and Japan, historically one of the world's biggest aid donors, shrunk its assistance due to a decadelong downturn in the Japanese economy. By 2004, according to a comprehensive analysis by Henry Yep of National Defense University, China's aid to the Philippines was four times as large as American aid to the Philippines, China's aid to Laos was three times as great as American aid, and China's aid to Indonesia was nearly double US aid. In Burma and Cambodia, Chinese aid vastly outstripped American aid, while in Central Asia, China now rivals Russia, the United States, and Japan in aid projects, such as its $600 million assistance to Uzbekistan. In Latin America, Beijing's aid rose from nothing ten years ago to at least $700 million in 2004. Between the mid-1990s and 2004, China's aid to Africa rose from roughly $100 million to $2.7 billion. Even in the remote Pacific, Chinese aid has become a major factor, with Prime Minister Wen Jiabao recently pledging $375 million in preferential loans to tiny island nations.[33]

Still a developing country, China could overplay its hand, making promises to other nations that it cannot fulfill. China's diplomatic style of signing many agreements during foreign visits by its top leaders earns it considerable initial goodwill and positive media coverage. But often the agreements are merely letters of intent. In Latin America and Asia, when officials from local boards of trade and investment follow up, they sometimes find that Chinese officials had laid no groundwork to put these letters into practice. Indeed, after Chinese leaders make promises of new aid during visits overseas, Beijing sometimes fails to follow through with the cash. Paul Marks, a China specialist at West Point, has spent years reading Cambodia's Chinese-language newspapers. The papers are full of stories hinting that Beijing, or provincial governments, or private groups in China, had made offers of aid to Cambodia that never came through—new schools that had not received their funding from Chinese sources, unpaid scholarships, Cambodian students who desperately wanted to study Chinese but had not gotten the money to do so.[34]

But while China's aid overall still does not always match that of other major powers, and while Beijing sometimes overpromises, it tries to make the most of the goodwill it receives from its funds, an approach Chinese scholars call the "maxi-mini" strategy, of getting the maximum return from the minimum outlay. After the Asian tsunami hit in December 2004, China eventually offered $95 million in assistance, one of its biggest-ever pledges of humanitarian aid, but still far less than Japan's assistance or US aid, which approached $1 billion. But because China is a new donor, Beijing seemed to win almost as much media coverage in Asia for its tsunami relief as did the United States and Japan. This has become a trend: China generates goodwill from its assistance partly because countries have become used to receiving money from Japan and America for decades, and China is a new donor. And China uses its aid for high-profile projects, like a new parliament building in Cambodia. "Providing a modern replacement for the current run-down headquarters of the Cambodian government will remind many in the Cambodian leadership who takes care of them," admits one US diplomat in an unclassified cable.[35]

The streets of Maputo, capital of the former Portuguese colony of Mozambique, look little different from those of many other sub-Saharan African cities. Open sewers overflow with rotting fruit, beggars and police harass pedestrians for money, and young mothers wander the streets in dirty rags carrying children on their backs. Yet Maputo also seems hopeful. After decades of brutal civil war, Mozambique has enjoyed peace since the early 1990s, and has built a nascent, if fragile, democracy. Taking advantage of the peace, Mozambicans have reconstructed the shattered economy of their capital. Young entrepreneurs in Maputo clinch deals over thimble-sized cups of coffee in the city's new cafés and plates of fresh grilled fish in the waterfront restaurants and bars lining the capital's wide public squares. The business district even has sprouted a small skyline of office towers.

In February 2005 I arrived in Mozambique. Walking amid the pink and green Mediterranean-style buildings of Maputo's oceanfront, signs of its Portuguese colonial heritage, I noticed one structure that stood out—an enormous, blocky building with an Asian pagoda roof nothing like the surrounding architecture. It was the Ministry of Foreign Affairs—built with Chinese aid, which is why it wound up looking like a giant slab of concrete topped with a pagoda.

In recent years China has become a major donor to Mozambique, not only constructing buildings, which China has been doing abroad since the 1960s, but also offering many other types of aid. Beijing has paid for an investment and trade-promotion center in Maputo, offered the country debt reduction, and promised significant other economic assistance, like more than $2 billion offered in May 2006 by China's Export-Import Bank to help Mozambique rebuild its power infrastructure, ruined by the long civil war.[36] Perhaps unsurprisingly, Mozambique now regards China as one of its most important allies outside of Africa.

Maputo shows how China's aid has not only grown but also become more sophisticated. In the past, many scholars associated China's aid with giant white-elephant projects, like large buildings and ministries and similar structures. Since the late 1990s, though, Beijing has developed comprehensive aid programs beyond funding buildings, so that projects like Maputo's Ministry of Foreign Affairs come along with other initiatives, like debt reduction and economic assistance and training programs for professionals from the developing world. In fact, Beijing will train some ten thousand African professionals annually; China already trains some three thousand professionals from the developing world each year, in programs organized by the Chinese Ministry of Commerce.[37]

As in Mozambique, around the world China also has more closely linked assistance to discrete policy goals, including mitigating concerns about China's economic rise, developing poorer parts of China, and increasing China's influence in places where other major powers, like the United States and Japan, seem to be losing influence. In Mozambique this means funding the trade-promotion center, which could help Chinese companies investing in Maputo. In Thailand it means Beijing using its aid to purchase surplus Thai agriculture, a way of conciliating Thai farmers worried about the impact of a looming Asean-China free trade agreement. Along the Mekong River in Southeast Asia, it means major new road-development projects that will link Southeast Asia to Yunnan, an impoverished province of southwestern China central to the Chinese government plan to boost the economies of western China.[38]

This aid helps Chinese companies, too—the roads will open routes to ocean ports for Yunnanese farmers and traders. Around the world, when Beijing scouts potential new infrastructure projects, this infrastructure construction winds up benefiting Chinese construction companies. Work on a $1.8 billion dam in Merowe, Sudan, for example, backed by export credits from China Export-Import Bank, will be farmed out to Chinese firms. Chinese companies can rely upon low-interest loans from Chinese banks and can bring cheap Chinese labor to implement the projects.[39]

In fact, Chinese aid also often comes tied to commitments to provide contracts to Chinese construction firms—a strategy similar to unpopular Japanese assistance programs in the past. In Angola, for example, 70 percent of Chinese-funded projects were reserved for Chinese companies.

China also has used its aid to cultivate important political actors. Beijing is building an informal kind of visitor program, creating opportunities for opinion leaders from the developing world to be wooed in China, including potential future heads of state like Cuba's Raúl Castro or young Vietnamese and Thai officials. Opinion leaders are brought to China for conferences, trips to study China's economic model, and contact with the Communist Party, which has aggressively built contacts with parties in the developing world—by 2005, the Chinese Communist Party had established official relations with thirty-nine political parties in Southeast Asia alone. In Cambodia, where Chinese aid will build a new prime minister's office and the Beijing Diplomacy Institute trains Cambodian officials from the ministries of tourism, foreign affairs, industry, and agriculture, several politicians say that the Chinese government also has directly provided funds to parties like the ruling party and its coalition partner.[40]

Some visitor programs may look little different from the kind of junketing for which Congress has long been notorious. "I look around the Parliament, and I see everyone I know taking trips to China," says the prominent Thai senator Kraisak Choonhavan. "If you're a Thai MP, it's the easiest thing in the world to get a trip to China for conferences or other events."[41]

In Laos, where Chinese aid built the capital's main drag and funded hospitals in Luang Prabang, the second city, Chinese junkets have proven even more popular. Some impoverished Lao officials—most take second jobs to supplement their meager government wages—receive sizable per diems when they travel to China for trainings on governance, environmental policies, counternarcotics strategy, and other issues, or when they attend China-sponsored seminars in Vientiane.[42] "Now our staff go to China as much as they can," says a top official in Laos's foreign ministry. "We have no money, and this is the only training we can get." Before I leave his office, he touches my arm and asks, "Do you think you have any books you could ship us?"

As China has become an international investor and world trader, the Chinese government has not only lifted restrictions on migration within China but also made it vastly easier for Chinese to leave the country for business and tourism. As Beijing relaxes immigration restrictions and encourages outward investment, Chinese businesspeople, traders, and workers leave China en masse. The fact that China has begun to protect some of its nationals abroad—in April 2006, the Chinese government airlifted more than three hundred people who had been attacked by rioters in the Solomon Islands, a Pacific nation, during a wave of anti-Chinese violence—also encourages Chinese businesspeople and laborers to feel comfortable moving abroad. One study of Chinese workers in Africa found that the number of Chinese registered in Sudan had tripled since the late 1990s, to roughly 24,000 in 2004, and the trade organization of Chinese labor contractors believes that the number of Chinese workers heading abroad is rising by nearly 20 percent per year; some will overstay their visa and never come home. Barry Sautman of Hong Kong University of Science and Technology found that one database of Chinese in Africa showed 137,000 Chinese residents on the continent in 2002, a number he believes out of date and vastly understated. In Nigeria alone, for example, Sautman found only 2,000 Chinese residents in 2001, but he estimated that some 50,000 Chinese had migrated to Nigeria by 2005, and that South Africa had as many as 300,000 Chinese migrants.[43] Since many of the Chinese migrants live more modestly than Western expatriates, they tend to earn the respect of local Africans—though in the long run, if the Chinese traders replace African businesses they may create resentment.

Asia has witnessed the largest number of Chinese migrants. In Thailand 120,000 Chinese migrants who entered the country in 2003 reportedly did not return home. In Cambodia, China has become the number one source of visitor arrivals, but Cambodia does not rank highly on Chinese tourists' itineraries, suggesting that most of these visitors are businesspeople, including many who do not return home.[44]

These new migrants are transforming the demographic makeup of China's border regions, like northern Southeast Asia, a wide swath of land from northern Burma to northern Vietnam. In these porous border areas, recent migrants from

China now dominate towns like Mandalay in Burma or Chiang Saen in northern Thailand or Luang Namtha in northern Laos. At a new glass-and-steel mall in Mandalay featuring almost exclusively Chinese products, Chinese teenage girls wander the floors in small groups. Outside the mall, wives of Chinese businessmen have opened hair salons, Chinese-style coffee shops, and stands selling fashion accessories; in one coffee shop, Burmese boys study Chinese-language books. The girls are part of the wave of 200,000 Chinese tourists and migrants who have come to Burma in recent years, mostly businesspeople from southwestern China and their families, along with laborers in town to work on infrastructure projects outside Mandalay funded by Chinese assistance. China's influence has become so prevalent in Mandalay, in fact, that locals call the town a "Chinese city," and some quietly resent the possibility that Chinese migrants dominate business in town.

Similarly, around Luang Namtha, recent migrants now run local markets and establish large agricultural estates, since Laos offers the kind of open land that is becoming almost impossible to find in China. "The Lao government is concerned about the Chinese influence in northern Laos, and they'll try to get people to go back to China," says one Western diplomat in Vientiane, Laos's capital. "But they don't have the resources to look for people." As a cable from the US embassy in Vientiane admitted, "the expanding Chinese presence in northern Laos . . . is nothing short of an economic offensive."[45]

This new migration of Chinese traders and laborers has had another effect. It has created a zone on China's borders in which Chinese currency is traded freely, despite the fact that it is not officially convertible. In Burma, Mongolia, Laos, Cambodia, and Vietnam, businesspeople use the renminbi as a de facto reserve currency, sometimes instead of the US dollar.[46] In northern Laos, migrant Chinese truckers and laborers now stop at the makeshift new bars and nightclubs lining the roadways, often just wooden shacks with tin roofs and signs in Chinese characters—though they all take renminbi. Inside, Lao and Chinese girls stand packed into one corner of the bars until the men pick them out, negotiate a price, and take them to grubby local short-time hotels or trailers for quick sex.

The lifting of restrictions on tourism from China also has allowed more Chinese to take their first vacations overseas. According to the World Tourism Organization, some 100 million Chinese will be traveling abroad by 2020, making China eventually the world's largest source of tourists. Today, Southeast Asia is the destination of choice for one-third of all outbound Chinese tourists. It will soon become the most important tourism market for Thailand, Singapore, Vietnam, and other Asian nations, and even more important in an era of terrorism, when Americans have grown increasingly fearful of travel abroad. Thailand alone hopes to receive four million Chinese tourists per year by the end of the decade.[47]

Many first-time mainland Chinese tourists, like the Japanese and Taiwanese before them, travel on short group tours. But as China becomes richer, average Chinese are breaking away from these group tours. They are traveling on their own on extended trips, spending like people from developed nations, and impressing citizens of host countries with their wealth and sophistication and taste. "The Billion Boomer generation—young, career-driven [Chinese] consumers—are spreading their wings," notes a report on Chinese tourism by the research group CLSA Asia Pacific Markets. "Luxury goods and cosmetics are the most sought after items" by these rich Chinese tourists, CLSA notes. In Hong Kong, mainland Chinese travelers now spend more per day than their Japanese counterparts; in Thailand, Chinese travelers already stay for as many days as Japanese tourists. Even in Paris, boutiques have added Mandarin-speaking staff to their coterie of English and Japanese assistants.[48]

The new migrants flocking out of China, the growth of Chinese business, the interest in studying Chinese, the Chinese aid projects, the influx of modern Chinese urban culture—in some places, like Mandalay, Burma, all these elements of soft power are coming together. China's soft power indeed has proven successful in many cities like Mandalay, allowing China in some cases to supplant the United States as the major external cultural and economic influence. But whether China can continue to enjoy this success without fostering more resentment in Burma—and elsewhere—is a far different question.

VI
Mr. Popular

Driving through the streets of Dili, the waterfront capital of the new nation of East Timor, I passed building after building littered with burned debris. The coastal road outside of Dili resembled an Iberian resort, with rose-and-white homes overlooking beach soccer games and waterfront palms, and Portuguese dance music blaring from car speakers. But the music concealed obvious pain. Rows of house frames lined the tarmac, mere skeletons of former dwellings, some still bearing char marks. For centuries, East Timor had been a sleepy outpost of Portugal's empire, and even when the Dutch surrendered the rest of the surrounding archipelago to create independent Indonesia, Lisbon maintained control of East Timor. But in 1975, after Portugal granted East Timor its independence, Indonesia immediately invaded the territory (with the tacit consent of the United States and Australia), launching one of the most brutal occupations in history before Jakarta allowed a referendum in 1999. After East Timor voted for independence in that referendum, the Indonesian military delivered a final blow, burning down much of East Timor, a swath of violence that forced more than 400,000 people from their homes, most of which were destroyed.[1]

During the Indonesian period, thousands of East Timorese fled into exile or escaped into Timor's mountains to wage a guerrilla battle against Jakarta's troops for an independent and democratic nation of their own. Their quixotic battle attracted global attention, partly because of Timor's tiny size—its entire population was less than 1.5 million people, yet it was battling giant Indonesia, with the world's fourth-largest population.[2] Honoring their struggle, in 1996 the Nobel committee awarded the Peace Prize to the Timorese leaders José Ramos Horta and Bishop Carlos Filipe Ximenes Belo.

When East Timor became an independent nation in 2002, after three years of UN administration, these former exiles and guerrillas became the leaders of their new country. In his bare, windowless office inside the East Timorese government complex—an Iberian-looking structure with a white frontage and long, shuttered windows—I met João de Câmara, director of the government division for multilateral affairs. When Indonesia invaded East Timor in 1975, de Câmara had fled into the hills to serve in the guerrilla resistance. Arrested four years later, he wound up in Jakarta, where the Indonesian government released him so that he could study law. "But then I was arrested in law school, and put back in jail," he says. "I was there in jail with Xanana Gusmão," the leader of the Timorese guerrillas. All told, de Câmara spent nearly two decades in Jakarta, either in jail or closely monitored by the Indonesian security forces.[3]

Where did fighters for freedom like de Câmara turn once they controlled their own destiny? To China. After Timor voted for independence in the 1999 referendum and was put on the path to nationhood under UN trusteeship, Chinese officials quickly cultivated the Timorese who would be leading the new country; some left-leaning Timorese had ties to China going back to the 1970s. Although in the past China had opposed virtually any UN-led intervention abroad, now Beijing deployed police as part of the UN mission to reconstruct East Timor. Beijing heavily advertised its peacekeeping, though its actual troop commitment to Timor paled next to those of other countries.[4]

China became one of the major donors in Dili, though Beijing does not actively coordinate its efforts with other major aid givers like Australia and the United States. Besides funding the construction of East Timor's foreign ministry, China paid for the Timor government to open a new embassy in Beijing and sponsored trainings for the biggest party in Timor. Meanwhile, a wave of Chinese migrants from the mainland have arrived in Dili, some encouraged by Chinese government policies that offer minimal assistance to come to Timor, others persuaded by word of mouth that Timor could be a business opportunity.[5]

China's ambassadors in Dili, Portuguese speakers able to communicate with Timor's Portuguese-speaking leadership, became some of the most active diplomats. More important, the savvy Timorese leadership saw in Beijing an opportunity to use China for its own ends, allowing Timor to avoid becoming dependent on either of its two giant neighbors, Indonesia or Australia. With their Portuguese skills, Chinese diplomats gained close access to Mari Alkatiri, independent Timor's first prime minister, who had spent the Indonesian years in exile in Portuguese-speaking Angola and Mozambique. Chinese officials could deliver an appealing message, emphasizing both nations' history of socialism—many Timorese leaders had begun their guerrilla careers as Marxists. China's domestic economic success helped as well, as did a vow never to bully small nations like East Timor.[6]

Rewarding China's diligence (and acting on Timor's need to find a friend outside Australia and Indonesia), Dili quickly established diplomatic relations with Beijing—in fact, China was the first country with which independent Timor established diplomatic relations. Foreign Minister Ramos Horta announced that China would be Timor's "closest possible ally," though Ramos Horta later said he had meant only that China and Timor should develop the closest possible relationship. Since then, the Timorese government has given Chinese companies permission to conduct seismic studies in Timor, putting these firms in position to play a role in extracting the resources of the oil- and gas-rich Timor Sea, which divides Timor and Australia, and which contains deposits that may be worth more than $30 billion.[7]

Though some former independence fighters seem concerned about Timor cozying up to China, Beijing appeared genuinely popular in Dili among average Timorese. Across the half-island, people praised China's influence, and many young Timorese tried to find ways to study Chinese in private classes. Educated middle-class Timorese who knew anything about the PRC knew that China had once been poor, like Timor, but somehow had become fabulously wealthy.

In East Timor, China's charm offensive is beginning to show results. Beijing has used a blend of pragmatic diplomacy, increased aid, and an implicit comparison between China and other major powers to woo elites and average people. Timor, like many countries, has seen China rising and has decided that it must make the most of this opportunity. But is China's charm working in other parts of the globe? Is Beijing truly becoming more popular, more of a model, more persuasive, more appealing? Have other nations resolved to make the most of China's newfound assertiveness?

Having traced China's goals for its influence, its strategies for building influence, and the tools it uses to cultivate that charm, it is possible to judge how successful Beijing has been in wooing the world. The clearest type of evidence is explicit evidence—evidence that directly demonstrates whether China's charm offensive is gaining ground.

Polls and opinion surveys offer one explicit measure of China's success. In 2005 the US embassy in Bangkok commissioned a study of Thai perceptions of other nations. This poll revealed that a majority of Thais believed that China would soon become their most important external influence and closest economic partner–a "development that few [Thais] perceive in threatening terms," the study reported. (Seven years ago, the study found, only 12 percent of Thais thought that China would wield the most influence in East Asia.) Eighty-three percent of Thais polled had a favorable opinion of China.[8]

Other studies concur. The comprehensive 2005 BBC poll of twenty-two nations, including developing countries like the Philippines, found that 48 percent of people thought China's role in the world was mainly positive. Thirty percent saw China's role as negative. "It is quite remarkable that, with its growing economic power, China is viewed as so benign, especially by its Asian neighbors that it could threaten or seek to dominate," noted Steven Kull, director of the organization that conducted the poll for the BBC. A follow-up poll released in February 2006 revealed positive public opinion toward China and deteriorating public opinion toward the United States in important developing nations, from Indonesia (60 percent positive for China) to Nigeria (68 percent positive) to Kenya (59 percent). Another study just of Latin America found that there was "ample support in Latin American public opinion, Argentina and Mexico partially excepted, for China's new role in world affairs."[9]

Anecdotal research suggests the same, though polls and anecdotes are not conclusive evidence, and need to be considered warily. In interviews with opinion leaders across Asia outside of Japan, I have found far less concern about China's growing influence than I heard during the late 1990s. Of course, this is partly because many Asians realize that China is growing powerful and that they cannot ignore China's influence. It is easy, however, to stumble across people furious over American policy, like the elderly Indonesian businessman who grilled me for thirty minutes about why America had allowed him to come lecture to business groups in the United States but barred his wife, a seventy-something woman, from accompanying him on the trip.[10]

Eventually, China's warm image may recede. One reason why the United States evokes such negative feelings in some countries is that many foreigners now feel they know the United States intimately. In places like Latin America, countries have two hundreds years of experience with the United States acting like a great power; even in Asia the United States has projected its power at least since the Second World War. Leaders and average citizens know America well, and in places like Latin America, some have come to associate the United States with interventions that backfired, causing economic and political misery. The fact that the international media focus on the United States further exposes America's faults to the world, like the Hurricane Katrina debacle or the controversy over the 2000 presidential election. "The image of the United States as a promised land—distant, exotic, and glamorous—has faded in the onslaught of familiarity with U.S. products, the media-portrayed image of America, and the vast numbers of people who have traveled there," notes a leading US business journal. And as American culture becomes so ubiquitous overseas, its exoticism and the excitement it inspires diminish, thereby undermining the glamour of the United States as a model of affluence and innovation. In post–World War II Europe, writes the German scholar Josef Joffe, "save for the tourists and soldiers, America was not a reality but a distant myth, as portrayed in soft brushstrokes on TV by series like *Lassie* and *Father Knows Best.*" Today, Joffe notes, "the entire world watches, wears, drinks, eats, listens, and dances American."[11]

By contrast, for countries outside of Asia, China remains something of a blank slate. After 1979 China retreated from the world and did not attempt to exert power across the globe, so a generation of African and Latin American policy makers had little experience with a powerful China. Though the international media cover China, it does not attract the kind of close attention that the United States draws. As a result, some opinion leaders can believe that China, unlike other major powers, will impose no conditions on other countries or pressure other nations to do what Beijing wants. They can believe that China's rise will truly be an uncomplicated "win-win," an opportunity but not a threat.

That honeymoon period will end. As China becomes more powerful, the world media will focus more intensely on the People's Republic. Some of China's own dirty laundry, like rising socioeconomic inequality or Beijing's crackdown on

Muslims in the western province of Xinjiang, will be beamed around the world. And as China becomes more powerful, other nations also will begin to see beyond its benign face to a more complicated, and sometimes negative, reality. Already, in one example, the South Korean media have highlighted statements by Chinese academics that seem to suggest that parts of ancient Korean kingdoms were actually not independent but rather subordinate to Chinese dynasties.[12]

Still, for now China is enjoying the honeymoon. China has gained popularity even in countries whose recent relations with Beijing had proved disastrous. In Cambodia the Maoist Khmer Rouge regime killed as many as two million Cambodians between 1975 and 1979. In one part of Phnom Penh, the Khmer Rouge turned Tuol Sleng, an old high school, into a laboratory of humankind's worst impulses, chaining prisoners to beds to stretch their limbs, applying shocks to their genitals, burning them with hot metal rods, or hanging them from hooks in the ceilings. (Signs posted at Tuol Sleng informed prisoners not to scream or commit other breaches of decorum.) China served as the Khmer Rouge's major foreign patron, sending it more than fifteen thousand military advisers. Beijing knew what was going on: former Chinese Vice Premier Geng Biao admitted that he suspected the Khmer Rouge was persecuting its opponents and putting them to death.[13]

In the decade after the fall of the Khmer Rouge, Cambodia had no relations with China, and even when the two nations restored ties, the relationship remained cool for a time. Cables obtained through the Freedom of Information Act from the US embassy in Phnom Penh suggest that China also pressured the Cambodian government not to create a tribunal to try former Khmer Rouge leaders. But today, opinion leaders across Cambodia look to China as a partner and model of development.[14]

China's appeal is reflected in another explicit sign of success. Chinese-language and -cultural studies have skyrocketed in popularity in the developing world, as average people come to see learning Chinese as vital to business and as providing a kind of popular cachet, the way English long has. In Argentina, the number of people studying Chinese reportedly tripled in 2005, and the new Mandarin program at the University of Buenos Aires enrolled more than a thousand students in just two years of operation. In Malaysia average daily readership of *Sin Chew Daily,* the largest Chinese-language newspaper, grew from 845,000 in 1999 to 1.1 million in 2004, despite a global downturn in newspaper reading. Financial analysts believe *Sin Chew*'s readership will continue to expand as more Malaysians study Chinese and become interested in news about China. Thailand has announced that every public school in the country should teach Mandarin, attendance at Laos's main Chinese-language school has more than doubled in the past five years, the demand for Chinese in Indonesia has become so great that the country faces a shortage of some 100,000 Chinese-language instructors, and in Cambodia one Chinese-language elementary school alone boasts more than 10,000 students.[15]

Though not a developing country, South Korea also reflects this trend. For centuries, Korea has enjoyed close links to China. Though history can divide the two nations, especially in debates over which parts of modern-day Korea and China historically belonged to each country, the shared heritage also unites them. As China has become South Korea's biggest trading partner, and growing numbers of Koreans visit China for holiday or business, private Chinese-language schools have blossomed in Seoul and other cities. Some 160,000 South Korean high school and university students now study Chinese, roughly 60 percent more than studied the language five years ago, and Chinese-language books and films sell well in Seoul, even as Korean soap operas and movies are hits in China. Chinese has begun to challenge English as the second language of choice in South Korean cities. Indeed, as the number of people studying Chinese grows, more Chinese companies expand abroad, and Chinese becomes the language most used on the Internet, Chinese may become a global second language, the way English is now—the language people want to learn after they master their own tongue. South Korea now sends more than 13,000 students per year to China, a figure equal to the total number of Koreans who studied in the United States between 1953 and 1975, the height of US–South Korean relations.[16]

Some elite Chinese universities have begun to challenge Western schools as destinations of choice for higher education, especially as China's provision of university scholarships has begun to be noticed in developing countries. Between 2002 and 2004 the number of Cambodian students in China grew by nearly 20 percent, the number of Indonesians rose nearly 50 percent, and the number of Vietnamese rose nearly 90 percent—even though the Vietnamese government, still suspicious of historic enemy China, has restrictions on the study of Chinese in Vietnam. Overall, the number of Southeast Asians who obtained visas to study in China nearly doubled between 2002 and 2004, and more than 1,600 African students now study at Chinese universities, many on Chinese government scholarships. "For a few years ahead, it will still be the United States as number one, but soon it will be China," one Thai student told the *New York Times,* explaining why he chose to study Chinese rather than English.[17]

In total, the number of foreign students enrolling in China has been increasing by 20 percent per year. By 2008, the Chinese Ministry of Education estimates, China's universities will enroll more than 120,000 foreign students, compared with some 8,000 twenty years ago. Some of these foreign students come from government backgrounds, as other countries encourage their diplomats and officials to learn Chinese. Singapore, for example, has launched a government effort to send as many top students on scholarships to China as to the United States. "As the Singapore government bolsters the number of scholarships to go to China for its brightest minds, it's going to become more prestigious for Ministry of Foreign Affairs people to have studied in China," says Eric Teo Chu Cheow, a former Singaporean diplomat. "Singapore will develop a cadre of diplomats with ties to China, just like we already have ones close to the US." Singapore proved visionary. In 2003 China trained nearly 1,500 people from 107 countries, primarily government bureaucrats and officials, in public management and technology.[18]

Desire for learning the Chinese language often sparks a greater interest in Chinese culture. "Chinese culture belongs not only to the Chinese but also to the whole world," Hu Jintao announced in 2003—revealing a conviction that other countries desire his culture, just as American leaders have always evinced. "It looks like being Chinese is cool," the publisher Kitti Jinsiriwanich told the *Wall Street Journal,* explaining his decision to produce a glossy new magazine about ethnic Chinese life in Bangkok and ethnic Chinese pop stars and rappers. His magazine had proven so popular, in fact, that high-rent advertisers like Nokia had tracked him down in his tiny office to hawk their wares. In other developing nations, publishers are launching similar efforts, which portray a glamorous Chinese lifestyle similar to what you might see in *Vanity Fair*'s depictions of the United States—a far cry from the drab peasant clothes of the Maoist era, or even from the wrenching poverty of rural China today.[19]

Meanwhile, interviews with artists across Southeast Asia suggest that many would be as interested today in training in China as in Japan or Europe or the United States, though they recognize that the Chinese government still imposes serious limits on artistic freedom. China has developed an art scene centered in places like Dashanzi, an art-oriented area of eastern Beijing where painters have gutted Maoist-era military equipment factories to put galleries and cafes inside the buildings' shells. A surprising recent report by UNESCO, the United Nations Educational, Scientific, and Cultural Organization, revealed that China has become the world's second-largest exporter of visual arts. China's scene is beginning to be recognized by collectors—the Beijing Art Fair now attracts nearly one hundred galleries from around the world, and one collector recently paid nearly $1 million at a Sotheby's auction for a painting by the Chinese contemporary artist Zhang Xiaogang, a high-water mark for modern Chinese art.[20] Not content to let Sotheby's control the market, Christie's has tried to muscle into contemporary Chinese painting, holding its first-ever auction of modern Chinese art in 2005.

As mainland China has developed an impressive literary scene, meanwhile, translators have been buying up Chinese works. In Vietnam, despite long-standing tensions with China, the Ministry of Culture's Publishing Department reports that novels by Chinese writers account for roughly half of all the foreign literary books translated in the country. Chinese-language television, music, and film are gaining wider audiences, too. Chinese-themed films have been sweeping cinemas in

Southeast Asia, so much so that the Philippines holds its own Chinese film festival. Chinese-themed films have won top prizes at the Manila Film Festival and attracted the interest of Hollywood studios, which are searching for joint-venture opportunities in China. Several Chinese movies have even begun to make waves internationally, like *Sanxia Haoren,* or *Still Life,* which won the Golden Lion for best film at the Venice International Film Festival in 2006. And across Asia, Chinese television serials have staked out viewerships alongside longer-established Korean and Hong Kong soaps, while Chinese pop singers, classical music stars, and film actors have become major figures in South Korea, part of a first wave of Chinese stars abroad—even as Korean stars, too, have become popular across Asia.[21]

In some developing nations, meanwhile, the print and broadcast media have become decidedly more positive toward China. In Thailand an analysis of elite English and vernacular media suggests that a decade ago many publications voiced concerns about China's economic power, human rights abuses, and designs on regions of Southeast Asia, but today it is nearly impossible to find any columnist or writer consistently critical of Beijing. Similarly, in Indonesia the media have been uncritical of China. This despite the fact that pan-Islamic issues dominate Indonesian newspapers' opinion pages, and Beijing's crackdown on Chinese Muslims in its western province of Xinjiang includes, according to Human Rights Watch, thousands of arbitrary detentions for "illegal religious activity." Yet Xinjiang rarely merits even a mention in the *Jakarta Post, Tempo,* or other top Indonesian publications.[22]

Partly, this reflects tough Chinese control of foreign news outlets, which limits coverage of Xinjiang and other problems in China. Partly, it reflects Washington's unpopularity: because the United States is still vastly more powerful on the world stage than China, American abuses of Muslims at Guantánamo Bay or Abu Ghraib make better-selling stories in the media than China's abuses. And partly, it may reflect success by Chinese diplomats in other countries in using their influence to prevent local reporters from writing stories that reflect badly on Beijing.

Elites in some developing nations also seem to have embraced China's growing soft power—they see in it opportunity for their companies and political parties. Across the developing world, mainland Chinese businesspeople and policy makers now are given the type of welcome and access once reserved for Americans or Japanese or Europeans. "Even Chinese diplomats well below the ambassadorial level, like the cultural and commercial attachés, get treated like royalty here," says one Malaysian scholar. When Hu Jintao arrived in Thailand in 2003, the Thais welcomed him with a state banquet at the royal family's palace, a rare honor. When Hu stopped in Brazil in 2004, Brazilian President Luiz Inácio Lula da Silva upgraded bilateral trade ties and decided to send Brazilian advisers to Beijing to study Chinese economics. "We want a partnership that integrates our economies and serves as a paradigm for South-South cooperation," Lula cooed.[23]

In the chaos of Indonesia's financial meltdown in 1998, many journalists focused on the implications of the crisis for Suharto, the sleepy-eyed dictator who had ruled Indonesia for three decades, maneuvering among his country's power bases like a masterful puppeteer. With Indonesia's currency free-falling, Suharto had approved fiscal austerity measures proposed by the International Monetary Fund. Austerity bit into average Indonesians' pocketbooks, and squatter camps of the newly poor spread across Jakarta. Students and democracy activists held open protests against the faltering government, unthinkable only five years before. By March 1998 Suharto seemed exhausted and ready to leave—which he did in May, handing power to his vice president, B. J. Habibie.[24]

With the spotlight on Suharto, many reporters missed an ominous trend. Though Suharto's government had imposed restrictions on the Chinese Indonesian minority, making it difficult for them to obtain financing from state banks and Indonesian citizenship, there had been no large-scale anti–ethnic Chinese violence in Indonesia for thirty years, partly because Suharto's authoritarian regime limited open protest. But in January 1998, as Suharto's grip on power loosened, Muslim leaders across the archipelago began demonizing the country's Chinese minority, telling young Muslims to "take back the wealth that is rightfully [yours]," as one academic studying the violence recorded. Religious leaders, army officers, and police further whipped up crowds of unemployed young men with anti-Chinese slurs and unsubstantiated reports that Chinese merchants were gouging customers on cooking oil and other staples. By February mobs had begun attacking Chinese-owned shops in the Javanese city of Pamanukan, screaming "Kill the Chinese" and "Chinese out"; some rioters ripped jewelry from the necks and arms of ethnic Chinese women in the streets.[25]

Violence spiraled. In February a meeting in the Al-Azhar mosque in Jakarta featured speakers calling on Indonesians to fight "traitors" in the country who were stealing the nation's wealth, leaving little doubt who they considered traitors. Mobs focused on ethnic Chinese–owned businesses like shopping malls and gold stores, and men on motorcycles led some of the rioters to selected Chinese-owned shops, where they locked the proprietors inside and burned the buildings to the ground. Perhaps as many as seventy thousand Chinese Indonesians fled the country, and many more escaped Jakarta for quieter parts of the archipelago, like Bali.[26]

At the time, the Chinese government did almost nothing to stop the rioting in Indonesia. During the Maoist period in the mid-1960s, when some Indonesian rioters had targeted Chinese Indonesians, Beijing had stepped in, offering refuge for ethnic Chinese fleeing the archipelago. Similarly, when ethnic Chinese refugees fled Vietnam in 1980, China sent ships to help them. But in 1998 Beijing said nothing for months about the Indonesian riots. More than two months after some of the worst violence, a Chinese foreign ministry spokesman belatedly announced, "China is concerned and sympathetic with the suffering experienced by the Indonesians of Chinese origin," but Beijing did not apply any pressure on Jakarta to protect Chinese Indonesians.[27] This callous approach alienated some diaspora Chinese, but, as interviews with Chinese officials suggest, it was part of a strategy by Beijing to assure its neighbors that it would not intervene in their affairs. The strategy worked: it made it possible for Indonesian leaders to genuinely believe Beijing was becoming more pragmatic and noninterventionist.

When one looks down from A. B. Susanto's penthouse office today, a view stretching over the elevated, manicured highways of Jakarta's financial district, it is hard to imagine that the chaos of 1998 took place less than a decade ago. Ushered into the office, I sit on a leather couch in one end of the sprawling room at Susanto's business strategy firm, the Jakarta Consulting Group, which counts among its clients many of Indonesia's most prominent companies. Susanto, who just returned from a lecture tour in Australia, had furnished his office, the size of two hotel suites, with large portraits of himself mounted on artists' easels and a coffee table covered in business books he had written. He settles his pudgy frame onto the couch opposite me, pulls off his gold cufflinks, and rolls up the sleeves of his crisp peach shirt.[28]

A. B. Susanto had long been a prominent Indonesian Chinese member of the Jakarta business community, but despite his wealth, until recent years he never became involved in politics. In the past five years, though, he began to sense a shift in views of Chinese Indonesians. After the riots in 1998, tensions calmed in Indonesia, and the country made the transition to democracy and developed closer ties to China itself, mitigating any (irrational) fear that Beijing would try to use Indonesian Chinese as a fifth column to undermine the Indonesian government.

"The population in Indonesia definitely has become more tolerant of ethnic Chinese—of ethnic Chinese politicians," says Susanto. In this new era of tolerance, several political parties wooed Susanto to run for Parliament in the 2004 Indonesian elections. He chose the National Awakening Party, and ran in 2004, one of at least thirty Indonesian Chinese running for Parliament in that election.

Though he did not win, Susanto was staying in politics.[29] In fact, he now felt completely comfortable in the political game, and was waiting for barons to come to him. "I've been asked to run for other offices, including vice mayor of Jakarta," Susanto said, though for now he had turned down all comers. "We can really exert our presence—we [ethnic Chinese] are not afraid to share some of our ideas anymore."

Analyzing the position of ethnic Chinese in the diaspora—men and women like A. B. Susanto—offers another explicit way to measure China's charm. Beijing has actively cultivated the diaspora, and sometimes has tried to use them as links between the developing world and China. And the ethnic Chinese's position, in society and politics, has been radically transformed in the past ten years. Diaspora Chinese, even powerful businessmen like Susanto, once avoided politics for fear of being tied to China's policies and negative image, and then being targeted by the majority in their nations.

But today diaspora Chinese increasingly advertise their Chinese heritage, like Americans living abroad in the 1950s and 1960s, a time when the United States' image in much of the world was much more positive, and advertising your American background might help woo business partners or persuade local politicians to side with you. Of course, many in the diaspora have little connection to mainland China, and many do not even speak Chinese; in this way, they are vastly different from Americans overseas, who obviously remained US citizens.

Still, even if the diaspora Chinese actually have little interaction with China, in many countries perceptions of China reflect upon perceptions of diaspora Chinese. In many cases the diaspora's identity now has taken on a positive connotation because China is no longer seen as a threat, and because, rightly or wrongly, some non-Chinese view ethnic Chinese as potential links to China.

In Indonesia, ethnic Chinese's fortunes have benefited from warming relations with Beijing, as well as from the democratization of Indonesian politics and society, which opened people's eyes to the history of Indonesia's discrimination. Over the past five years, Chinese Indonesians like A. B. Susanto have become even more integrated into Indonesian society. They now celebrate Chinese New Year, outlawed under Suharto, and visit China for vacations. Banned by Suharto from creating political organizations, Chinese Indonesians today have founded ethnic associations and self-help groups that assisted ethnic Chinese victims of the 2004 tsunami. Along with Susanto and the thirty parliamentary candidates, more than one hundred Indonesian Chinese ran for regional legislatures in 2004. Perhaps the greatest sign that Indonesians are more willing to accept their Chinese minority? A Chinese Indonesian nearly won the Indonesian version of *American Idol.*[30]

Other developing nations have witnessed similar shifts in public opinion toward diaspora Chinese. Shortly after coming to office in 2001, former Thai Prime Minister Thaksin Shinawatra paid a visit to China. Bringing with him a delegation of Thai business and political elites, Thaksin arrived in Beijing before continuing on to Meizhou, the area of Guangdong province that Thaksin's ancestors had left for Thailand. The prime minister's visit befuddled the farmers in Meizhou, who probably remembered Thaksin's relatives about as well as anyone in Poland would remember the Kurlantzick family, which emigrated to America a century ago. But the Meizhou residents played along in the spirit of goodwill, staging a lion dance and chatting with the prime minister in Hakka, a dialect spoken in southern China.[31]

Returning to Thailand, Thaksin emphasized his ethnic Chinese background and touted his ability to bridge relations between Bangkok and Beijing. Playing up his heritage, Thaksin led some of the largest delegations to the Boao Forum, China's World Economic Forum–like summit, and ultimately pushed for a closer Thailand-China strategic partnership. Beijing responded, providing funding for the Sirindhorn Center, a new Chinese-language and cultural facility located at Mae Fah Luang University in northern Thailand, and signing an agreement promising to increase bilateral trade between the two nations to $50 billion by 2010. Today other prominent Thai politicians tout their Chinese background, partly because they believe it will open doors to China, and partly because it seems popular with a public that views Beijing as cool, rich, and attractive. "Every time we sit down with the Chinese [officials], all the Thai are always tracing their ancestry," says Kraisak, the Thai senator.[32]

Meanwhile, few Thais accuse local Thai companies with close links to Beijing of favoring the People's Republic, even as some Thai firms and Thai leaders receive criticism for their alliances with Western companies or Western countries. When Thailand tried to negotiate a free trade deal with the United States in 2006, more than ten thousand protesters greeted the negotiating team during their meetings in Chiang Mai, a city in northern Thailand. Demonstrators fought with police and burned the Thai negotiator Nit Pibulsongkram in effigy, complaining that he was too American, because he had formerly been the Thai ambassador to the United States and had family links to America.[33]

Contrast this with average Thais' response to news about Charoen Pokphand, the agricultural giant that was the first foreign investor in China. CP, I learned, is quietly building warehouses across Bangkok to import Chinese goods; some of those Chinese agricultural imports probably will displace Thai farmers. CP's chief reportedly examined prospective hires' facial features to see whether they have ethnic Chinese ancestry. CP has advised the Thai government on its relations with China, and reportedly even helped the Chinese government with its overseas lobbying efforts.[34]

But China is now seen as Thailand's close friend, a friendship facilitated by China's diplomacy, aid, and cultivation of diaspora Chinese in Thailand, and because Thailand sees the benefits of latching onto China's rising economic star. So few Thais lash out against Thailand's trade negotiations with China, or Thai companies that benefit from close relations with Beijing. The Thai media rarely criticize CP for being "too Chinese." When I asked many Thai opinion leaders whether they were concerned that CP might benefit at the expense of Thai farmers, most seem befuddled at the question. Not a single one said yes.

VII
Goal Oriented

These are the early days of China's charm offensive, which can make it difficult to draw hard and fast conclusions, but there are other ways, beyond what we saw in the last chapter, to measure Beijing's successes and failures. Results of opinion studies, interest in Chinese culture and language, respect for Chinese officials, and treatment of diaspora Chinese are explicit, relatively obvious signs of China's charm success. It is also possible to look at *implicit* signs of China's success—by recalling China's goals, and then examining whether it is achieving its goals.

China has hardly enjoyed unchecked success in achieving its goals, and it still faces many significant obstacles. Since China's soft power also contains coercive elements, it can be hard to tell how much China is pulling other nations and how much it is pushing. Nor has Beijing consistently used its power to compel other nations to take actions not already in their own self-interest; other countries may use aspects of Chinese soft power to their own benefit.

Still, by examining China's goals, we can infer that China has enjoyed some success wielding soft power. China's goals include maintaining peace and stability on its borders, portraying itself to other nations as a benign and constructive actor, possibly becoming a model of development to other nations, obtaining resources needed to power the Chinese economy, isolating Taiwan, and demonstrating the possibility that it can eventually become a great power—one day even an equal of the United States.

Beijing has built peaceful relations with most of its neighbors, creating the kind of stability China long has desired. As China has become more popular, leaders across Asia could not rally domestic political support by persisting in disputes with Beijing. Beijing has settled most of its border issues, which previously threatened its peaceful relations.[1]

China also has begun to convince developing nations that it can be a constructive player in global affairs. To be sure, Asian nations like Vietnam clearly still harbor fears that China seeks to dominate the region; countries like Vietnam build ties with other Asian nations, and with the United States, to counterbalance Beijing. China's neighbors have some reason to worry: the history of interactions between China and the rest of Asia stretches back millennia, and gives little reassurance to other Asian countries. As the historians John King Fairbank and Merle Goldman write, historically China viewed the nations of Southeast Asia as inferior vassal states. China carried out a foreign policy in which it sought to dominate these countries without militarily controlling them; other Asian countries offered the Chinese court lavish gifts, probably to keep Beijing from invading.[2]

These memories have not vanished, from the minds of either Chinese leaders or their neighbors. As Chinese foreign policy specialists recently told the former intelligence officer Robert Sutter, secret Chinese Communist Party documents consistently refer to a goal of having China be the leader in Asia.[3]

Still, other nations are balancing less against China than in the past. Only a decade ago, after China's military staked a claim to the South China Sea, fearful Southeast Asian nations united to condemn Beijing's actions. Today, the Southeast Asian nation closest to the disputed sea, the Philippines, has established closer military ties with China—a decision, Philippine politicians agree, it can make only because the Philippine public has grow more enthusiastic about China's influence. Indeed, a Pentagon-sponsored report obtained through the Freedom of Information Act noted, "Philippine officials and scholars generally have a very positive view of China." They are not alone. As a panel of Asian experts convened by the National Bureau of Asian Research, America's leading Asia research group, concluded, "Southeast Asian states generally perceive China's rise as more of [an] opportunity." "The majority of Asian states currently view China as more benign than malign, and are accommodating themselves to China's rise," agrees George Washington University's David Shambaugh, in one of his most recent studies of Asian reactions to China.[4]

This appeal could boost Beijing's influence, just as American popularity after the Second World War allowed leaders from a range of nations to ally with the United States, since appearing close to America helped them in their domestic political environments. In democratic nations like the Philippines or Thailand, China's appeal today allows leaders in the region the political space to move closer to China, since public sentiment supports warming relations. In Thailand, for example, former Prime Minister Thaksin Shinawatra's aides believed that their boss's touting of ties to China helped him win votes among businesspeople and other elite sections of society.[5] In less democratic nations, like Venezuela, where a small circle of leaders makes decisions, China's appeal to those elites may serve the same function, allowing them to build consensus on warming relations with Beijing.

In South Korea, meanwhile, some government officials told former intelligence officer Sutter that they were concerned about how popular China was becoming among South Korean legislators and the general public. One internal poll of incoming South Korean legislators, they warned, showed that 63 percent viewed China as the most important nation for Seoul. Though these officials wanted to make relations with the United States the top priority of Seoul's foreign policy, they said that "they faced a difficult challenge in achieving these tasks in the face of widespread South Korean public opinion, and the opinion of recently elected legislators, that gave China the top priority in South Korean foreign policy and took a dim view of the United States."[6]

Many of these leaders already display greater comfort working with China. In the run-up to the December 2005 East Asia Summit, a pan-Asian forum on economic and regional political issues, semiauthoritarian Malaysia consulted closely with China on EAS policy making, reflecting the warmth between the Malaysian and Chinese governments.[7] Some Asian countries eventually may consider upgrading their strategic partnerships with Beijing to formal alliances. Again, if they have more comfort working with Beijing, it is because China has become less threatening, and more popular, with elites and with the general public.

Some of this warmth clearly comes from other countries' fear of getting on Beijing's bad side—they have no choice but to deal with China's rising strength. "This government sees

China as the power that will engage Asia and dominate the destiny of Asia," leading Thai commentator Kavi Chongkittavorn told the *Washington Post.* Similarly, Cambodian Prime Minister Hun Sen in 1988 wrote, "China is the root of all that is evil in Cambodia," remembering that Beijing had supported the murderous Khmer Rouge in the 1970s. In 2005 as China poured in aid to Cambodia, Hun Sen announced that Phnom Penh's relations with Beijing were "entering into the best stage in history." "The People's Republic of China has achieved this amazing volte-face through a patient and economical application of military and development assistance, loans, investment, and the cultivation of the Sino-Khmer community," admitted a classified cable sent by former US Ambassador to Cambodia Charles A. Ray. Similarly, partly because of China's dominance of trade with Thailand, a Thai foreign ministry official, Sihasak Phuangketkeow, was careful to tell the *Washington Post* that Thailand's relationship with the United States was "not more special than relations with China."[8]

Some countries now appear comfortable enough with China's rise that they do view it as a model of development. In places like Vietnam or Iran, where regimes are attempting to maintain control while growing the economy, policy makers seem convinced that if they learn from China, they can duplicate China's success in promoting development while forestalling political liberalization. In Vietnam younger policy makers have adopted what they call a "Chinese model" of slowly opening the economy while retaining control of the political system. Across the border, policy makers in Laos see China as a source of inspiration. "We see that the economy of China has grown, and we think that there are lessons for Laos's economy from China—the building up of socialism while also having sustained economic growth," said one China specialist at Laos's foreign ministry.[9]

Iran and Syria provide even clearer examples of the appeal of the China model. In Syria, the leadership has openly touted its desire to move toward a Chinese model of development. In Iran conservatives from the office of Supreme Leader Ayatollah Khameini have traveled to China to study the Chinese development model, and the applicability of the China model to Iran became a major topic of debate in the 2005 Iranian elections.[10]

In Latin America and Africa, the China model of state-directed growth and poverty reduction holds appeal as well. China successfully advertises its model of development as a contrast to the neoliberal, free-market Washington Consensus, which failed many developing nations. In a poll taken in 2002, after a decade of weak growth in the region, a mere 35 percent of Latin Americans said that the state should allow the private sector to control economic activity, showing the level of frustration with free-market economics and its supporters in the West. Another study showed that support for democracy was declining sharply, with more than 50 percent of Latin Americans agreeing with the statement "I wouldn't mind if a nondemocratic government came to power if it could solve economic problems"—a sentiment that could prove amenable to China's model of economic liberalization combined with political control.[11] Perhaps unsurprisingly, then, Brazilian President Lula has sent teams of advisers to Beijing to learn from China, while Raúl Castro has traveled to China on numerous occasions, spending long periods learning at the side of China's former Premier Zhu Rongji. According to the Cuba expert William Ratliff, Raúl invited one of Zhu's top advisers back to Cuba, where he gave lectures to hundreds of top Cuban officials and executives.

Similarly, in Africa many opinion leaders tout the Chinese model as a solution to the continent's long history of underdevelopment. According to Barry Sautman, the specialist on China-Africa relations at Hong Kong University of Science and Technology, one leading Nigerian writer has argued that "China has not allowed any . . . World Bank to impose on it some neoliberal package of reforms. . . . Their strategy has not been a neoliberal overdose of deregulation, cutting social expenditure, privatizing everything under the sun, and jettisoning the public good. They have not branded subsidy a dirty word." Even the head of the African Development Bank announced, "We can learn from [the Chinese] how . . . to move from low to middle income status."[12]

Even democracies that historically have placed communal rights above a Western emphasis on individual liberties can find things to admire in China's model. I Wibowo, a specialist on Chinese studies in Indonesia, which is still struggling to recover from the Asian financial crisis, says, "Indonesians might not know much about China, but they know that China has been successful in making their economy grow, [and] they see China as a model"—a place where some individual sacrifices have created prosperity. "There's great admiration of China," agrees Dewi Fortuna Anwar, former assistant minister for foreign affairs in the Indonesian government. "Indonesians look at China and see a situation Indonesians would like to emulate." Next door in Malaysia, "China's model of government mobilizing society for economic gain, while keeping down tension—this is attractive here," says Gavin Khoo, a research fellow at the Asian Center for Media Studies, a Malaysian think tank. "There is little emphasis on individual rights and freedoms here, even among average people."[13]

The Chinese vision of diplomacy, in which countries

rarely intervene in each other's affairs, also appeals to elites and populaces in some democracies—particularly in freer nations like India and Thailand and Brazil and Mexico, which face serious rights problems at home. India, for example, has earned criticism from American policy makers for its crackdown in Kashmir, as has Thailand for its brutal battle against a Muslim insurgency in its deep south. Indeed, many of these countries, like Thailand, chafe at American criticism of their human rights records. "China doesn't lecture . . . on democracy, human rights, or deregulation," argues Frank Ching, a leading Hong Kong–based commentator on China. "As a result, [countries are] wooed more successfully by China."[14]

The appeal of the China model, of course, depends on China's continuing to post astounding growth rates. Any slippage would cost it dearly in soft power; in the old Soviet Union, when sympathetic foreign visitors actually came to the USSR and saw how poorly its economy was performing, they often became far less enthusiastic about the potential spread of the Soviet model around the world. China clearly faces obstacles to long-term growth. China's banking sector remains riddled by nonperforming loans and shady deals with state-linked enterprises—several state recapitalizations of the banking sector have failed. Only three years ago, one of China's largest financial institutions, China Construction Bank, was insolvent, and while the Chinese government estimates that its banking sector faces roughly $130 billion in bad loans, most Western analysts believe the true number is far higher. Meanwhile, China faces an income divide between its prosperous eastern half, which has attracted most of the foreign investment and has cities like Shanghai that rival New York, and the interior, rural areas, which look more like Africa, with farmers struggling to eke out any income and living in simple huts without modern amenities. "The income gap . . . has exceeded reasonable trends," the Chinese news wire Xinhua admitted in 2005. Rising income inequality has sparked waves of protest in China: even China's public security minister admitted that there were some eighty-seven thousand "mass incidents" in China in 2005, up from fifty-eight thousand in 2003.[15]

In poorer countries like Laos, Cambodia, Kazakhstan, North Korea, and even the Russian far east, the appeal of China's model, of life in China, is more than an abstract idea: people want to get to China itself. This isn't a new concept for Americans or Europeans, who expect to see millions of foreigners coming to the United States or the European Union to make a better life for themselves and their families. Mexicans and Central Americans look to the United States as an example of a successful, wealthy neighbor and a place to make money; Moldovans and Ukrainians now see the European Union the same way.

This is how many Laotians and Burmese and Cambodians and North Koreans see China today—as a promised land, even though China's per capita gross domestic product, outside of a few rich eastern cities, remains low compared to the United States or the European Union. In Africa, Latin America, and parts of Asia, many people already perceive China as a wealthy nation, because they hear about China's economic progress and see Chinese business delegations jetting into town to buy up their resources, and because they know far more about wealthier Chinese cities like Shanghai than they do about poor interior areas of China.

Just as Central Americans want to get to the rich United States, some of these people want to get to China. In Burma laborers tell of developing plans to sneak across the porous border at night and then stay in China permanently. In far western China, Kazakh, Pakistani, and Uzbek traders flock to the bustling Chinese markets, and then often stay on, trying to blend into western China's ethnically diverse society. In Laos, Laotian women search for Chinese husbands, whom they believe might take them back to China. To Laotians, "China kind of symbolizes modernity—they move to Jinghong [a city in southwestern China] and they can go to shopping malls, live a modern life," says Antonella Diana, an anthropologist at Australian National University specializing in Laotian perceptions of China. "Lao citizens want to strategically get married to Chinese [even though this does not guarantee Chinese citizenship] because it's a way to enhance your living standards," she says. "They view China as . . . a ticket out of their lives."[16]

As we have already seen, Beijing's state-linked companies are amassing stakes in numerous foreign oil and gas fields, though they are far from matching the holdings of major Western companies like ExxonMobil. Still, China's skillful resource diplomacy has allowed Beijing to diversify its base of oil and gas suppliers. In 1995 China obtained more than half its crude oil from just two nations, Indonesia and Oman. By 2003 Beijing obtained 16.8 percent of its oil from Saudi Arabia, 13.8 percent from Iran, 10.3 percent from Oman, and smaller percentages from other nations.[17]

Foreign leaders now sometimes sell resources to China because dealing with Beijing is less politically dangerous than selling to Western firms. If they sell resources to American companies, leaders find themselves vulnerable to accusations by political opponents of being too pro-American. As one survey of the Middle East by Mamoun Fandy, then of Rice University, discovered, Arabs "find in Beijing a counterweight" to American power.[18]

In contrast with several years ago, when Beijing could only pick off small oil fields in second-tier countries, China has built inroads with the most important suppliers, like Saudi Arabia. In January 2006 Riyadh and Beijing signed a landmark deal expanding oil-sector cooperation between the two nations. China National Petroleum Corporation, one of China's major oil companies, has rapidly set up offices in Saudi Arabia, and the Saudi government also is considering creating a strategic reserve of Saudi Arabian oil in China, which Beijing might be able to rely on the way Washington relies upon America's strategic reserve. Trade between the two countries is rising by more than 50 percent per year, and Saudi businesspeople and officials have been impressed that Chinese diplomats take the time to learn their language. "Their Arabic is fluent. They don't even talk slang," one Saudi businessman marveled about his Chinese hosts.[19]

Though some energy analysts believe that China may have overpaid for resources, the price of a barrel of oil has more than doubled since 1999, and global reserves of cheaply obtainable black gold are decreasing, as major fields in countries like Saudi Arabia reach maturity.[20]

Though China's declared policy is noninterference, and though many nations have found that China does not make as many demands as the United States, Beijing has begun to get what it wants from its foreign relations. In fact, China has skillfully used soft power to influence nations to act according to Beijing's wishes.

In a dramatic shift, China has subtly begun to dominate the internal dynamics of regional organizations in Asia. These groups have begun to shape their decision making to accommodate Beijing, making choices they know will please China.

Take the most prominent example. The Association of Southeast Asian Nations, the most important regional group, is of course supposed to take its interests into account first, making decisions based on Southeast Asia's needs. But several Southeast Asian countries, like Burma, Cambodia, and larger and wealthier Thailand, have developed such close ties to China that they often seem to be considering Beijing's interests while they are making decisions in Asean.

Indeed, Southeast Asian diplomats say that in the past three years, consensus at Asean meetings often is delayed as member nations analyze how Beijing will react to any decision. "A lot of Asean countries clearly take into consideration what the Chinese think—and info quietly gets leaked back to Beijing about who's on their side," says one senior Southeast Asian diplomat. "Asean nations are trying to figure out what China wants ahead of time."[21]

China also has begun leveraging its influence with individual nations. In Zambia, where China is one of the largest investors in the local copper industry and one of the biggest sources of aid, the Chinese ambassador in 2006 warned that Beijing might cut off diplomatic ties if voters picked an opposition candidate known for protesting China's poor labor policies and threatening to evict Chinese companies from the country. The ambassador's comments, which sent shock waves through the local media, marked the first time in the post-Mao period that China had overtly tried to influence an African election.[22] The effort may have been a success: the opposition leader lost the presidential election.

In Cambodia, too, China uses its soft power to force Phnom Penh to take actions it might not otherwise choose.

China has become the most important foreign influence and aid donor in Cambodia, and Cambodian Prime Minister Hun Sen shuttles to and from Beijing constantly. Yet by 2006 it also was clear that China's decision to dam upper portions of the Mekong River, which runs down through Southeast Asia, could have a disastrous impact on Cambodia. In some parts of the river, water levels had fallen so low that the Mekong had turned into flat plains. China had refused to join the Mekong River Commission, the main organization monitoring the river, and continued blasting and damming its sections of the waterway. China even commissioned an environmental impact assessment of its dams that was the ecological equivalent of a drive-by shooting—a one-day trip in which scientists saw virtually nothing. "Hun Sen knows what China is doing," said one Cambodian scientist. Like the prime minister, the scientist was convinced Chinese dams on the upper part of the Mekong River were drying up Cambodia's Tonle Sap, the biggest freshwater lake in Southeast Asia, which is fed by the Mekong and provides the major protein source in Cambodia.[23]

Still, said one senior Cambodian environmental official, every time Cambodians complain privately to the Chinese about the Mekong River, a Chinese delegation visits countries in Southeast Asia, offers promises of aid, emphasizes how popular China has become, and makes promises to uphold environmental standards. "They know Asian leaders can go back to their people and say, 'We have this commitment from China,'" he says—it will appear that these leaders are building relations with China, which average people support. And Beijing's aid goes far in poor nations like Cambodia. As a result, the official said, Hun Sen had publicly declared that Chinese dams would pose "no problems" and instructed his diplomats not to make any complaints about the Mekong.[24]

As China becomes more aggressive, however, it could squander its own gains. "The Chinese diplomats I've dealt with have become increasingly sure and proud of their status, and disdainful of Southeast Asian nations," says one Singaporean diplomat. As the Chinese diplomats abandon their style of appearing to listen to every nation's concerns, he says, they will lose some of their appeal. In Singapore, one of the Southeast Asian nations more skeptical of China's charm offensive, China's growing diplomatic assertiveness has suggested to some Singaporean officials that China's charm is merely a facade, one reason why Singapore has boosted defense cooperation with the United States in recent years. Similarly, says James Wong, a leading Malaysian commentator, "The Chinese angered many Asians by so openly confronting Japan at the East Asia Summit," where China's delegation refused to meet Japan's delegation and Beijing pressured other attendees to disregard any proposals backed by Tokyo.[25]

Beijing also flexes its muscles to isolate Taiwan. Countries are dropping Taiwan partly because they desire closer relations with Beijing and partly because they fear offending China. Either way, for many nations cutting ties to Taiwan now makes sense—it hurts very little but pleases China enormously. In Latin America, where Taiwan retains nearly half of its formal allies in the world, China's economic success, aid, and broader popularity have in recent years swayed Dominica and Grenada to switch recognition to Beijing, while Guatemala has opened commercial relations with China, often the first step toward recognition. Latin American nations have prevented Taiwan from obtaining observer status at the Organization of American States, the region's most important international grouping.[26]

Matters could get worse for Taipei. If Panama switched

recognition to Beijing, other Central American nations probably would follow, since Panama is the most important nation in Central America still recognizing Taiwan. In 2004, during Panama's presidential election, one leading candidate announced that if elected he would open ties to Beijing. Though he lost, his position cannot have reassured Taipei, and several prominent Latin America scholars believe that within a decade Taiwan will retain no formal allies in Central or South America.[27]

In Africa, another region where countries still recognize Taiwan, the die seems cast as well. The Central African Republic and South Africa switched recognition to Beijing in the 1990s. In 2003 Liberia switched to China, and in late 2005 China won over Senegal, one of the most important democracies in Africa, even though Taiwanese President Chen Shui-bian had taken a personal tour through Senegal touting the importance of new democracies sticking together. In 2006 Chad cut diplomatic ties to Taiwan. "We are losing the people sympathetic to us," admits Joanne Chang, formerly one of Taiwan's top representatives in Washington.[28]

Governments are slashing even their informal links to Taiwan. In the 1990s leaders from many developing countries that officially recognized Beijing hosted Taiwanese leaders for quiet meetings and traveled to Taipei for informal visits, as former Malaysian Prime Minister Mahathir Mohamad and former Singaporean Prime Minister Goh Chok Tong did in 1997. They also allowed Taiwan to open informal embassies abroad, normally known as Taipei Economic and Cultural Offices. Cambodia was one of the first to push the Taiwanese out. In 1998 Cambodian Prime Minister Hun Sen announced that he did not want a Taiwanese informal embassy in Phnom Penh, depriving Taipei of this important forum. Other Asian countries halted the informal diplomacy routine. In 2002, after Beijing publicly exposed a visit by Taiwanese Vice President Annette Lu to Bali, the Indonesian Foreign Ministry announced it knew nothing of her visit—surely a lie—and refused to let her come to Jakarta, where she probably had planned some informal meetings with the government. Shortly after the Jakarta incident, the Philippine government announced that it would refuse any visit by Taiwan's president. The following year, after China blasted Lee Hsien Loong, then Singapore's deputy prime minister, for making an informal visit to Taipei, Malaysia announced it would bar any ministers from trips to Taiwan.[29]

Chinese diaspora organizations have become wary of Taiwan as well, and the allure of Taiwan has faded. Over the past decade, Taiwanese companies have relocated large chunks of their factories abroad to China: by the period between 2002 and 2004, nearly half of Taiwan's entire outward investment went to China.[30] At the same time, Taiwan's opposition group, the Democratic Progressive Party, grew in strength and ultimately defeated the long-ruling Kuomintang in the presidential election of 2000, putting itself in power for the first time.

These changes may have helped Taiwanese businesses and benefited Taiwanese democracy, but they damaged Taiwan's precarious soft power. Taiwan's investments in other parts of the developing world plummeted as Taiwanese firms moved to China. Meanwhile, the Kuomintang had spent decades building up links to ethnic Chinese organizations around the world and to leading politicians—women and men like the Philippines' former President Fidel Ramos, whose father had been Philippine ambassador to Taiwan and who himself had built close relations with the Kuomintang leadership.[31]

After nearly two decades in opposition, the Democratic Progressive Party came to power with weak ties to foreign leaders and to the ethnic Chinese diaspora. Still, the DPP quickly cashiered many of the Kuomintang-era diplomats, costing Taiwan years of experience and strong links to diaspora Chinese organizations.[32]

Taiwan has paid a price. Diaspora Chinese organizations have started holding international meetings specifically to denounce Taiwan, like the 2004 get-together in Bangkok, where some one thousand ethnic Chinese held a two-day meeting entitled "Global Overseas Chinese Congregation of Anti-Taiwan Independence." Obviously aware of the vast potential of trade with China, they are making decisions in their best interest. The Chinese Chamber of Commerce in Panama has moved closer to the PRC, pushing for the Panamanian government to switch diplomatic ties and formally recognize Beijing. When Chen Shui-bian has visited Panama, other diaspora Chinese groups like the China Council for Peaceful Reunification have announced that they did not welcome his visit. In the Philippines, Ellen Palanca, a China expert at Ateneo de Manila University, closely monitors these trends. "The Filipino-Chinese business community historically was very pro-Taiwan, but in the past five years they've started to become more pro-PRC," says Palanca. Like many Filipino analysts, she believes that the influence of pro-Beijing Filipino-Chinese tycoon Lucio Tan has swayed the diaspora Chinese community.[33]

Countries have proven willing to isolate other perceived enemies of China—again, both because they desire warmer relations with Beijing and because they fear cooler relations. At the request of Beijing, Cambodia in 2002 barred the Dalai Lama from attending a Buddhism conference. Later, the South Korean government essentially refused the Dalai Lama a visa.

Similarly, China seems to have persuaded other countries to crack down on the Falun Gong, the spiritual movement that frightened Beijing in the late 1990s by holding coordinated nationwide demonstrations, some of the largest in China since the 1989 Tiananmen movement. Soon after, Chinese security services arrested thousands of supposed Falun Gong members, sending them to labor camps and sometimes executing them. China then targeted the group's actions overseas. In 2001 the Thai government, under pressure from Beijing, forced Falun Gong to cancel an international meeting in Bangkok. Explaining Thailand's actions, the country's police minister bluntly told reporters, "We want to keep good relations with China." Thailand established a precedent, and in the following years, Indonesia prohibited marches by Falun Gong supporters and sentenced Falun Gong activists to jail, and Malaysia filed charges against Falun Gong adherents.[34]

The ultimate test of a country's influence is its ability to create a string of friends around the world; great powers build relationships spanning continents. China has begun creating an alternative pole to Western democracies in international organizations and global diplomacy. On Iran, on North Korea, and on many other issues, the United Nations Security Council now faces a long-term serious divide among its five permanent members. China, along with Russia, can increasingly assemble a bloc that can stop US, British, and French action against oil and gas producers, like Sudan or Burma, or simply halt action against authoritarian states, like Belarus and North Korea, even if those countries do not possess petroleum.

China has assembled these coalitions to protect itself as well. In 2004 the United States sponsored a resolution at the United Nations Commission on Human Rights, the global body's main rights watchdog, prodding China toward greater openness and respect for human rights. China proposed a motion urging "no action" on the Americans' idea—a motion calculated to prevent a potentially embarrassing debate and vote on China's rights record. The no-action resolution passed, with the support of twenty-seven nations. Half of those countries were from Africa, including Sudan, Eritrea, and Zimbabwe. Many had benefited from aid and targeted investment from China, and few wanted to see any human rights resolutions levied against Beijing.[35] China had set a precedent: it now had enough allies that it could beat back any future challenge at the Commission on Human Rights.

VIII
Wielding the Charm

Mong La, a village in northeastern Burma, lies more than three hundred miles from the nearest city, has no air links with the world, and sits in one of the poorest, most mountainous regions of one of the poorest nations in the world. Towns near Mong La lack electricity, paved roads, running water. In these towns' simple huts of thatch and wood, naked, hungry-looking children squat in the dirt, fighting over scraps of food.[1]

An unlikely place for an Asian version of Las Vegas. But in the late 1990s, that is exactly what Mong La became. Fueled by investments from the United Wa State Army—a nearly twenty thousand–strong militia group operating in northeastern Burma, situated in a region of Burma with few laws—Mong La proved an ideal spot for casino gambling. Beginning in 1998 businesspeople with links to the UWSA, allegedly along with the Burmese government, constructed garish casinos in the one-lane frontier town, complete with Vegas-style neon billboards, tons of fake marble, and croupiers in tuxedos. The formal attire worked in the casinos, but the dealers seemed strangely out of place when they left the gaming palaces to walk Mong La's narrow dirt streets.[2]

The casino tycoons brought in Vegas-style entertainment, too—with a twist. Casinos built up Mong La dance revues and staffed them with "ladyboys" imported from Thailand, known as *katoeys* in Thai—either transvestites or, more commonly, transsexuals who had undergone sex-change operations at one of the Bangkok hospitals. The ladyboys played all the dance roles and then posed afterward for photos with patrons. For a few bucks, gamblers could shoot photos of themselves fondling the dancers' surgically altered body parts.[3]

On any weekend night in the late 1990s, more than a thousand visitors from China streamed into Mong La, getting little trouble from either the Burmese or the Chinese customs authorities. By one estimate, Mong La received as many as 350,000 Chinese tourists a year. In town, where Mercedes taxis ferried gamblers from one Mong La hotspot to the next, the Chinese visitors could spend more than $12,000 each at some of the city's more exclusive tables. After an evening of gambling, Chinese punters would hit one of the large karaoke halls, where they could sing Chinese, Thai, Korean, or English songs, hook up with platinum blond Eastern European prostitutes, or drink hundreds of dollars worth of imported Scotch, before retiring to the lavish hotels that had appeared almost overnight in town.[4]

According to one estimate, the Mong La casinos grossed as much as $5 billion in revenues between 1998 and 2004. (By comparison, Burma's entire annual gross domestic product has been estimated at $7.5 billion.)[5] Some of that money helped build Mong La's services and infrastructure: the city offered a better electric grid than Burma's decrepit capital, Rangoon. Even better, Mong La created jobs for many local villagers.

But much of the Mong La casino profits were plowed back into corrosive activities. One cut undoubtedly went to the Burmese military junta, which the international monitoring group Freedom House ranks as one of the world's worst regimes. Since the Burmese junta reportedly spends less than one-half of one percent on health care, but devotes some 40 percent of the budget to its military, it is unlikely that much of the regime's casino money ever helped average Burmese.[6]

One cut undoubtedly went to the UWSA itself, a drug-running private army the US State Department has called the world's "most heavily armed narco-traffickers." The money probably helped the UWSA flood amphetamines and heroin into neighboring countries like Thailand, Laos, and China. (The Golden Triangle region of Burma and Laos is the world's second-largest source of opium poppies, the precursor to heroin.) The drugs created an epidemic of amphetamine users in Thailand, where as many as two million Thais used the drugs, 3 percent of the entire population. The heroin seeped into southwestern China, which soon faced an epidemic in border cities like Ruili, where junkies shot up openly on city streets, and needle sharing and prostitution led to rising HIV rates.[7]

As Mong La was prospering, China was becoming vastly more influential in Burma. After the United States imposed sanctions on Burma in 1997 and 2003, American companies avoided the country, and China became Burma's major source of investment and aid.[8] Chinese businesspeople flowed into northern Burma, and Beijing received Burma's leaders on lavish state visits, even as Europe and the United States banned top Burmese leaders.

In the fall of 2003 China started to use that influence to do some good in Burma. Worried about the flow of drugs out of northeastern Burma, and angry that Chinese officials were blowing state money at overseas casinos, including in Mong La, the Chinese government's attitude toward Mong La and other casinos on China's borders changed. Beijing restricted visas for travel to Mong La, forbade Chinese to stay overnight in the one-time casino capital, and even massed troops on the Burmese border. China instituted tough measures on travel by senior cadres to casinos in other countries, like North Korea, where one Chinese official reportedly had lost more than $300,000 in state funds and other monies. One Chinese media outlet reported that because of the crackdown, "103 overseas casinos in counties surrounding Yunnan, Guangxi, Heilongjiang, Jilin and other provinces and autonomous regions had been shut down." At the same time, China cracked down on drugs entering from Burma, prodding the Burmese government to fight narcotics within its borders and stepping up enforcement cooperation.[9]

Cooperation produced results—Chinese police started seizing heroin along the border. By the spring of 2006 Mong La no longer resembled a frontier Vegas. Most casinos had closed their doors and boarded up their windows, though some were launching online gambling operations to survive. No one sang in the karaoke halls; no one slept in the hotels. No one shopped in the stores full of fake brand name clothes. Even the dancers had gone home to Thailand, though an occasional solitary *katoey* still wandered the empty streets.[10]

Mong La, along with the Chinese government's response, reveals one side of Beijing's growing influence in the world. China could use its growing power to promote positive change, like fighting narcotics in Burma and cooperating with its neighbors to stop drug trafficking and the spread of HIV.

But only a few hundred miles from Mong La, China has

used its influence in a vastly different way. Chinese companies, including many with close government links, have decimated Burma's northern forests, which are supposedly protected from logging, and which have been called "very possibly the most biodiverse, rich temperate area on earth."[11]

With soaring demand for housing in China's cities, and with China's own forest cover depleted or protected, China's builders needed new sources of lumber. In Kachin State, the far north of Burma, the Chinese companies found a solution. Between 1984 and 2005, according to one report, the number of Chinese logging companies operating near Kachin State rose from four to more than one hundred. Investigators for the watchdog group Global Witness reported seeing "vast quantities of timber" stockpiled in towns along the China-Burma border. Nearly all that felled timber probably was illegally cut.[12]

China itself has some of the world's weakest environmental controls, and Beijing has repressed green activist groups, fearing they could spark broader protests against the government; in October 2005, China arrested members of Chinese activist group Green Watch. Given this background, Beijing and Chinese provincial governments seemed unlikely to intervene in the deforestation of its neighbor, though China officially had signed international bans on illegal logging. "By taking action [to fight deforestation], the government of the PRC can demonstrate that it takes its responsibility as a regional and global power seriously, and provide leadership for other timber importing countries," Global Witness argued. But China did nothing of the sort. Chinese officials seemed to encourage the illegal timber trade, with local leaders allegedly encouraging the cross-border cutting.[13]

By 2005, Global Witness reported, "large tracts of forest adjacent to the China-Burma border have been almost entirely logged out," mainly by Chinese companies. Its estimate suggests that 98 percent of Burma's exports of felled timber to China come from illegal sources, such as supposedly protected forests. Global Witness further reported that revenue from the timber trade was funding low-intensity local conflicts inside Burma.[14]

Burma is not unique. Global Witness believes that half of China's total felled timber imports—wood from not only Burma but also many other nations, including Indonesia—come from illegal sources. Overall, between 1997 and 2005, China's imports of forest products more than tripled in volume, with illegal wood accounting for much of that.[15]

Today China is a rising power whose role in the world's future remains unclear. Beijing could wield its soft power responsibly. As one analysis by the US National Intelligence Council suggests, in the coming years China may "remain an authoritarian state . . . but respect the rules of the order, work within the existing framework [of international institutions] and seek to change it by peaceful and legitimate means." American leaders unsurprisingly urge China to go in this direction. "China has a responsibility to strengthen the international system that has enabled its success," said former Deputy Secretary of State Robert Zoellick, a longtime Asia hand, in a major policy address in September 2005. China should "recognize that the international system sustains their peaceful prosperity," Zoellick added.[16]

Some Chinese officials seem to agree with Zoellick. After all, Beijing argues that it wants only peace and harmony in the world; the Chinese government's 2005 white paper on foreign policy claims, "To achieve peaceful development is a sincere hope and unremitting pursuit of the Chinese people." As Fu

Ying, the former Chinese ambassador to the Philippines and current envoy to Australia, notes, "Throughout history, the rise of most of the world's large countries was inevitably the result of bullying, weakening, and exploiting other countries." China, Fu Ying argues, will be different. Or as one Chinese diplomat told me, if China is truly going to become a world leader, it will have to use its soft power to serve the global good, and it must use the United Nations and regional groups to solve serious problems.[17]

Yet as China's soft power grows, its influence also could prove disastrous in other countries—an obstacle overseas to environmental protection, to better labor policies, to corporate governance. Whichever way it goes, of course, in a more interlinked and globalized world, where countries can utilize much faster tools of communication, China's influence will spread faster than that of other rising powers, like the United States, Germany, and Japan, did during the early twentieth century.

China could essentially wind up exporting its own domestic weaknesses. Before China became a major player on the world stage, its internal policies were a potential nightmare for people in Shenzhen or Guangzhou or Shenyang. Today Chinese policies could be a nightmare for people in São Paolo or Guatemala City or Surabaya.

Consider China's labor policies. Most Chinese companies still do not treat their employees well at home, and developing countries have few of the tools necessary to enforce labor rules on powerful multinationals, whether from America or China. Chinese companies have no experience dealing with independent unions, since the All China Federation of Trade Unions, an organization controlled by the Communist Party, runs all unions in the country, and the government sometimes jails people who try to start independent unions.

Most Chinese corporations do not know how to interact with nongovernmental organizations, activists, shareholder groups, and other groups overseas. Many Chinese heavy industries, such as coal mining, have horrible safety and environmental records. Being a coal miner in China must rank among the world's most dangerous occupations; thousands of Chinese miners die in accidents each year, often because their employers did not purchase even minimal safety equipment.[18]

There are clear positive signs of how China will use its soft power. Beijing seems ready to embrace multilateral institutions. In the past decade, besides enthusiastically joining regional groups and creating its own multilateral initiatives, Beijing has sent Chinese peacekeepers or police under the UN flag to desperate places like Haiti and Liberia and East Timor. In Liberia, China has contributed some six hundred men to the UN mission, and today China has more troops participating in UN peacekeeping missions than any other permanent member of the Security Council.[19]

China also has begun to mediate other nations' disputes—a task of responsible great powers. This is a significant change from China's recent past, and can scarcely be overstated. If Beijing is to begin playing a role as a mediator of conflict, joining with the United States in solving many problems, it could dramatically transform power dynamics in Asia and elsewhere.

In some cases, China has proven a proactive mediator. On most days, the street outside the Thai embassy in Phnom Penh, Cambodia's capital, fills early with pedicab drivers shuttling old women to market and Thai diplomats greeting local businessmen with modest bows. But one winter day in 2003, a far different crowd gathered outside the Thai mission. For centuries, Thailand and Cambodia have bickered over their borders, their ancient history of wars and incursions, and their modern-day politics.

In January 2003 Cambodian newspapers misquoted a Thai television pop star as calling Cambodians "worms" and questioning whether Angkor Wat, Cambodia's gargantuan ancient temple complex, should be returned to Thailand, which controlled the temple at several points in history. Stoked by the report, and by Cambodian politicians' anti-Thai comments, mobs attacked Thai-owned businesses across Phnom Penh, causing millions of dollars worth of damage and forcing many Thai citizens to evacuate the city on Thai military aircraft.[20]

Hundreds of young Cambodian men ran toward the Thai embassy, where they smashed through the mission's glass doors. Inside, they pulled down pictures of Thailand's beloved king, Bhumibol Adulyadej, and stomped on his face. Thailand's ambassador scrambled out the back of the embassy, hopped over the guard wall, and ran down to the river, where he escaped the rioters, James Bond style, in a speedboat. Nothing angers a Thai more than an insult to the country's monarch, who has led Thailand through fifty years of political turbulence. When the Philadelphia *City Paper,* a local free weekly, once ran a throwaway advertisement for a local bar portraying the Thai king as a hip-hop star, the Thai deputy consul in America warned that the ad could disrupt US-Thai relations, and Thais from Bangkok deluged the paper's offices with angry phone calls and thousands of emails.[21]

Not surprisingly, images of Cambodians stomping and burning the Thai king's picture infuriated Thailand's population. In response, Thailand moved an aircraft carrier near the Cambodian border and threatened to send commandos into its neighbor's territory. A border war seemed possible. "Cambodia must burn," one Bangkokian told *Time* magazine. "This is the worst incident in international relations between Thailand and Cambodia," Thailand's prime minister announced.[22]

Both countries needed someone to broker their feud, and Cambodia has poor relations with the United States. So the two sides turned to Beijing. After the Chinese ambassador in Phnom Penh issued a statement asking Cambodia and Thailand to cool down, Chinese Vice Foreign Minister Wang Yi called in the Thai and Cambodian representatives in Beijing and helped them lay out their grievances. In private, several diplomats told me, the Chinese minister warned the neighbors to normalize relations as soon as possible, or risk angering China—something neither Cambodia nor Thailand wanted to do, since both are increasingly reliant on trade and aid from China. Chastened, the two sides began to patch up their relationship, with Cambodia's own king, Norodom Sihanouk, sending a personal apology to the Thai monarch. By March 2003, Thailand and Cambodia had reopened their customs posts, and their relationship had normalized.[23]

China has started mediating even more important disputes. In October 2002, after a decade of supposedly cooperating with international efforts to monitor its nuclear program, North Korea admitted that it had been secretly enriching uranium. Soon after, a top North Korean official, Li Gun, took US Assistant Secretary of State Jim Kelly aside at a meeting in Beijing. Li Gun nonchalantly informed him that the North, one of the most closed and unpredictable countries in the world, possessed nukes and might be willing to sell them to other nations.[24]

With few levers to pressure North Korea, and no access to high levels of dictator Kim Jong Il's isolated regime, the United States and North Korea's Asian neighbors turned to China, Pyongyang's longtime ally and major provider of aid, food, and energy. Beijing pushed North Korea and the United States to hold bilateral talks. Later China volunteered to host six-way talks on the North Korean nuclear program involving Beijing, Moscow, Pyongyang, Seoul, Washington, and Tokyo. The former US envoy to North Korea, Charles Pritchard, admitted that without China's help, there would have been no six-way talks at all. And when the North Koreans balked at coming to the table, Chinese officials engaged in rounds of shuttle diplomacy to bring them in and also handed North Korea increased aid. At the same time, top Chinese officials invited Kim to booming southern China in order to study China's economic reforms, potential models for remaking North Korea's Stalinist economy. To support reform, China stepped up training for key North Korean bureaucrats, teaching them about modern economic management.[25]

After several rounds of discussions, when North Korea declared that it would withdraw from the six-party talks, Beijing openly expressed anger with the North. To put more pressure on North Korea, Beijing reportedly shut off an oil pipeline to Pyongyang for three days in 2003, then cracked down on North Korea's banking in the Chinese territory of Macau.[26] Again, China simultaneously offered new disbursements of aid to North Korea, and when North Korea tested a nuclear weapon, China agreed to the major step of imposing sanctions on Pyongyang, temporarily cut off oil exports to North Korea, and sent a high-level delegation to Pyongyang to try to defuse the crisis, bringing the North back to the bargaining table.

Beijing wasn't shy about taking credit for its diplomacy. "With respect to the nuclear issue on the Korean Peninsula, China has worked tirelessly with the other relevant parties, and succeeded in convening and hosting" the talks, noted the 2005 government white paper on Chinese foreign policy. Even some impartial observers agreed. "I think we should really focus on the positive aspects of [the six-party talks], including the absolutely rightful role of China," said Aleksandr Ilitchev, a Russian UN expert on North Korea.[27]

Getting Pyongyang to the table helped China's appeal with other countries, too. Since the talks began, South Korean President Roh Mun-Hyun, a former human rights lawyer who has led Seoul toward Beijing's orbit, consistently has looked to China for cues on how to handle North Korea.[28] Asian news outlets, meanwhile, typically portrayed China as a rational actor mediating between two angry, unbalanced nations led by madmen—North Korea and the United States.

Besides mediating disputes, China has utilized its charm in other positive ways. Over the past five years, as China has developed a serious heroin problem in parts of the country, it has worked not only with Burma but also with many other nations in battling drugs. According to America's Drug Enforcement Administration, Chinese authorities "clearly understand the threat posed by drug trafficking." Beijing has signed several UN drug conventions, hosted major multinational meetings in China on drug control, and started training Asian prosecutors on combating transnational crime like drug trafficking. Working with Asian neighbors and with the United States, the Chinese authorities in 2003 busted one of the biggest drug syndicates, an organization known as "125."[29]

Beijing also has taken a proactive stance on fighting trafficking in human beings. "The Chinese authorities . . . have become relatively progressive on issues of human trafficking," says Heather Peters, an expert on trafficking who has worked for several UN agencies. Peters says the Chinese government has supported her efforts to teach women in Chinese border regions about HIV and other sexually transmitted diseases. Beijing also has put pressure on China's neighbors to participate in these educational programs. In 2004 China created a joint effort with Vietnam to fight human trafficking along their common border—an effort that included educational campaigns and stepped-up law enforcement.[30]

Meanwhile, after facing international criticism in 2003 for initially covering up the outbreak of SARS disease in China, an outbreak that soon spread across the world, the Chinese government has begun using its influence to promote cooperation in fighting dangerous diseases. As avian flu became the latest potential pandemic to emerge from Asia, Beijing responded. China vowed to help other countries develop bird flu early warning systems and to work with international organizations to strengthen quarantines. Later, in January 2006, China hosted a global donors' conference on fighting avian flu.[31]

China's growing soft power also is having some economic benefits. China's enormous consumption of resources offers an opportunity to developing countries, and they are trying to make the most of China's needs for oil, gas, minerals, and other commodities. China now drives trade in Asia, a role the United States and Japan historically filled, and China's commodity demands are allowing Latin American and African nations to run trade surpluses and potentially use the money to build stronger social and educational institutions. These surpluses forestall the kind of debt that once crippled many developing world economies. They have another benefit, too—feeding China's economy creates jobs, reducing the kind of social unrest that in many Latin American countries has driven migrants north toward the United States.

Even countries facing intense competitive pressure from

China understand this opportunity. Though Mexico's industries compete directly with China's, a comprehensive opinion survey taken in 2004 shows that few Mexicans worry about China—"the development of China as a world power rank[s] at the bottom of the list of threats that Mexicans consider critical." Malaysia has run trade deficits with China, but a study of Malaysian businesspeople found that "in spite of the purported threats of free trade from China, the majority of the private sector respondents views China positively." While Malaysia's previous prime minister warned, "China is an economic threat for Southeast Asia," the current Malaysian leader, Abdullah Badawi, an advocate of the China–Southeast Asia free trade deal, asserted that "Malaysia does not feel threatened by the emergence of China as an economic powerhouse."[32]

Yet China's exports also may threaten developing nations' industries. China's exports overlap by more than 50 percent with those of countries like Thailand and the Philippines, foreign investment in developing regions like Latin America that compete with China fell by half in the early 2000s, and nations like Laos import eight times as much as they export to China. Since joining the World Trade Organization in 2001, China has displaced Mexico as the second-largest exporter to the United States; nearly 225,000 workers in Mexican *maquiladoras,* factories near the US border, may be endangered by competition from Chinese manufacturing. One study of Thailand-China economic relations found that Thailand already runs a trade deficit with China of more than $1 billion annually, and Vietnam's Ministry of Trade warns that the country's trade deficit with China will soon top $2 billion.[33]

In the long run, developing nations may become less sanguine about trade with China if leaders perceive Beijing as an unfair competitor, due to China's labor practices, dumping, undervaluation of its currency, and state support for certain industries. China's labor costs in producing clothing, to take one example, are roughly one-half Mexican labor costs.[34] Many of China's overseas investments are made by state-owned companies, which do not necessarily have to prove their profitability to shareholders. And though cheap Chinese goods are welcomed by some poor consumers in the developing world, who cannot always afford Western products, Chinese companies have been accused of dumping low-quality, sometimes pirated goods on markets across Africa, Latin America, and Southeast Asia, taking a loss at first in order to win market share.

Some foreign leaders are beginning to respond. In October 2005 Brazil's foreign minister told reporters that Brazil has not reaped the new investment from China it had expected when it granted Beijing market economy status, and Argentine leaders expressed frustration that imports from China were growing at more than three times the rate of exports to China. In response, Argentina's government imposed new nontariff barriers on categories of Chinese imports. In fact, though the international financial press has highlighted European Union and US actions against Chinese exports, nearly two-thirds of trade investigations against China in 2005 actually were initiated by developing countries. Brazil alone has imposed at least twenty antidumping clauses and safeguards against categories of Chinese exports. In Ecuador the government has passed laws to limit Chinese investment, and potential competition from China was a reason why Central American nations signed a 2005 free trade agreement with the United States, since they believed that it might entice some garment companies to keep production in the hemisphere rather than switching to China.[35]

Similar complaints have begun to surface in Asia and Africa. Though China has promised that trade would be a win-win proposition, like other major powers it also has tried to protect its own population from some of the negative effects of slashing trade barriers. Even as Chinese agricultural products flood into Thailand, Thai farmers have faced difficulty selling their products to China, encountering high value-added taxes and other obstacles. "Breaking into China's market is not as easy as some might think," admitted one Thai academic studying Thailand-China trade relations. Across northern Thailand, farmers now question whether it was wise to sign a free trade deal with Beijing, and farmers, textile companies, and small manufacturers in Vietnam, Cambodia, Malaysia, and Indonesia express the same fears of trade with China.[36]

This difficulty of trading with China, and the suspicion that China is acting rapaciously, may be seeping into local perceptions of Beijing. In Nigeria militants in the Niger Delta have warned Chinese investors that they will be "treated as thieves" robbing Nigerians of their valuable oil resources—a charge the militants previously laid against Western companies. In the Nigerian commercial capital of Lagos, police have begun expelling recent Chinese migrants from local markets because Nigerians complained that Chinese goods are undercutting local products. In Zambia the populist politician Michael Sata has rallied support among the poor by claiming that Chinese imports are undercutting Zambian products, while Zambian companies cannot export any finished goods to China. "Chinese investment has not added any value to the people of Zambia," Sata declared. Responding to his rhetoric, Zambians have targeted Chinese shops in Lusaka, the capital.[37]

China's growing soft power also could lead it to export its environmental problems. Within China, environmental protection is almost nonexistent, and despite a government campaign for more sustainable development, most officials, focused on keeping up growth rates, care little about the ecological consequences of construction and industrialization. As the China environmental expert Elizabeth Economy has revealed, Beijing has demonstrated little commitment to river and watershed preservation within China, destroying the Yangtze River and other major waterways. Two-thirds of Chinese cities fail World Health Organization standards for air quality, by far the worst rate of any large country. Several cities rank among the highest rates of airborne carbon monoxide in the world.[38]

This environmental recklessness spreads across borders as China's global influence grows. Ten years ago, China's environmental mismanagement was a problem for a citizen of polluted Lanzhou city or someone living along the Yangtze; today it is a threat to citizens in Burma or someone living along the Amazon. Besides the logging of its neighbors, China may fund a massive Burmese dam that could proceed without adequate environmental studies, and China's Export-Import Bank reportedly declines to sign environmental guidelines commonly adopted by credit providers from Western countries. In northern Laos, according to a consultant with the Asian Development Bank, a major aid donor, Chinese firms tasked to build part of the country's new highway simply refused to produce any environmental impact assessment. "The Chinese just went ahead and did their part of the road, without any assessment," said the consultant, who worked on the highway, "They would just never talk to me."[39]

China also has ignored fears about the impact of Chinese dams on the Mekong River—Beijing has silenced critics, and continued building dams and blasting parts of the river. While China stalls, scientists estimate that fish catches in part of the river have fallen by half; the giant Mekong catfish, a monstrous creature that can top six hundred pounds, soon may become extinct. Whole stretches of the Mekong, which must support a growing human population that could double within thirty years, are becoming too dry for farming.[40]

In its aid, infrastructure building, and business deals, China also demonstrates little respect for transparency and other aspects of good governance. In other words, how Chinese companies act at home reflects how they may act overseas. In Cambodia local activists accuse both the Cambodian government and Wuzhishan LS, a Chinese state–linked firm, of forcing hundreds of villagers off their land in a Cambodian province called Mondulkiri, and replacing them with large-scale agriculture. Critics contend that Wuzhishan then sprayed the area, which includes ancestral burial areas, with dangerous herbicides. "The government and the company have disregarded the well-being, culture, and livelihoods of the . . . indigenous people who make up more than half the population of the province," announced the United Nations' special representative for human rights in Cambodia.[41]

Wuzhishan's behavior so infuriated locals that despite the Cambodian government's usual rough treatment of demonstrators, villagers took to the roads in Mondulkiri to protest. Five hundred villagers tried to march to the local capital to petition the governor, while another pack of six hundred launched a demonstration. Local police officers fired water cannons into the crowd, knocking several women unconscious. One group of Mondulkiri ethnic minority protesters even seized Wuzhishan's trucks and blockaded roads with old tree branches, backing off only after Cambodian police armed with AK-47s threatened to jail them.[42]

More generally, the state-led business model China suggests to the developing world could undermine the rule of law in Africa or Latin America or poorer countries in Asia. To be sure,

American or European or Japanese companies also sometimes abdicate corporate responsibility, cook their books, or hand out bribes. And some Chinese companies operate transparently at home and abroad, install quality management, and practice corporate responsibility. China's true private sector, that group of companies without ties to the state, boasts several high-quality multinationals that operate with real oversight and modern corporate boards.

But for the most part, Western and Japanese firms are private companies separate from their governments. These companies have some degree of accountability to their shareholders and boards, offer the public information about their environmental and labor practices, and can be sanctioned, whether by America's Foreign Corrupt Practices Act or similar legislation in other countries, by the media, or by democratically elected legislatures. When Enron collapsed in a mountain of supposed fraud, American prosecutors indicted its corporate leadership, and the US Congress passed tougher laws on corporate accounting policies. When the US oil company Unocal allegedly contributed to forced labor in a pipeline in Burma, Burmese villagers affected by the oil project sued Unocal in an American court and won a settlement from the company estimated at more than $30 million.[43]

Chinese firms generally do not operate under the same burdens of oversight. As Minxin Pei of the Carnegie Endowment has found, the Chinese state and state-linked companies still account for nearly 40 percent of China's Gross Domestic Product, control more than 50 percent of industrial assets, and dominate more than 60 percent of the financial sector. Chinese firms with state links often display poor corporate governance, including a lack of transparency. China's own official news agency revealed in 2004 that some four thousand corrupt officials had fled the country, carrying with them $50 billion in state money.[44] Chinese courts and prosecutors rarely apply the kind of scrutiny to Chinese firms that the United States did to Enron; according to Pei, one study of twelve thousand Chinese, across several provinces, found that people perceived China's judiciary to be one of the five most corrupt public institutions in the country.

Yet at least Beijing has to play by some rules. Constrained by its need to demonstrate rule of law in order to maintain China's attractiveness to investors, Beijing has managed to prosecute the most egregious white-collar criminals in China, like senior officials at the Bank of China accused of stealing nearly half a billion dollars.[45] Driven by the need to keep the population placated through consistent economic growth, and unable to repress all interest groups in such a large and diverse country, Chinese officials have used the state-dominated model of development to do considerable good. Though corruption ravages Chinese officialdom, the central government and provincial governments have used enough of the state's wealth to pull hundreds of millions of people out of poverty.

In the poorest parts of Africa, Asia, and Latin America—where the rule of law often simply doesn't exist, the media are far less sophisticated than Chinese financial publications, economic policy makers are not insulated from politics, and leaders have no problem stealing all, rather than part, of the state's wealth—the state-dominated China model of development could be an invitation to disaster. In parts of Africa, Asia, and Latin America, the China model could be an entrée for already rapacious governments to act even worse. In Indonesia, for example, one reason why Chinese companies have success winning deals, admits an oil executive, is that the Chinese companies basically bribe whomever they need to pay. This behavior only adds to graft in one of Asia's most corrupt nations—angering local good-governance activists, who then blame China for their problems.[46]

The small Peruvian town of San Juan de Marcona, an old port on the Pacific long since bypassed by larger harbors, offers a window into some of the problems that occur as China exports labor and environmental policies to poor nations. In 1992–1993, Shougang International Trade and Engineering, a Chinese state steel company, purchased Hierro de Peru, a state-run iron mine near San Juan de Marcona, for roughly $118 million. At first, residents of San Juan de Marcona, a town of thirteen thousand people, welcomed the Chinese company's investment, sure that it would revitalize the dismal economy in the town, some two hundred miles away from the capital, Lima. The Chinese company promised to invest $150 million in the mine to modernize its facilities.[47]

The locals' delight soon faded. Even as Shougang's profits rose due to strong prices on the international market for metals, the company did little to improve the mine or its safety facilities, spending only $35 million. The mineworkers in San Juan de Marcona began to complain. They complained about serious environmental problems, like Shougang's alleged dumping of chemical waste in the nearby ocean, killing the fish around town that provided a source of protein. They complained about lax safety standards, charging that the mine lacked safety harnesses and workers suffered many accidental electrocutions. They complained about their dismal pay. "Shougang has turned us into slaves," one local told a reporter, complaining that her husband worked fifteen hours per day at the mine for roughly fourteen US dollars, less than half the average miner's salary in Peru.[48]

The Peruvian government began to investigate. Peru's Labor Ministry recorded 170 accidents, including two fatal ones, at the mine in one year alone. Peru's government slapped a $14 million fine on Shougang for failing to spend the money to improve the mine. The company paid the fine, but its managers still didn't improve working conditions, probably because paying fines seemed cheaper than spending money to upgrade. Shougang had no background experience of dealing with protests or unions, and the Peruvian government would not take more steps to punish the company. "There is a culture problem," Peru's minister of mines told Reuters. "The Chinese managers see their way of doing things as discipline, while the workers see it differently."[49]

Eventually, the relationship between the miners and the company deteriorated so badly that the employees could not control themselves. Starting in 2001 the miners began going on strike nearly every year; at some points, more than one thousand strikers demonstrated at one time. In 2004, a year when Shougang's parent earned a record profit of $150 million, the strikers blocked local roads accessing the mine, asking for a raise of eighty-five cents per day and better safety conditions. Some angry locals reportedly covered the town's walls in anti-Chinese graffiti and threatened the mine's management.[50] The following year, strikers again walked out of work, this time complaining that the company, which is supposedly responsible for providing water to the town, paid for only four hours of water per day.

The miners' activism got them nothing. When their labor unions protested too much, Shougang simply fired them. To fix their problem, the company brought in imported laborers from China to replace them, a common practice among Chinese companies investing overseas. Or it hired temporary Peruvian workers, whom it employed without offering them any benefits at all.[51]

Exporting China's own poor standards on labor issues, the environment, and corporate governance could foster blowback against Beijing in many other countries: in one ranking of eighty nations' adherence to corporate responsibility, China placed sixty-sixth, below other developing economies like India.[52] The Chinese government probably realizes this, one reason why China recently has hosted high-profile meetings on issues like corporate responsibility, such as the United Nations Global Compact Summit in Shanghai in November 2005.

Foreign opinion leaders and the general public realize that China could export its domestic problems, a recognition that could limit China's soft appeal. Local workers have protested Chinese firms' labor policies not only in Peru but also in South Africa, the Pacific Islands, and Zambia, where one miner told reporters that his Chinese managers "make me work seven days a week [and] pay me $30 a month." In South Africa trade unions have warned the government that it must control Chinese investment, and trade union leaders tore off their T-shirts during a meeting when they discovered that the shirts had been manufactured in China, thus potentially in factories with minimal labor standards.[53]

Foreign populations also recognize Chinese firms' low safety standards. In Zambia, where a Chinese firm runs the Chambishi copper mine, and where locals had been overjoyed that the company had revitalized Chambishi's decrepit infrastructure, forty-nine miners died in an accident in April 2005. Soon after, the dead miners' families complained that they had received no compensation at all, and Chambishi's Chinese managers stayed away from the men's funerals for fear of being attacked. "The Chinese don't put safety concerns . . . as that important," one professor at the University of Zambia told the *Chicago Tribune*.[54]

Though China's demand for resources is powering some African and Asian and Latin American economies, local opinion leaders also recognize the potential environmental consequences, like the deforestation of Southeast Asian nations like Indonesia and Burma, and African nations like Gabon. In Thailand, Laos, and Cambodia, activists and some politicians have aggressively campaigned against China's damming of the upper portions of the Mekong River, while Filipino activists have launched a campaign against China's poor environmental standards in mines it has purchased in the Philippines. In Brazil, nongovernmental organizations like Amazon Watch warn that Chinese investments could damage Amazonian indigenous groups and their native environments.[55]

Even as China's corporate governance could undermine labor and environmental standards in other countries, China's aid policies could undermine efforts by Western governments and international financial institutions to demand better governance and environmental regulation from aid recipients. Led by the World Bank, international development specialists have moved toward an aid model that distinguishes between governments that fight corruption and those that do not. This model tries to impose some transparency, so that aid benefits a wider spectrum of people in the developing world. America's Millennium Challenge Corporation, which offers aid to countries that "rule justly, invest in their people, and encourage economic freedom," offers one example of this trend. The World Bank's anticorruption strategy, a priority of new bank President Paul Wolfowitz, offers another example of this trend of setting more stringent conditions before granting aid.[56]

Committed to this new, tough aid model, in late 2004 the World Bank threatened to suspend hundreds of millions of dollars worth of assistance to Cambodia because of Phnom Penh's allegedly rampant corruption and its crackdown on civil liberties. The United Nations' special representative in Phnom Penh warned of an "increasingly autocratic form of government and growing concentration of power in the hands of the prime minister."[57]

Five or ten years ago, Cambodia would have had to comply with the World Bank and the donors' demands. Not now. "Western governments would like to use their assistance to [Cambodian Prime Minister] Hun Sen to put pressure on Hun Sen, so he turns to the Chinese," said Sokhem Pech, a leading Cambodian academic. Beijing then rewards Hun Sen. On a visit to Cambodia in April 2006 Chinese Premier Wen Jiabao promised Phnom Penh $600 million worth of loans and grants. Meanwhile, the World Bank did not cut Cambodia off, perhaps because it feared that it would then have no influence in the country. Foreign diplomats in Cambodia say that Western donors now feel they have no choice but to continue assisting the Cambodian government in order to maintain some leverage over Phnom Penh's human rights record and political future. Similarly, in neighboring Laos, after the World Bank considered withholding support from a new dam project called Nam Theun 2 because it could potentially destroy the local environment, China made it clear that it would help finance the dam instead. Worried that China's backing could result in an environmental disaster, the bank agreed to support the dam.[58]

Africa, the biggest recipient of foreign assistance, has become perhaps the most glaring example of the potentially corrosive consequences of Chinese aid. After Western donors withdrew aid from the autocratic government of the Central African Republic in 2003 following a coup, China stepped in, providing key assistance to the regime.[59] As a result, the Central African regime has been able to tighten its rule.

Eventually, this Chinese assistance could lead average citizens in Africa, and in other regions, to question whether Beijing really is a power that does not interfere in nations' affairs. After all, if China uses its influence to support elites in countries like the Central African Republic or Cambodia, to the detriment of average people, it is very clearly interfering.

Beijing's assistance has proven even more critical in the southwest African nation of Angola, where China's demand for resources, foreign aid, and commitment to noninterference all come together. During three decades of civil war, a tiny elite in Luanda, Angola's capital, siphoned off revenues from the country's oil deposits, the second-largest in Africa. The elites holed up in Luanda's seaside mansions, ringed with barbed wire and protected by private security companies, and they used the oil money to fund the ongoing conflict and line their own pockets. Meanwhile, most of Angola's twelve million citizens lived in dire poverty, earning less than two dollars a day and surviving in shacks made from tin and old bricks and scrap metal, built on top of each other across Luanda's shantytown sprawl. One corruption watchdog, Global Witness, reported that one-third of Angola's state revenue goes missing, essentially meaning that it has been siphoned off. An Angolan newspaper found in 2003 that the nation's president, José Eduardo dos Santos, had somehow become Angola's richest man.[60]

In 2002 Angola's government and the rebels finally laid down their arms, paving the way for free, competitive elections in the future. Peace also offered an opportunity for foreign aid organizations to get back into the country and help rebuild the shattered social services and decrepit oil infrastructure. To ensure that Angola used aid money wisely, the International Monetary Fund tried to force the government to agree to provisions that would slash graft and improve economic management.[61]

Angolan government ministers at first seemed receptive to loans linked to intensive, on-the-ground monitoring by IMF staff designed to ensure that the aid and oil money actually got plowed into social programs. Angola even promised to join Britain's Extractive Industries Transparency Initiative (EITI), a program designed to monitor how resource wealth gets spent. By the beginning of 2005 IMF officials had reason to believe that they stood on the verge of a financing agreement with the country.[62]

At the last moment, the Angolan government broke off talks with the IMF. China had stepped in, offering Angola loans and credits for reconstruction that may be worth as much as $6 billion. The Chinese money came with no conditions for accountability—only an agreement to use Chinese firms for the reconstruction—and no demands like the EITI program.[63]

For the Angolan leaders, though perhaps not for average Angolans, China's policies jibe with their own disdain at Westerners trying to tell them what to do. (One reporter for the *Financial Times* remembered an executive at Angola's state-owned oil company ranting at him after the journalist asked a question about transparency.)[64] International corruption watchdogs warn that the Chinese assistance, given with no conditions, will allow the Angolan government to revert to its old habits, skimming the petroleum cream for itself. Already Angola has backed off its EITI commitment and postponed a mission by the World Bank designed to teach the country about transparency.

Some of the Chinese cash may even go directly to the

government, funding progovernment propaganda in advance of the national election—and offering a sign to other African leaders of what they can get by joining up with Beijing. "The African [leaders] are very welcoming of the Chinese," the South African economic analyst Dianna Games told reporters. "They feel it's easy money. In Angola in particular, the Chinese don't ask many questions."[65]

IX
America's Soft Power Goes Soft

Even as China has wooed the world, America has alienated many of its oldest friends. Australia, where legislators jeer President Bush, is but one example. In the 2005 BBC poll of twenty-two nations, not only did 48 percent of people believe that China's role in the world was mainly positive, only 38 percent thought the United States had a positive influence on the world, about the same number as for Russia, a near-authoritarian regime run by a dour former KGB man. The follow-up BBC poll in 2006 displayed similar results. In some of these nations, Osama bin Laden enjoyed higher favorability ratings than the United States—a trend that led former US Ambassador to the United Nations Richard Holbrooke to wonder, "How can a man in a cave outcommunicate the world's leading communications society?"[1]

Although China's soft power rise does not depend on an American soft power decline, plummeting American appeal could contribute to China's growing appeal. But before we examine, in the next chapter, how China's appeal can affect the United States, we must understand why and how America's brand has been tarnished. The tarnishing began in the 1990s, after the United States had vanquished the Soviet Union in the Cold War and seemed at the peak of its power. The trend became worse after 2001—so bad that dislike for American policy has often mutated into hatred of American culture, people, and companies, and, sometimes, American values themselves.

After the fall of the Berlin Wall, America seemed to have no competitor for global soft power. Representative democracy and free-market capitalism were now spreading throughout the world, and leaders of newly democratic countries looked to the United States for cues on how to build their political systems. President Bill Clinton, the symbol of US-style democracy, was welcomed overseas like a rock star, as on a trip to former enemy Vietnam, where the president waded through crowds of jubilant Vietnamese as if he were the pope.[2]

America's rivals couldn't keep up. The former Soviet Union was preoccupied with itself—disintegrating into chaos and discovering capitalism and democracy, all at the same time. China remained weak and, in the wake of the Tiananmen crackdown, had become a pariah in much of the world. The European Union struggled to unite with the former communist Eastern European nations. Though Japan had built itself into an economic colossus, Japanese culture, outside of its business models, had little impact on the wider world. (Today, with Japan in economic decline, its culture actually has become more popular internationally.)

Meanwhile, American companies' dominance in information technology powered the US economy and placed US businesses at the leading edge of the 1990s Internet revolution and of the process of international integration that came to be called globalization. American music, film, and television dominated local markets in nations ranging from India to Indonesia. English was becoming the universal language of business, and companies around the globe copied American management style, shareholder capitalism, and other corporate practices.

But with the Cold War won, Americans seemed to look inward, as if tired of the world's burdens. For nearly a decade, America turned to its own problems, debated its own culture, and feasted on its own scandals, highlighted by the Clinton impeachment trial. "Since World War II, America has accumulated huge, huge reservoirs of goodwill all over the world," said Kishore Mahbubani, Singapore's former ambassador to the United Nations and one of the world's most respected foreign policy thinkers. In part, Mahbubani believes, America built this goodwill by serving as a beacon of morality and democracy. In part, it built this goodwill by leading in the creation of institutions during the Cold War, like the United Nations, designed to integrate the United States with the globe and to create a multilateral order in trade, aid, and diplomacy. "But, unfortunately, at the end of the Cold War, when there was a massive opportunity for America to take advantage of these reservoirs of goodwill to build a better world, America did the opposite thing: it walked away from the world," Mahbubani continued.[3]

The numbers do not lie. Throughout the 1990s the White House and Congress slashed programs that had bound America to the world. Washington hacked up the Foreign Service and stopped paying America's share in international institutions like the United Nations. Several blue ribbon studies revealed that the US government cut funding for foreign affairs programs from more than $5 billion in 1994 to $3.64 billion in 2000. Because of this, from 1994 to 1997 the State Department could replace only 53 percent of the staff it lost through retirement, resignation, and death. According to one report, these cuts resulted in "decrepit facilities" at US embassies that put American diplomacy "near a state of crisis."[4]

Washington eviscerated US public diplomacy, the government-funded programs designed to influence public opinion abroad. State Department international exchange programs had introduced future foreign leaders like Afghanistan's Hamid Karzai to the United States. Libraries and American Centers operated by the United States Information Agency (USIA) had offered foreigners a window into American society. US government–sponsored tours by artists and musicians had brought jazz, Pop art, and many other American trends to foreign audiences. Now Washington was destroying those success stories. "We cut out a lot of what we do well," admitted Lloyd Neighbors, a former public affairs officer at many American embassies. "We wound up closing our United States Information Service libraries." Indeed, State Department funding for educational and cultural exchange programs declined every year between 1993 and 2002. By the late 1990s the United States Information Agency, once the main outlet of public diplomacy, had roughly half as much staff as it had in the 1960s.[5]

American leaders also turned away from Washington's commitment to multilateralism. The United States failed to ratify the Kyoto Protocol or the International Criminal Court, and President Clinton did not expend much political capital trying to push for their ratification. This was an initial sign that the United States would no longer support the multilateral institutions it had helped create after the Second World War. At the same time, the Clinton administration refused to intervene in the genocide in Rwanda, further undermining Washington's credibility as a moral actor. That the world's sole remaining superpower would not lift a finger to help in times of great crisis, even as it slapped sanctions on nations like Burma and Pakistan, created a legacy of resentment. America had put itself in the worst possible position, appearing demanding of other nations but unwilling to provide the world with help or moral leadership.

Worse, as democracy swept through the world, the United States did not embrace many of the actors newly empowered by democratization. As regions like Latin America and Africa made the transition to democracy, conservative elites, many of whom had studied in the United States, could no longer dominate politics. Long-suppressed popular movements, from indigenous groups in Latin America to religious parties in Turkey, came to the fore, gaining power at the ballot box. The United States could have worked to gain the trust of these new actors. It could have leveraged the fact that America's democracy promotion had helped empower them. Instead, Washington chose to continue dealing primarily with elites in most developing nations, who tended to be more conservative, even repressive.

Later, during the Bush administration, this ignorance of how democratization had changed other nations' relations with America would come back to haunt the White House. Democracies like Chile and Turkey would prove accountable to their own people—people who did not want to support the war in Iraq and other White House objectives.

This retreat from the globe seemed to enjoy popular support among the American public. Numerous studies showed declining interest among Americans in global events and foreign aid: polls taken in 1993 and 1997 revealed that just one out of eight Americans thought that the United States should be the globe's single leader. Despite the fact that much of the United Nations' peacekeeping force is staffed with soldiers from low-income countries, in a poll of Americans taken in 1995 by the Program on International Policy Attitudes (PIPA), the majority of respondents were convinced that America offered more than its fair share of troops to United Nations peacekeeping.[6]

During the Clinton years, the White House did pay close attention to one element of foreign policy—international economics. Clinton seemed personally fascinated by economic globalization, and his top economic policy makers, like Treasury Secretaries Robert Rubin and Larry Summers, were attuned to international business, finance, and trade. But American intransigence on many free trade initiatives fostered ill will abroad. American business leaders and politicians seemed to ignore fears that, because of globalization, US film and media and consumer products would overwhelm local industries. The free market–oriented, neoliberal economic model promoted by the United States and by Washington-based international financial institutions failed to deliver strong growth to many poor nations. "The 1990s turned into a period of severe disappointment as free markets led to rampant corruption and unfulfilled expectations in Latin America," argues Cynthia Watson, an expert on Latin America at the National War College.[7]

Across the world, as America's cultural and corporate power grew unchallenged, many average citizens began to see globalization essentially as Americanization. If they saw it this way, they often viewed American-led globalization as a threat to their societies and national identities—one reason why the antiglobalization activist José Bové became an overnight celebrity in 1999 by smashing up a McDonald's franchise in the French town of Millau. Of course, even as they worshiped Bové, the French remained among the world's biggest consumers of Ray Kroc's products—the kind of schizophrenia and desire for American products and culture that could eventually allow the United States to rebuild its global soft power.[8]

Some foreigners also linked globalization with unwelcome elements of the United States' social model, including laissez-faire capitalism. This fear of adopting American-style socioeconomic models grew as ever fewer foreigners perceived the United States as a meritocracy—perceptions sparked by Americans' late-1990s worship of the stock market and Internet start-ups at a time when much of the developing world was facing financial crises.[9] These perceptions would only grow stronger in the 2000s. Foreigners first witnessed revelations of American executives living plutocratic existences while average American workers' incomes stagnated, then, in 2005, saw the savage poverty revealed by Hurricane Katrina.

By the end of the 1990s nations also had other models to look toward—other models of successful development. During the Cold War, the United States had held itself up in contrast to the Soviet Union, whose totalitarian system and stagnant economic development made America look more efficient and successful. With the Soviet Union gone, the "American Dream" was matched up against other models, like China and the European Union, not against the villainous USSR.

As the 1990s came to a close, then, the United States had squandered many of its Cold War gains, though it remained more popular than it is today. Too many foreigners no longer noticed US foreign aid: one study of Moroccans showed that "older focus group members recalled US food aid and libraries in their youth, but they said no one sees US aid now."[10] The fear of American-led globalization exploded, resulting in violent anti-US and antiglobalization protests at meetings of the International Monetary Fund, the World Trade Organization, and the World Bank in places like Quebec City, Genoa, and even in the United States—in Seattle in 1999.

Since 2001 America has turned this resentment against the United States into outright anger. Shifting from the neoisolationism of the 1990s, the White House has become intensely engaged with the world. But in the process, it has alienated many former friends and sparked worries about Washington's excessive involvement in other nations' affairs.

To start with, tough security measures launched in the wake of September 11 made it harder for foreigners to obtain American student, work, and tourist visas, or to apply for political asylum in the United States. No one doubts that America had to bolster security after September 11. But tighter security was bound to alienate foreigners. The cost of applying for a US visit visa quintupled between 1998 and 2004, and new security restrictions slowed reviews of visa applications. Not surprisingly, the State Department's refusal rates for all forms of visas rose between 2000 and 2003.[11]

The security measures were understandable, but the White House made significant mistakes in public diplomacy. Under an increasingly partisan board of governors, the Bush administration prodded Voice of America, long the flagship of US broadcasting abroad, to become less impartial. Management demoted Voice of America's news director, a move some at VoA suspect was punishment for the director's refusal to air positive coverage of the war in Iraq. This demotion threatened VoA's image as an impartial news broadcaster. Meanwhile, the administration's new broadcasting efforts, like Radio Sawa, a pop music station aimed at average people in the Middle East, failed to have much impact on Middle Easterners' opinions of America, because they shied away from serious news. "Radio Sawa has failed to present America to its audience," argued a draft report by the State Department's inspector general obtained by the *Washington Post.*[12]

More broadly, the administration did not develop an effective public diplomacy strategy, even more important in an age when globalization can instantly spread rumor and anti-American sentiment around the world, and when tight security measures at American embassies overseas make it even harder for US diplomats to meet foreigners and promote America's appeal. When I visited the US embassy in Jakarta, where the mission indeed faces a serious terrorist threat, I passed through rings of barbed wire, barriers, and numerous security checks to meet my contact, who had had to preclear me for entry the day before.

Ultimately, though most American diplomats joined the Foreign Service to meet people in other countries, security measures will only put them at an increasing disadvantage compared with diplomats from countries that do not feel as threatened by terrorism. The war on terrorism also stretches the US Foreign Service, since it must staff large missions in Iraq, Afghanistan, and other hotspots in the war on terror. "It didn't help that the US didn't have an ambassador in Australia for eighteen months [between 2004 and 2006], even while the Chinese were making inroads," said Allan Gyngell, a former senior policy adviser to the Australian prime minister.[13]

There was no shortage of warnings: every think tank and advocacy group in Washington seems to be issuing reports on how to improve America's image abroad. Reported the Government Accountability Office, the US government watchdog,

"Public diplomacy efforts generally lacked important strategic communication elements. . . . These elements include having core messages, segmented target audiences, [and] detailed strategies and tactics."[14]

The White House realized that it needed one figure to command public diplomacy. But by 2006 the Bush administration already had picked its third public diplomacy czar, the White House confidante Karen Hughes. The first two public diplomacy czars, the advertising executive Charlotte Beers and the longtime diplomat Margaret Tutwiler, quit after short tenures. Once in place, Hughes embarked on "listening tours," primarily in the Muslim world, in which she preached about America but did strikingly little listening. When confronted with difficult situations amid skeptical foreigners, Hughes just resorted to platitudes, informing a Turkish audience, "I am a mom, and I love kids. I love all kids."[15]

To its credit, at least the Bush administration has tried to revive the Foreign Service and foreign aid. The White House has developed an innovative new program for delivering aid to well-governed poor nations, the Millennium Challenge Corporation. Though the first MCC head appointed by the administration, Paul Applegarth, was criticized for his poor management, the MCC at least demonstrated to developing nations that America was back in the aid game. Meanwhile, Secretary of State Condoleezza Rice decided upon an ambitious restructuring of the US Foreign Service. Under the realignment, Rice would shift some one hundred Foreign Service officers away from overstaffed but comfortable posts in Western Europe and place them in important, if less comfortable, developing countries. She also vowed to reopen many one-person Foreign Service missions in important outposts of the developing world, like Alexandria, Egypt, and Medan, a provincial city in Indonesia. Just having one US diplomat on the ground in these places could prove vital for extending the American government's presence.[16]

Washington's near-exclusive focus on terrorism in the years after September 11 only adds to alienation overseas. In a small number of foreign countries seriously threatened by terrorism, such as Israel and Singapore, this focus on terror makes sense. But in many countries where terrorism is not a threat, an almost exclusive focus on counterterrorism by the world's biggest power, which should be able to focus on many issues at once, seems unwise. At meetings of the Asia Pacific Economic Cooperation (APEC) group in Chile in 2004 (APEC includes several Latin American nations), President Bush focused on counterterrorism cooperation and weapons of mass destruction. Yet most APEC nations, like Chile, have only limited interest in terrorism issues, and APEC originally was supposed to just discuss issues of economics and business. So the president's focus at these APEC events, and at many other summits, befuddled some foreign opinion leaders. As the Malaysian lawyer and columnist Karim Raslan told the *New York Times,* Washington's "obsession" with terrorism had become irrelevant to average people in Asia. "We've all got to live, we've all got to make money," Raslan told the *Times.* "The Chinese want to make money, and so do we."[17]

Meanwhile, the White House and Congress ignored economic globalization, an ignorance symbolized by tin-eared treasury secretaries and congresspeople transforming the war on terror into economic demagoguery, for example, by attempting to block a Dubai company from operating six US ports, though there was no evidence this would compromise security. When Chile's neighbor, Argentina—held up as an example of neoliberal economics during the 1990s—melted down into an economic crisis in 2001 and 2002, the Bush administration did not respond. Instead, the White House poured scorn on the Argentines. "They have been off and on in trouble for seventy years or more," Treasury Secretary Paul O'Neill remarked about Argentina. "Nobody forced them to be what they are."[18]

On a one hundred–degree day in Phnom Penh in January 2006, I saw firsthand how the US government's lack of interest in economic globalization and its focus on terrorism was costing America friends. Outside one of the offices of Cambodia's Ministry of Commerce, I met Mean Sophea, a squat middle-aged man with small eyes and a broad forehead. It was a weekend, but he had been rushing from meeting to meeting, and now he dabbed his slick forehead with a mound of paper napkins.[19]

Mean was in charge of trade preferences in the Cambodian Ministry of Commerce, which meant that he was one of the people responsible for studying how tiny Cambodia could compete in the global economy. He had few resources at his disposal; he kept all statistics on Cambodia's textile exports on a laptop computer. When I asked for information about Cambodia's economy, I didn't need to make a formal request: he simply called up files from his hard drive and burned me a CD of the government's economic data.

From outside the building, Mean led me up a narrow staircase that stank of old fruit and into a small office that reminded me of every other bureaucrat's office I had ever seen in the developing world. The only decoration was a garish, faux-Impressionist painting of Angkor Wat, Cambodia's famous twelfth-century temple complex. A small fan shuddered and sputtered. Mean's assistant kicked the fan. The fan stopped moving at all. Sweat dripped off my forehead onto the linoleum-covered floor.

In 1999 Cambodia had signed a unique trade agreement with the United States, the first to link duty-free access to American markets with labor standards in factories overseas. Under the deal Cambodia and the International Labor Organization together would certify that the workers in Cambodian garment factories received fair pay and decent labor conditions. The better these conditions became, the more Cambodia would be entitled to export garments duty free to the United States. In theory, the better these conditions became, the more Western companies would be interested in importing from Cambodia, since they would receive preference in selling Cambodian goods to America and could advertise to American consumers that they had not used sweatshop labor.[20]

This agreement worked—at least at first. Cambodia's garment industry gained jobs, won foreign investment, and cultivated major buyers like Nike. According to the Asian business expert Sheridan Prasso, the agreement led to large increases in foreign companies' purchase of Cambodian garments, and in 2003 garments accounted for 97 percent of Cambodia's exports and earned one-third of the country's entire gross domestic product. While the United States had purchased $1 million in Cambodian textiles in 1996, it bought $1.1 billion in 2003, making America the biggest market for Cambodian goods. The garment industry fed Cambodian families and built Cambodians houses back in their hometowns. By the early 2000s, 25 percent of Cambodia's population depended in some way on garment workers' wages.[21]

But in January 2005, according to a World Trade Organization decision, the world eliminated quotas for garment imports—quotas like the duty-free access to America enjoyed by

Cambodian goods. After January 2005 Cambodia would face the same duties as bigger rivals like Indonesia and China, which have many more workers, lower wages, and worse labor conditions.[22]

Since the Clinton administration had pushed Cambodia to sign the 1999 agreement, Mean and other Cambodian trade officials thought that the White House now should help Cambodia's garment makers survive by continuing to give them preferential access to America's markets. "We need US help. We need quota-free access for garments, or our garment makers will die," Mean pleaded with me. "We must have help."

Mean's pleas didn't get him anywhere. Washington had developed a closer relationship with Phnom Penh in recent years, but the cooperation centered on counterterrorism. The Cambodian government started cooperating in 2003, arresting alleged members of the Al Qaeda offshoot Jemaah Islamiah. The United States then helped Cambodia participate in a multinational counterterrorism exercise. But counterterrorism assistance should not have been the extent of the relationship. Several savvy American politicians, like former Arizona Congressman Jim Kolbe, had realized how the United States could build greater goodwill in poor nations. Kolbe had proposed the Tariff Relief Assistance for Developing Economies Act. This bill would have given Cambodia and thirteen other poor nations duty-free access to the United States.[23] But the bill didn't go anywhere. Perhaps in the run-up to 2006 midterm congressional elections, American legislators didn't want to alienate the United States' own tiny, and shrinking, textile sector, which still had some lobbying clout.

In the first three months of 2005, after the elimination of garment quotas, Cambodia's garment factories suffered, and some closed.[24] Looking for help, Mean had turned to China, which had been cultivating the Cambodian cabinet for nearly a decade. Mean personally feared that Cambodia might be overwhelmed by Chinese imports—China's giant textile sector competed directly with Cambodian garments. Still, on the advice of one of his superiors, he had taken a study trip to the booming southern Chinese city of Guangzhou, where Chinese officials told him that they would soothe Cambodia's pain by considering lifting tariffs on certain Cambodian exports. The Chinese loaded him with reports about efficiencies attained in China's garment factories, and he rolled some of these management buzzwords off his tongue, trying the phrases out as if they were new toys—"supply chain," "labor-management relations."

Mean smiled briefly, then frowned again. "But how can we sell garments to China? China itself produces garments much cheaper than we do." His voice rose and he stood up, and then sat down again. "They use cheap labor, even forced labor," he said. "I don't know. I don't know what to do."

Worse than the White House's indifference toward economics, the excesses of the war on terror, like abuses at Guantánamo Bay, undermined the attractiveness of American values, since that attractiveness rested in part on perceptions of the United States as a humane and lawful actor—as compared with, say, China. These excesses also undermined American attempts to promote democracy and human rights abroad, since repressive nations could always turn the spotlight back on the White House's own unattractive policies. "The treatment of prisoners at Guantánamo and in Iraq, and US policies in other corners of the Muslim world . . . have all undercut US moral standing in the region," reported one panel of Asia experts.[25]

China's annual report on America's human rights record

captured how America had lost some of its ability to criticize. For years Beijing has been producing this document to rebut American criticism of Chinese abuses. In the past China used the report to make mild complaints about problems like income disparity in America. But now Beijing had more than enough ammunition. "In 2004 the atrocity of US troops abusing Iraqi POWs exposed the dark side of human rights performance of the United States," noted China's 2005 report. "The scandal shocked . . . humanity and was condemned by the international community."[26]

The White House also eviscerated multinational institutions, from the Kyoto Protocol to the Comprehensive Test Ban Treaty on nuclear weapons. The Bush White House reportedly even opposed a United Nations treaty to promote cultural diversity, which has strong support around the world, particularly in nations proud of their local film and music industries. To take one of the saddest examples, as the *New York Times* reported, Washington considered cutting off aid to impoverished nations like Niger—a relatively pro-US Muslim country in Africa that has suffered repeated famines—if they supported the International Criminal Court, which the White House opposed. By comparison, the United Kingdom's government, which also went to war in Iraq, continues to back international institutions ranging from Kyoto to the International Criminal Court. The United Kingdom's global image has remained strong.[27]

A freer international media now magnified Washington's mistakes. Satellite television stations like Al Jazeera, which tend to be skeptical of the United States, have spread through formerly media-poor regions of the world. These globalized media have made the White House's actions—for good or ill—instantly accessible to people around the globe. In one study of

Moroccans', Egyptians', and Indonesians' views about America, no one in the focus group had a positive thing to say about the US president, and the authors reported that "among educated, otherwise polite young women, reactions to the mention of America included 'Go to Hell' and 'I hope God will destroy them.'"[28] Some Moroccans, Egyptians, and Indonesians even compared President Bush to Satan.

American policy today is as unpopular as at any point in the United States' modern history. Some anti-Americanism has become so strident it is almost comical. In one recent poll of South Korea, a country the United States continues to help defend against nuclear-armed North Korea, roughly half of young South Koreans surveyed said that their nation should support *North Korea* if Pyongyang and Washington were to go to war.[29] Only 11.6 percent thought that South Korea should back America in a North Korea–United States conflict.

Evidence of American unpopularity is both wide, as suggested by broader polls, and narrow, as revealed by specific weaknesses in American appeal. The Council of Graduate Schools, an organization of American universities, found that the number of international graduate school applications to US universities fell 28 percent between 2003 and 2004, its first decline in more than thirty years. Applications dropped 5 percent further between 2004 and 2005. France now receives more applications for asylum than does the United States.[30]

What is more important, unlike previous periods of unpopular American policy, when people in many countries distinguished between their dislike for US foreign policies and their personal respect for American people, American values, American culture, and American companies, today these distinctions are disappearing. In the early 1980s many countries criticized Washington's decisions to increase rhetorical pressure on the Soviet Union and to deploy new nuclear missiles in Europe, but American culture, companies, and people remained popular. A 1983 Gallup poll revealed that many Europeans disdained President Ronald Reagan's policies but approved of the American way of life.[31]

That has begun to change. In a 2002 poll of forty-three nations, majorities of people in thirty-four of the countries were unhappy with the growing influence of America—not just American policy—on their nation. In another study, large percentages of respondents in eighteen nations had a declining view of American *people* between 2002 and 2005.[32]

Foreigners also seem to be losing interest in America's core values—like the idea of America as a land of opportunity, an idea that vanishes if foreigners believe that the United States is no longer a meritocracy. In a 2005 Pew study of people from sixteen countries, in which respondents were asked, "Suppose a young man who wanted to leave this country asked you to recommend where to go to lead a good life—what country would you recommend?" most of those polled placed other nations above America as choices for emigration. US companies took a hit, too. Even in relatively pro-American countries in Western Europe, recent studies suggest that some consumers avoid American brands, and a study by Anholt-GMI, an organization that ranks the "brands" of nations, found that respondents from a range of nations ranked the United States only eleventh overall in terms of its cultural, political, popular, and business attractiveness.[33]

This unpopularity matters. Even without China on the scene, America's declining popularity decreases Washington's soft power, and potentially makes the United States more likely to resort to force rather than persuasion to meet American objectives. One recent bipartisan report on American diplomacy concluded as much, warning that if the "downward spiral [in diplomacy] is not reversed, the prospect of relying on military force to protect US national interests will increase."[34]

In just the past four years, the impact of American unpopularity has become clear. With America so unloved, and with American leaders having failed to understand how democratization in Africa, Latin America, and Asia had changed international relations, the United States was unprepared for the run-up to the war in Iraq. At the time, many leaders of democracies felt that they could not support the US-led war in Iraq, for fear of the popular backlash against them if they joined the coalition. So Chile, Mexico, and Turkey did not support the US intervention. Similarly, even though Indonesia clearly faces a serious domestic terrorism problem—a problem highlighted by the 2002 Bali bombing—Indonesian leaders for years refused to publicly support the US-led war on terror or to openly cooperate with Washington on counterterrorism.[35]

These countries' decisions had serious consequences. Unlike in the past, when the United States could twist arms among these countries' leaderships and get what it wanted, now Mexican and Chilean and Turkish leaders had to be accountable to their electorates. Without the votes of Mexico, Chile, and others, the United States failed to get the United Nations Security Council to endorse war against Iraq, a decision that made the conflict look illegitimate in the eyes of many nations, and ultimately made it difficult for Washington to persuade countries to contribute to Iraq's reconstruction. Because Turkey refused to provide a base for the invasion, there was no initial US troop presence in northern Iraq, giving Kurdish militias rein to push Sunnis and Shia out of their homes and setting the stage for deadly interethnic conflict in northern Iraq.[36]

In Indonesia, the government's refusal to cooperate with American counterterrorism efforts deprived Jakarta of intelligence, and allowed terrorist groups to proliferate, taking advantage of Indonesia's weak rule of law to establish themselves across the archipelago. FBI agents working in Indonesia complained about a lack of coopcration from local authorities, and then–Indonesian President Megawati Sukarnoputri failed to appoint a national counterterrorism coordinator. Eventually, Indonesia's policies rebounded against it, and against the United States. A string of post-Bali bombs in Indonesia further scared off tourists and investors and targeted American companies like the JW Marriott Hotel in Jakarta, where a 2003 attack killed twelve people.[37]

By the end of 2006, more than three years after the invasion of Iraq, the White House still had not succeeded in restoring America's popularity, even in longtime allies like Turkey. The isolationism of the 1990s had set the stage for America's declining soft power, undercutting America's ties to the world. While the United States reengaged with the world in the 2000s, the style of its reengagement—unilateral action, bellicose rhetoric, public diplomacy that seemed all style and no substance—only further alienated many countries. As Karen Hughes was setting off for her first listening tour, a congressional panel pulled no punches, capturing all of these trends in American declining appeal. The panel reported, "America's image and reputation abroad could hardly be worse."[38]

Of course, America still possesses numerous strengths, including core values and ideals that remain attractive to many foreigners. America could draw upon these strengths to stage a comeback, to potentially combat China's influence, and win back the world; in some countries, like Indonesia, the United States has already come back from the depths of its unpopularity. But until America uses those inherent strengths, Beijing will be able to wield its soft power to push back against American power and, potentially, to threaten American interests.

X
What's Next?

On June 14, 2001, China, Russia, Kazakhstan, Kyrgyzstan, Tajikistan, and Uzbekistan founded the Shanghai Cooperation Organization, or SCO, an organization focused on Central Asia. At the founding summit, the members declared that the SCO would be devoted to enhancing regional economic, cultural, and security cooperation. As the Chinese foreign ministry put it, in a rambling statement, the SCO would "strengthen mutual trust and good-neighborliness and friendship among member states, developing their effective cooperation in political affairs, the economy and trade, science and technology, culture, education, energy, transportation, environmental protection and other fields."[1]

The rest of the world paid little attention to SCO's founding; most American officials dismissed it as a useless talk shop. As the Central Asia scholar Greg Austin wrote, "The Shanghai Cooperation Organization has been ridiculed in many Western commentaries . . . for its apparent lack of focus and lack of achievements." But between 2001 and 2005, Central

Asia went from an obscure region of Muslim-majority "'Stans" to one of the world's most vital regions. As diminishing global oil reserves and growing energy demands pushed up world oil prices, the resource-rich Central Asian states—Kazakhstan alone produces more than one million barrels of oil per day—became, comparatively, even resource-richer.[2] After September 11, the region's land borders with Afghanistan, and its old Soviet bases, placed it in the center of the fight against Al Qaeda. US Secretary of Defense Donald Rumsfeld suddenly had to bone up on his Uzbek. Foreign reporters descended on cities like Tashkent and Dushanbe to cover the battle for Central Asian oil and the links between Central Asian radicals and Al Qaeda members holed up in Afghanistan and Pakistan.

After September 11, Washington secured basing rights in Central Asia, though some of the region's leaders appeared concerned that the United States would use its presence to help topple their governments. As it became clearer that the war on terrorism had no end in sight, it also became clearer that the Pentagon wanted to keep a semipermanent garrison of US troops at Central Asian bases. For its part, Beijing was not pleased with the idea of American soldiers permanently stationed next door, and its paranoia only grew after democratic revolutions in the former Soviet states of Georgia and Kyrgyzstan. Combined with the democratic revolutions, American troops stationed in Japan and South Korea, and American defense relationships with Singapore, Mongolia, the Philippines, and Thailand, having US soldiers in Central Asia made some Chinese strategists feel surrounded. "As the war on terrorism continues in Afghanistan, [the] US military presence in Central Asia has become a reality. However, the United States will never be satisfied with this reality," wrote the Chinese commentator Gao Fuqui. "The entrance of the United States into

Central Asia serves as a springboard from which to contain the rise of China."[3]

China had been cultivating Central Asia before the world discovered the region. Beginning in the mid-1990s, Chinese officials like then-Premier Li Peng courted Central Asia's leaders, promoting Chinese investment and trying to boost trade through proposed border free trade zones. Supporting China's charm offensive, the Chinese government invested in public diplomacy in Central Asia and increased its aid programs. Beijing established a Confucius Institute for Chinese-language and -cultural studies in Uzbekistan. It created programs to train Central Asian officials and politicians, and promised the 'Stans that Beijing would fund a $1.5 billion highway linking China to Central Asia.[4]

Once the SCO was formed, China could use the multilateral organization for leverage as well, to present itself as a natural leader of the region, or at least a regional coleader with Russia. China would be the friend who would not interfere in domestic politics, even as American officials touched down in Central Asia to make demands for basing rights. Chinese investment also received local media coverage, which molded perceptions of China. At the same time, America's image plummeted—in one Pew poll, a majority of people in Uzbekistan did not want American ideas and customs spreading to their country.[5]

China's appeal seemed to be working in Central Asia. Just as important, China's rise offered the Central Asian nations leverage to pursue their own national self-interests—with China becoming a major player in the region, countries that resented growing US influence now had another power to turn to. By 2005 China was ready to use its subtle influence in Central Asia to support the region in taking a clearer stand against

America. Before the 2005 SCO meeting, China quietly offered increased aid to Central Asian nations. After the Uzbek government cracked down on opposition in 2005—a crackdown that culminated in the massacre of more than four hundred people in the city of Andijan—and American officials criticized the Uzbek regime, China quickly backed the Uzbek policies, hosting Uzbek leader Islam Karimov for a state visit to Beijing, where China feted him with a twenty-one-gun salute.[6]

In July 2005, at the Shanghai Cooperation Organization summit, SCO countries warned against any countries—clearly meaning America—"monopolizing or dominating international affairs" and demanded that Washington provide a timeline for withdrawing American forces from SCO member countries. Soon Uzbekistan rescinded America's basing rights. Now Washington was paying attention to the Shanghai Cooperation Organization. General Richard B. Myers, chairman of America's Joint Chiefs of Staff, resorted to tossing a kettle-calls-the-pot-black charge at Moscow and Beijing: "It looks to me like two very large countries were trying to bully some smaller countries" in Central Asia, Myers told reporters. "China's interest in building relations with Central Asia is not startling given its long history in the region, but the agility and creativity it has exercised in doing so has taken many by surprise," admitted Bates Gill and Matthew Oresman, China specialists at the Center for Strategic and International Studies, a Washington think tank.[7]

The story of the Shanghai Cooperation Organization teaches several lessons—lessons about China's growing global influence, and potentially about the future of China's relations with the United States. In a short period of time, and under the US radar, China amassed significant soft power in Central Asia through aid, formal diplomacy, public diplomacy, investment, and other tools. Even as China's role in Central Asia expanded, the region became far more important to both China and America. Central Asia became critical to America for its energy reserves and its role in the war on terrorism. Meanwhile, Central Asia became crucial to China for its resources, its support for China in international organizations, its trade potential, and its geostrategic position.

In some respects, Chinese and American interests coincide in Central Asia—and around the world. Many of China's interests, as we have seen, are only natural—peace, access to resources, friends, and allies. China's soft power often has benefited the United States. In Central Asia, Beijing has helped prod the Central Asian governments to round up suspected terrorists, promoted regional economic cooperation, and become a growing market for Central Asian goods, potentially reducing economic instability. But sometimes China's interests conflict with American interests, including America's own alliances, need for energy, and commitment to democratization. When China discovers that its interests do not overlap with America's, it now has the tools to build allegiances to Beijing—and it can find countries looking for a great power to balance their relations with America. In the worst-case scenario, China might use its soft power to subtly prod countries to choose between itself and the United States.

As China becomes more powerful, it has begun to face international pressure, as an important nation, to use its soft power more responsibly. In one sign of growing engagement with the United Nations, Beijing recently sent some one thousand peacekeepers to southern Lebanon after the Israel-Hezbollah war. Beijing's Foreign Ministry has created a new department for external security affairs, to handle larger peacekeeping duties and other tasks like protecting Chinese citizens abroad.[8]

Despite its unconditional aid to countries like Angola, China also is thinking about working with other aid donors so that its assistance does not undermine World Bank or IMF programs supporting good governance. In some respects, China's aid fills gaps—China constructs roads and bridges across Africa and Latin America, where most major donors abandoned funding infrastructure decades ago, and it often produces infrastructure far more cheaply than contractors working for Western aid organizations. China may make its aid programs more transparent and sophisticated. In crises like the Asian tsunami, China has coordinated with other donors. On other occasions, in Cambodia and East Timor, Chinese officials were invited to meetings of all major donors, and began attending, showing their interest in working with other countries. Beijing also has quietly told aid specialists that it wants to build a Chinese version of the United States Agency for International Development (USAID), a permanent aid bureaucracy.[9] Building a Chinese USAID would make Chinese aid more accountable, since it would create an independent organization full of aid specialists rather than relying on the Chinese Ministry of Commerce—which simply links assistance to China's immediate political and economic needs—to disburse aid.

Beijing also may be warming to the idea that Chinese support for authoritarian regimes can create instability—instability that, in the long run, doesn't benefit China itself. In Burma the junta's backward, erratic rule has not only created the drug and HIV crises that threaten China but also endangered local Chinese businessmen, who never know when the political situation will turn violent or whom they must pay off to keep operating.

Fearful of Burma's instability, Chinese officials have not only cracked down on gambling and drugs in the China-Burma frontier but also pushed for political reform inside Burma. According to several Burma watchers, Chinese officials have held quiet meetings with activist organizations battling the Burmese government, bringing these opposition figures to China for talks. During the most recent visit of Burma's prime minister to China, Chinese officials pushed Burma to improve its dialogue with opposition groups, with Wen Jiabao calling for "reconciliation" in Burma. "China is increasingly circumspect in its defense of Burma," one diplomat told the Burma analyst Larry Jagan. Even more surprising, Beijing has allowed Burma's human rights crisis to be placed on the agenda of the UN Security Council, a momentous decision for a country skeptical of allowing the United Nations to meddle in other nations' affairs.[10]

The Burma example may become representative—China may increasingly use its soft power to promote stability in places where the United States has little influence. Having China, along with the United States, prodding these countries means that leaders in places like Burma or North Korea cannot write off the pressure as merely an American initiative. China is especially likely to use its influence when Beijing fears that instability in another nation could spill over into China, either by spreading drugs and disease (Burma), or by causing massive refugee flows (North Korea), or by exacerbating terrorism (Central Asia)—and when those countries do not possess significant amounts of oil, gas, or other resources.

China's soft power can help the United States in other ways. As we have seen, by providing a new, growing market for developing nations' commodities, China has allowed African, Asian, and Latin American countries to amass large positive balances of trade (at least for now), pay off some of their debts, and reduce potential financial instability. Even Chinese competition with Latin American and Asian exports could have a positive impact, tangentially benefiting the United States. In Latin America, competition with China is leading nations to address their own obstacles to economic competitiveness, for fear of losing foreign direct investment to China. These are problems often cited by US firms operating in Latin America as obstacles to better business. In Africa growing Chinese competition is providing a similar wake-up call, especially in more developed economies like South Africa or Kenya. Similarly, the China–Southeast Asia free trade agreement has forced the region's leaders, who have many of their own bilateral grievances, to think of Southeast Asia as a unified economic bloc, and to move faster on a free trade agreement linking ten countries in Southeast Asia. Again, lower trade barriers within Southeast Asia would benefit American multinationals—companies like Ford that have developed regionwide supply chains in which they make some parts in Thailand and other parts in the Philippines, then ship completed automobiles to dealers in Indonesia.[11]

Some Asian leaders believe that China's soft power will have its greatest impact not on the United States but on Japan. Japan, which also focuses on cultivating influence in Asia, certainly has found itself on its back foot. During its own period of stunning economic growth, from the end of the Second World War until the early 1990s, Japan failed to cultivate soft power. Japanese companies did invest heavily in Asia, helping nations like Thailand grow from making toys and shoes to building computers and personal digital assistants. Japan lavished aid on the developing world as well. During the 1990s and early

2000s, Indonesia, Japan's largest aid recipient, often received nearly $1 billion in assistance from Tokyo each year.[12]

But Tokyo seemed to believe that this cash alone would win friends. Though aid and investment helped to improve Japan's image, during its economic boom Japan never became an object of cultural interest, a draw for emigrants, or a model of development. With only a small diaspora in the developing world, Japan could not undertake the kind of outreach to overseas Japanese that China can with diaspora Chinese. And Tokyo, chastened by shame over its World War II history, was loath to advertise Japan with high-profile public diplomacy. "We don't need to do the kind of official visits to show what we're spending in aid in a country," one Japanese diplomat told me.[13] The Japanese foreign ministry did not heavily advertise its aid programs, or hold out Japan as a model, or take the lead on regional trade agreements.

Without unsubtle advertising, however, average people in other nations often do not know where the donated vaccines for their children or the new road for their town came from. Too often, Tokyo does not even try to leverage the fact that it is a democracy to appeal to average people in the developing world, making it hard for Japan to differentiate itself from China. After the Burmese government refused in spring 2006 to release opposition leader Aung San Suu Kyi from house arrest, every democracy on the UN Security Council wanted to put more pressure on the Burmese regime. Alone among free nations, Japan argued that the United Nations should do nothing.[14]

As a result, Japan did not build as much goodwill among leaders or average citizens as one might have expected, given the size of its aid and investment. Few opinion leaders in a place like the Philippines had genuinely warm feelings toward

Tokyo; even fewer had lived or studied in Japan. During the 1980s and the early 1990s, as China remained weak and Japan's economy boomed, these mistakes did not matter much. And of course, Japan did not directly compete with America's soft influence, since Tokyo and Washington were close allies. But when Japan's economy sank into decadelong stagnation in the 1990s, and China began to exert influence and subtly prod other nations to pay less attention to Japanese leadership, Japan's past missteps grew in importance.

By the late 1990s and early 2000s a combination of factors further undermined Japan's soft power. As the United States became more unpopular, Japan, a close American ally, suffered by association. With no room for flab in their overseas operations, Japanese companies shifted investments away from other parts of the developing world and toward China. Worried about popular anger within Japan over Tokyo's lavishing money abroad while the domestic economy tanked, the Japanese government slashed foreign aid: in its 2005 budget Japan's Finance Ministry cut overseas development assistance for the sixth straight year. Meanwhile, the conservative Japanese leader Junichiro Koizumi, prime minister between 2001 and 2006, alienated other nations in Asia by visiting the Yasukuni Shrine, a controversial Tokyo memorial that commemorates more than two million Japanese war dead but also explicitly honors fourteen veterans convicted of class A war crimes by a post–World War II court. Next to the controversial shrine stands a museum that downplays Japan's behavior in the war, like its massacre of some 300,000 Chinese civilians in Nanjing.[15]

China skillfully played on this anger, condemning Koizumi's visits and using Yasukuni against Japan in public settings. (China's spotlighting of the Yasukuni situation, of course, helps the Communist Party at home, by directing potential popular anger toward Japan and away from the Beijing government.) As Japan has pushed in recent years for a permanent spot at the UN Security Council, one of Tokyo's most important goals, China has repeatedly brought up the Yasukuni visits to remind the world of Japan's wartime aggression and to persuade Asian nations not to support a permanent Japanese seat. During a summit in South Korea held in 2005, China's foreign minister, Li Zhaoxing, wondered, "What would European people think if German leaders were to visit [shrines] related to Hitler and Nazis?"[16]

By the early 2000s Japan was hemorrhaging influence in the developing world. "In the 1980s, the US ambassador would be lucky to see [Malaysian Prime Minister] Mahathir Mohamad and the Japanese ambassador was there three times a week—not anymore," says one American policy maker. Indeed, when China proposed a free trade deal in 2001 with ten Southeast Asian nations, Japan appeared caught off guard. Suddenly China, not Japan, was driving trade talks in Asia, and many Asian opinion leaders perceived Tokyo as lagging and out of touch. When nations in Asia and Africa that had been major recipients of Japanese aid refused to back Tokyo's bid for a UN Security Council seat, the message came home: the Japanese foreign ministry realized how badly it had slipped. Japan belatedly acceded to Southeast Asia's Treaty of Amity and Cooperation, but because China had signed on first, Japan received little press coverage for this decision. Japan came up with a framework for a free trade agreement with Southeast Asia but did not take discussions very far, partly because Japan's farmers resisted opening markets.[17]

Opinion leaders across Asia already believe that China's charm eventually will overwhelm Japan's fading influence, especially as Japan's population ages and its investments abroad decline. "The Chinese are just moving much faster than the Japanese," said Ajit Singh, the former secretary general of Asean. "The Japanese are mired in bureaucracy and now they're always looking over their shoulder" at China. Even American policy makers sympathetic to Tokyo admit as much. "It's amazing how much influence Japan has lost," marveled one senior American policy maker.[18]

But China's growing soft power will threaten the United States as well: the emergence of China's soft power is already having a strategic impact on US foreign policy. China could wield its influence in a growing clash over resources. Like China, the United States needs continued access to oil and gas, since estimates suggest that America could be importing nearly 70 percent of its oil in two decades, up from just over 50 percent today. Oil and gas do not trade on a completely free market, tend to be controlled by state-linked companies—and may be running out. Stores of easily accessible petroleum, like the fields in Saudi Arabia, could be dwindling. Colin Campbell, the former chief geologist for Amoco, argues that 2006 may have been the peak production year for oil, after which reserves and production will hit a long downward slope.[19] With oil becoming scarcer, Latin American and West African and Asian oil remain among the cheapest for the United States, and the easiest for American companies to refine and use.

The United States cannot afford to lose access to these reserves to any potential competitor. As we saw in Chapter 7, China has enjoyed success in winning access to oil and gas, and Beijing views energy as a zero-sum game. "For China's leaders, energy security clearly is too important to be left to the markets," argues the Asia energy specialist Mikkal Herberg, who believes competing US and Chinese demands for energy will eventually lead to a clash over resources. "The Chinese are seeking to achieve assured sources of supply in Latin America through a strategy that focuses on securing the entire supply chain in critical industries," believes R. Evan Ellis, a Latin America specialist.[20] "This strategy of 'vertical integration' involves using strategic purchases and investments to ensure an acceptable amount of leverage over . . . all elements of the supply chain."

In Venezuela, for one, China not only promises new investment and aid but also provides Hugo Chávez with a potential alternative consumer to the United States, which has endured frosty relations with Caracas. For now, Venezuela, home to the largest oil reserves outside of the Middle East, remains reliant on shipping its oil to the United States, and China has resisted suggesting that it will lead Caracas to shift its oil industry toward Beijing. But Venezuela eventually may wean itself off of American markets. Chávez has announced plans to double oil exports to China, and Venezuela is building its shipping fleet, making an investment in long-term growth in exports to the People's Republic.[21]

Beijing does not want Chávez to openly tout his China connections—in 2005 China's ambassador in Venezuela pointedly told reporters that "the natural markets for Venezuelan oil are North and South America." But though China has been cautious about directly threatening American access to oil, as Beijing's energy needs skyrocket, it could find itself with little choice other than to compete with the United States. Already, the Chinese state-linked oil company Sinopec has expressed interest in upgrading a pipeline from Venezuela that would run through Panama and to the Pacific, orienting Venezuela toward China, and Chinese companies have helped Venezuela become less dependent on American technology in other industries, including telecommunications.[22]

Any major shift in Venezuelan oil shipments could badly damage America's economy. Caracas sends some 1.3 million barrels of oil a day to the United States, making it America's fourth-largest supplier of crude. According to Michelle Billig, a former analyst at the US Department of Energy, in June 2004, after a strike in Venezuela decreased the country's oil production, Venezuela's shipments to America crashed. "Over the next three months," Billig says, "the [Venezuelan] crisis kept some 200 million barrels of oil and gasoline from the world market," forcing the price of a barrel of oil to a twenty-one-year high.[23]

If Venezuela shifted to sending more oil to China, it could set a model for its neighbors as well. As with Venezuela, China's socialist history, and its long-standing outreach to populist groups in the developing world, offers Chinese leaders residual bona fides in dealing with leftist leaders in nations like Bolivia or Ecuador. If Latin countries run by populist leaders see that Venezuela shifts to supplying China and does not suffer economically, other leaders, like Bolivia's Evo Morales, would recognize that they too could use relations with China to reduce America's dominance in the Western Hemisphere without damaging their own economies.

Getting deep into Latin American oil also could draw the Chinese military into the region, which would clearly challenge American power. This scenario lies in the future, but in a 2004 white paper explaining its defense planning, Beijing, in a departure from past strategy, accepted the idea that the Chinese military could become engaged in power projection abroad to protect economic interests and secure strategic assets.[24] If this idea of power projection becomes a central component of Chinese military strategy, and if China comes to see its assets in Latin America—resources and ports, access to pipelines—as vital, the People's Liberation Army may seek closer relationships with many Latin American militaries.

A similar situation could unfold in Nigeria, the fifth-biggest supplier of oil to America, which like Venezuela has a political elite sensitive to the idea that it is selling the country's resources to rich Western nations. This is a criticism leveled at the Nigerian government by opposition groups and armed radicals operating in the Niger Delta, which pumps two million barrels of oil per day yet remains one of the poorest parts of the country. Beijing has enjoyed initial success in Nigeria, leveraging the idea that China, as a nonmeddling, developing nation, could be a better partner than Western states; China has won some $4 billion worth of preferential Nigerian exploration rights. If Beijing builds on its initial success in Nigeria, once again China will come into direct conflict with America's need for vital resources.

China might be able to apply the type of appeal it uses in Venezuela and Nigeria to producers in the Middle East, who also see in China a potential alternative consumer. As the energy analyst Erica Downs writes, Chinese scholars now argue that Beijing could utilize "opposition to American hegemony" to improve relations with leaders in the Middle East. By partnering with China, these regimes would reduce domestic criticisms that they are too pro-American. Saudi officials have begun speaking openly about potentially cutting off oil to the United States—presumably if America's image in the Muslim world declines so much that Riyadh cannot afford an alliance with Washington.[25]

America's demand for oil, when combined with a reduction in exports from Venezuela or Nigeria, could have even more dangerous consequences. Facing a world in which oil producers now have another large consumer, the United States has abandoned some of its own commitment to promoting democracy, for fear of alienating autocratic oil states. After delivering a speech in May 2006 in which he blasted President Vladimir Putin for destroying Russian democracy, Vice President Richard Cheney jetted off to Kazakhstan, a dictatorship whose oil production could nearly triple by 2015, and where the United States wants the Kazakhs to build a pipeline that would bypass Russia. In Kazakhstan, Cheney "expressed [his] admiration" for the country's "economic and political development." Soon after, the administration invited Kazakh leader Nursultan Nazarbayev to visit the White House, though the State Department's own report on human rights in Kazakhstan put it simply: "The government's human rights record remained poor."[26]

Meanwhile, Secretary of State Condoleezza Rice hosted Teodoro Obiang Nguema Mbasogo, who has ruled Equatorial Guinea with an iron grip since a coup in 1979. Obiang also appears extraordinarily corrupt—as documented by the journalist Peter Maass, Obiang is accused of depositing at least $13 million into accounts at the shady Riggs Bank in Washington. As the two leaders together met the press, Obiang seemed uncomfortable—at home, he could toss pesky reporters in jail—but Rice held his hand. "You are a good friend," Rice cooed.[27]

China's soft power also could help it push countries to decide between Washington and Beijing. Already, partly due to China's improving image, which makes other countries comfortable with closer ties to Beijing, nations in Asia, as well as in parts of Africa and Latin America, are using Beijing as a hedge against American power. China could take advantage of these changes. As these shifts are occurring, right now Beijing has supported only nations, like Uzbekistan, looking to break away from closer ties to the United States, but in the future it could more aggressively push countries to make those decisions.

China is already trying to draw upon its charm to push back against American power in Asia. Even as it publicly accepts America's presence in the region, Beijing has helped initiate multilateral forums, like the East Asia Summit, that exclude the United States. Similarly, Dennis Blair, then commander of American forces in the Pacific, proposed in 2001 that Asia create what he called "security communities" in which the United States would increase its defense cooperation with Asian nations to create a kind of informal regional security organization. But many Asian nations vetoed the idea, in part because China quietly applied pressure on them to reject it.[28]

In the Philippines, defense officials told me that China is pushing for much closer military relations, the kind of strong defense ties the Philippines enjoys with America now. If Beijing were to develop this close cooperation with Manila, the Philippines' cooperation with the United States would almost certainly decline, since it would be difficult for Manila to have close security ties with both powers. "The Chinese would like joint military exercises [with us], huge defense assistance," says one Philippine official.[29] Five years ago, Philippine defense planners would have balked at this idea. But as China becomes more popular in the Philippines, he says, this is no longer out of the question, because the Philippine public could be sold on close defense ties with Beijing. "China-Philippines defense cooperation can be expanded," he said. "My gut feeling is that the Philippine public would support this."

In the future, China could prod countries like the Philippines or Thailand, which are already using China as a hedge, to downgrade their close relations with the United States, or could push countries like Singapore to stop providing basing rights for America. It could pressure countries not to intervene if the United States and China were to go to war over Taiwan, as it has done with Singapore, protesting angrily and threatening to impose economic sanctions when Singaporean Deputy Prime Minister Lee Hsien Loong visited Taiwan. China's protests obtained results: Lee later promised that Singapore would not support Taiwan in a war, if Taiwan provoked the conflict by making moves toward independence, as China often accuses it of doing.[30]

China might even drive a wedge between America and its closest allies. For fifty years, Australia has been bound to the United States through the ANZUS treaty, which states that any armed attack on a country covered in the treaty would endanger all the countries, compelling them to come to the besieged nation's assistance.

But as we have seen, Australians no longer feel so warmly toward America, an alienation captured in the 2005 poll by Australian research organization the Lowy Institute, in which only half the Australians surveyed had positive feelings about the United States. At the same time, China has aggressively wooed Australia, sending its finest diplomats, building up cultural exchanges, offering a strategic partnership, and aggressively promoting the importance of China's demand for natural resources to the Australian economy. China has become Australia's second-largest trading partner, behind Japan, and Australian mining companies like BHP Billiton have posted record profits—in February 2006 BHP Billiton announced the highest half-year profit in Australian history. Australia's close commercial relationship has received major coverage in the Australian media, making China seem more benign.[31]

As in Central Asia, China's soft power has begun to help it gain harder objectives in Australia. With Chinese consumption becoming crucial to the Australian economy, and China itself becoming vastly more popular, Australian politicians have started to back away from ANZUS. At a press conference held in Beijing in August 2004, Australian Foreign Minister Alexander Downer told reporters, "The ANZUS obligations could be invoked only in the event of a direct attack on the United States or Australia." Downer continued, with his comments clearly suggesting that Australia would not help the United States fight a war with China over Taiwan. "Some other activity elsewhere in the world . . . doesn't invoke it." A surprised US State Department issued a sharp rebuke and sent six cables to Canberra to ask the Australians for an immediate explanation of Downer's comments, and Australian leaders publicly repudiated Downer.[32]

China has tried to build on this potential Australian-US divide. In March 2005 a top Chinese Foreign Ministry official suggested that Canberra "relook" at the ANZUS treaty and reinterpret it so that Australia would not be compelled to help defend Taiwan. "We all know Taiwan is part of China, and we do not want to see in any way the Taiwan issue become one of the elements that will be taken up by bilateral military alliances," he warned. Just to make sure there was no misunderstanding, he added: "If there were any move by Australia and the US in terms of that alliance that is detrimental to peace and stability in Asia, then [Australia] has to be very careful."[33]

Iran. Uzkbekistan. Sudan. What do all these countries have in common? Freedom House ranks all of them as "not free," its lowest possible rating.[34] Governments in all of these places show little respect for human rights. And China courts all of them, selling its model of controlled development and assisting them to build the same model.

This is the most dangerous part of China's soft power—the most dangerous to the world, and, potentially, to American influence. Despite its smooth highways and flashy shopping malls and reams of Starbucks, China remains an authoritarian country, a Leninist regime if no longer a Marxist one. Despite promises of reform, under Hu Jintao China actually has proven less tolerant of domestic civil society than under Jiang Zemin. "Plans by some officials to ease regulations and give more room to civil society, including grassroots groups, appear to have been shelved," says Human Rights Watch in its annual report on human rights in the PRC. Despite media coverage suggesting that Chinese officials are allowing more popular protests, the US State Department recently reported, "There was a trend [in China] towards increased harassment, detention, and imprisonment by government and security authorities of those perceived as threatening to government authority."[35]

Though China may be backsliding on reform, American leaders and foreign policy elites in other free societies have embraced the idea of promoting democracy. When the Berlin Wall fell, America was led by George H. W. Bush, a traditional realist wary of interfering in other nations' affairs, except in cases of overwhelming American security interests. Since the end of the Cold War, the elder Bush's brand of realism has all but perished, even in the wake of the disastrous Iraq war. The idea that rich nations should use their power both to intervene in humanitarian disasters and to reform autocracies has migrated from the creed of a select few American thinkers once perceived as naïve idealists to the core of the United States' national security strategy. As Western leaders witnessed—and often ignored—genocides in the 1990s, nations realized that they had to intervene in catastrophes like those in the Balkans and Rwanda; otherwise, these mass killings would happen again, and dangerous leaders in the developing world would lose any respect for the threat of foreign power. As the post–Cold War era's failed states bred civil conflict and havens for terror like Afghanistan, world leaders recognized that developed countries could not isolate themselves from the unrest of the developing world.

Just ten years after George H. W. Bush left office, America's National Security Strategy announced, "The events of September 11, 2001 taught us that weak states, like Afghanistan, can pose as great a danger to our national interests as strong states." To defeat terror, the National Security Strategy promised, America would "actively work to bring the hope of democracy . . . to every corner of the world." Many liberals, too, agreed that helping create strong civil societies and democratic systems in the developing world is not just a good in itself—it is the key to security, to combating instability and terror. Subscribers to this belief included foreign leaders like Britain's Tony Blair and Germany's Joschka Fischer and members of both major parties in the United States. Even John Kerry, who during the 2004 presidential campaign heaped criticism on the White House for its mismanagement of the Iraq War, bought into the idea of using American power to promote democratization. "Kerry and his foreign policy advisors are not doves," the writer Paul Starobin noted in a 2004 profile of the Democratic candidate. "They are liberal war hawks who would be unafraid to use American power to promote their values."[36]

Academics provided rigor to these theories. In one prominent study, Harvard professor Alberto Abadie found that nations with the highest levels of political freedom had relative few incidents of terrorism. Another study, by the economists

Alan B. Krueger and Jitka Maleckova, demonstrated a link between terrorism and the lack of civil liberties within societies.[37]

Beijing's support for authoritarian regimes, stemming from its vow of noninterference, runs exactly contrary to this American foreign policy. Though their interests sometimes overlap, fundamentally the United States and China do not agree on how diplomacy and international affairs should be conducted. And though Beijing can be persuaded to support better governance in places, like Burma, with limited resources and such horrendous regimes that they breed instability in China, it is much harder to persuade China to act against terrible governments with oil, like Sudan, or whose policies have no direct impact on China itself, like Zimbabwe. In the future, China's ability to support its friends will only grow stronger as China builds its global soft power.

In the spring of 2005 once-prosperous Zimbabwe, which because of government mismanagement now boasts the world's worst inflation, held a dismal election. As election day drew near in Harare, Zimbabwe's capital, President Robert Mugabe's goons detained hundreds of activists and opposition politicians. On election day, when thousands of opposition voters claimed that they had been physically prevented from going to the polls, Mugabe unsurprisingly won a smashing victory, then announced that he could remain in power until he was one hundred. (He was eighty-one at the time.) The US embassy in Zimbabwe announced that its election monitoring had uncovered "several patterns of irregularities that raised concerns about the freeness and fairness of the process."[38]

After the election, Mugabe further consolidated his power, launching what the Zimbabwean government called "Operation Drive Out Trash." As part of this campaign, the state evicted from their homes hundreds of thousands of urban poor, who tended to be opposition supporters, then forced the poor people to burn down their own houses.[39]

During the sham elections, no major international power would endorse the Zimbabwe vote—except China. Beijing didn't just endorse the election; it may have actively helped Mugabe win. During the run-up to the election, China offered planeloads of T-shirts to Mugabe backers, sent the Zimbabwean government jamming devices to be used against independent radio stations, and provided Zimbabwe with riot-control gear. "Providing African countries with aid without any political strings within our ability is an important part of China's policy toward Africa," Hu Jintao confirmed in a speech.[40]

China's assistance went along with Mugabe's broader "Look East" policy of cultivating Beijing, under which the government helps students at Zimbabwe's public universities learn Chinese, and Zimbabwean officials tout China's economic model as a solution for their nation's financial woes. Beijing responded by promoting a trade deal with impoverished Zimbabwe and sending economic advisers to Harare. China even hosted Mugabe for a state visit, where one of China's leading universities honored the Zimbabwean leader, who had alienated his entire region, for his "brilliant contribution" to global relations.[41]

Mugabe appeared ecstatic over his good fortune. "The Chinese are our good friends, you see," he told one interviewer, barely able to contain a smile. At a rally held on Zimbabwe's independence day at a stadium in Harare, Mugabe declared, "We have turned east, where the sun rises, and given our back to the West." Many in the crowd, forced to attend the rally, did not agree, but Mugabe paid them no mind, warning that state security forces would "descend mercilessly" on anyone who questioned him.[42] As he spoke, Chinese fighter planes looped over the stadium, which had been built for Zimbabwe by China.

Few Western nations have tried to pressure Beijing to back off of its support for Mugabe. On Iran, however, a much more dangerous actor, Europe and the United States have tried to persuade China to work with them. But Iran is a major source of oil for China, providing some 14 percent of Beijing's imports, and unlike Burma or North Korea, which sit on China's borders, domestic events in Iran do not directly affect China.

Since the election of hard-line president Mahmoud Ahmadinejad in May 2005, Iran has become more unstable and threatening. Under Ahmadinejad, the Iranian government has cracked down on writers and even bloggers, purged Iran's civil service of its most moderate members, and called for Israel to be "wiped off the map." At the same time, Ahmadinejad has become more aggressive in touting Iran's nuclear program, which many Western experts believe is designed to build weapons; Ahmadinejad prevented inspectors from visiting suspected Iranian nuclear sites, called Iran's nuclear program "irreversible," and oversaw new tests of Iranian missiles. Ahmadinejad even presided over a bizarre event on Iranian state television, in which the president celebrated Iran's nuclear ambitions by speaking in front of men dressed in traditional Iranian costumes, who danced around a silver box Ahmadinejad claimed held enriched uranium.[43]

With Iran defiant, the Bush administration, along with Britain and France, pushed for a UN Security Council resolution that would require Iran to stop its uranium enrichment or face such potential consequences as multinational sanctions. But the Chinese Foreign Ministry stood fast. Although Beijing expressed concern about Iran's nuclear ambitions, China opposed any efforts by the Council to censure Iran. The Beijing

People's Daily newspaper announced, "The real intention behind the US fueling the Iran issue is . . . to pave the way for regime change in that country." At the same time, China expanded its oil interests in Iran, tying itself closely with Tehran by proposing a $100 billion deal to develop a new Iranian oil field. Although China later quietly applied pressure on Tehran, working behind the scenes to come up with a nuclear compromise, it still refused to accept any intervention in Iran's domestic affairs.[44]

Even in cases of genocide, China seems willing to choose noninterference when the crisis does not threaten its immediate interests. By the fall of 2003 veteran Africa watchers had begun warning of impending disaster in the western Sudanese region of Darfur. Local villagers told foreign aid workers that the Arab *janjaweed,* militias reportedly backed by the Sudanese government, were attacking black tribes. The janjaweed, they said, were trying to wipe out entire tribes, destroying their towns, possessions, and even their tools.[45]

Over the next year, janjaweed attacks escalated. The World Health Organization reported that as many as ten thousand people were perishing per month in Darfur. United Nations monitors sent to the region in April 2004 came back with tales of massacres, gang rapes, and worse. By September 2004, then–Secretary of State Colin Powell told the Senate Foreign Relations Committee, "We concluded—I concluded that genocide has been committed in Darfur."[46] In response to the crisis, the UN Security Council passed a resolution in September 2004 condemning the killing.

China, the major consumer of Sudan's oil and most important foreign partner, did not budge. (China National Petroleum Corporation owns 40 percent of Sudan's oil consortium.) Beijing allegedly did nothing to stop its state-linked oil companies from removing populations of average Sudanese to replace them with oil installations. It worked at the United Nations to water down condemnations of the Sudanese government. China's UN ambassador, Wang Guangya, pushed the United Nations to change a resolution from calling for "further action" against Sudan's government to considering "taking additional measures." Beijing then threatened to veto any subsequent resolutions that imposed sanctions on the Sudanese leadership. As China's Deputy Foreign Minister Zhou Wenzhong said, "Business is business. We try to separate politics from business. Secondly, I think the internal situation in the Sudan is an internal affair, and we are not in a position to impose upon them."[47]

Over the following years, the situation deteriorated further. Sudanese soldiers blocked access to some of the Darfurian refugee camps, ensuring that even larger numbers of people would die. Human Rights Watch estimated that at least two million Darfurians had been driven from their homes.[48] Casualty counts skyrocketed, and the crisis spilled into other countries, destabilizing neighboring Chad. By the spring of 2006, the Sudan expert Eric Reeves estimated that more than 450,000 people had died in Darfur, and nearly 90 percent of the black villages in Darfur had been ruined. Reeves further concluded that communities would never rebuild, since the janjaweed had murdered an entire generation of Darfurian men.

Still China did not budge. On a visit to the United States in April 2006, Hu Jintao offered no concessions on China's support for Sudan. Chinese foreign ministry officials repeatedly emphasized that they opposed any economic sanctions on Sudan, no matter how grave that regime's offenses.

Citizens of authoritarian regimes like Zimbabwe or Sudan are not the only ones who suffer from China's influence; China's support for dictators damages American interests. For years, the United States and its allies had tried to pressure Mugabe to loosen his control of the political system, and Zimbabwe was proving one of the world's major tests of whether the United States and its democratic allies could actually help transform other societies. Western countries had slapped sanctions on Zimbabwe, and the Commonwealth of Nations, the association of former British colonies, had suspended Zimbabwe from the group. But with China's support, Mugabe could ignore Western pressure.

In August 2005 Mugabe said as much. In a televised speech, he ruled out any talks between himself and the political opposition—talks favored by many foreign powers, including neighboring South Africa. "I am aware there are shrill calls from many quarters," the Zimbabwean leader said. But, he said, Harare would not bow to pressure, since "our Look East policies are beginning to assume a concrete form . . . transform[ing] our economy in a fundamental way."[49]

In other countries, too, China's backing of dictators makes Washington look weak and reduces pressure on unstable, rogue actors like Sudan or Venezuela or Iran. In Sudan, China's decisions not only condemned tens of thousands of Darfurians to death but also helped demonstrate to the world that the United States, the world's biggest power, could not stop genocide. (To be sure, some critics have argued that the Bush administration did not press hard enough for tougher UN action against Sudan, but it tried far harder than China.) In Chávez's case, China's backing actually helps boost his regional profile. This adds prestige Chávez can use to convince other leaders in Latin America, like his fellow populist Bolivian President Evo Morales, to follow Chávez's autocratic policies.

In Iran, China (aided by Russia, which has significant interests in Iran) also serves as the major impediment to further pressure, and to keeping nuclear weapons out of the hands of the Iranian regime. China is effectively prolonging the Iranian nuclear stalemate, making it more likely that Tehran will acquire nuclear weapons and reducing pressure on a dangerous actor. In this way, Beijing again weakens Washington's global influence, since the United States talks tough but the world sees that it does not have the appeal to persuade enough nations to support its pressure on Iran.

In the long run, however, China's relations with countries like Sudan could come back to haunt Beijing. If countries like Sudan or Zimbabwe ever made the transition to freer governments, China could face a sizable backlash for its past support of authoritarian rulers, just as the United States now faces left-leaning governments in Latin America resentful of past US backing for conservative Latin dictators. This is one reason, perhaps, why Chinese officials have begun cultivating contacts with opposition activists in countries like Burma. "Don't you think that if Burma became a democracy all the leaders might remember who helped keep them in jail before?" asked one Burma activist. "There could be an immediate popular backlash against all the Chinese businesses and officials in Burma."[50]

Locals angry over China's propping up bad governments already have attacked Chinese businesspeople in the Pacific Islands, Venezuela, Burma, and elsewhere. If the killing in Sudan continues, and if China is perceived as doing nothing to help solve the Darfur crisis while taking out vast quantities of Sudanese oil, protesters eventually might wind up directing violence at the thousands of Chinese who have come to Sudan to set up businesses or work in the oil industry.

Even China's old comrades have turned against Beijing. In the Philippines, the New People's Army, a communist insurgent group, once based its rhetoric on Mao's teachings and exempted Chinese businesspeople from its attacks. In the 1960s and early 1970s Beijing even provided support for the NPA. But China cut off its aid to the NPA long ago, and now NPA soldiers threaten Chinese companies coming to the Philippines as well. The NPA views them as no different from other firms—as equally guilty of "stealing" the Philippines' resources.[51]

XI
Responding to the Charm Offensive

In a short period of time, Beijing has proven that it can shift its foreign policy quickly and woo the world, often focusing on countries America has alienated. China has drastically changed its image in many parts of the world from dangerous to benign. It may already be the preeminent power in parts of Asia, and it could develop China-centered spheres of influence in other parts of the globe, like Central Asia or Africa. Even longtime American allies like Australia have moved closer to Beijing.

But these changes do not mean that China's soft power yet approaches America's, or that the United States will not remain the essential power in world affairs. They do not mean that the United States will never recover its lost appeal. As Joseph Nye notes, the United States recovered from a similar decline in its international soft power in the wake of the Vietnam War, partly by reemphasizing American values that appeal to the world.[1]

The United States still enjoys several crucial advantages over China. America remains the world's unchallenged military power. Military power does not necessarily ensure soft influence—North Korea retains a massive army but few people are listening to North Korean music. But military power, if used correctly, can complement soft power. Military power can be deployed for humanitarian missions that then improve a nation's popularity, like American relief efforts after the 2004 Pacific tsunami. The tsunami demonstrated that only the United States has a sufficiently sophisticated military to move aid overnight. And the tsunami response, combined with aggressive American public diplomacy that highlighted the relief effort, clearly altered opinions of the United States, even among some of the most anti-American groups. In Indonesia you did not have to look hard to find strident anti-American sentiment before the tsunami hit: after the September 11 attacks, Indonesian Vice President Hamzah Haz declared that the terrorist attacks might "cleanse the sins of the United States." After seeing American marines delivering relief to the shattered province of Aceh, one of the most devoutly Muslim parts of Indonesia, many Indonesians changed their minds. A survey of Indonesians taken in January 2006 found that unfavorable views of America had dropped from 48 percent in 2004 to 13 percent. "There has been an incredibly deep emotional connection between America and Indonesia since the tsunami," Indonesian President Susilo Bambang Yudhoyono told the audience during a dinner in 2005. "When the USS Lincoln and the USNS Mercy ended their humanitarian mission in Aceh and Nias [another part of Indonesia], they left behind thankful patients, tearful friends, and a grateful nation."[2]

Military power also can help defend allies and friends, thereby improving popular and elite opinion. Only the United States has the blue-water navy, basing agreements around the world, and rapid reaction forces to come to the aid of any friend threatened by conflict. Elites in most foreign countries, including China, recognize this, and understand that it will be decades before Beijing has the potential to perform a similar role. The 2005 study of Thailand commissioned by the US embassy, which revealed growing warmth toward China, also showed that "The US has always been the prime choice as a security partner." Even elites in countries that fought recent wars with the United States understand that only America can act as the global policeman. "Vietnam sees the US as the only superpower that can really influence major events, and so Vietnam must deal with the US," said one official from Hanoi's Institute of International Relations, the Vietnamese government's think tank.[3]

The United States also remains the world's preeminent economic power. For all its staggering growth, China remains a developing country, with a gross domestic product per capita of less than $7,000, calculated using purchasing power parity. America's GDP per capita, by comparison, now tops $40,000. At least for now, American investment dominates foreign direct investment in developing countries. The United States' dynamic economy and relatively open door to immigration allow US companies to remain world leaders in technology. This technology reflects back on America as a land of innovation—even in global polls where respondents do not support American policy, majorities usually express admiration for American science and technology.[4]

Although Chinese-language studies and Chinese culture

have become more popular, they remain no match for American popular culture. The United States stands as the biggest source of film, television, popular music, and fiction and nonfiction books. Average people across the developing world still prefer to send their sons and daughters to universities in the United States, which they consider the best schools in the world. In a 2006 ranking of the world's top universities conducted by Shanghai's Jiao Tong University, which examined quality of education, quality of faculty, and research output, American schools took eight of the top nine places.[5]

Most important, the United States still offers a political and social model, a set of values, which can appeal to average people around the world. China's values—noninterference, respect for other nations' internal affairs, economic gradualism directed by the state—can enjoy appeal. But China's values appeal only to specific groups: elites in authoritarian nations; average people in countries like Venezuela or Iran that equate the American model with the failing Washington Consensus or American interventionism; populaces in states willing to trade away some degree of political freedom for Chinese-style growth rates. China cannot offer average people a comprehensive, inspiring vision of how to build a free, rights-oriented political system and economy, a vision that remains popular in many parts of the world. In studies of Asian populations taken by the East Asia Barometer, a comprehensive project examining opinion in nine countries, majorities in every nation said that they desired democracy rather than any other type of political system. "If America does live up to its values, it will find states in Asia who can and will cooperate," notes Simon Tay, a leading Singaporean commentator.[6]

Even in less free regions of the world, studies show the same trend. In Pew polls taken in 2005, more than 80 percent of people in Muslim nations like Morocco, Jordan, and Lebanon believed that Western-style democracy could work in their countries. They clearly desired American-style democratic freedoms, including freedom of the press, multiparty systems, and freedom of expression.[7]

China also may not be able to build its soft power indefinitely. As we have seen, greater familiarity with China will expose many countries to the People's Republic's flaws. China's promises of aid and investment could take years to materialize, yet Beijing has created heightened expectations about its potential as a donor and investor in many countries. China's exportation of labor, environmental, and governance problems alienates average people in Asia, Latin America, and Africa. China's support for autocratic rulers in countries like Zimbabwe and Sudan angers civil society leaders and opposition politicians. If Beijing seems to be dropping its preference for noninterference and "win-win" relations, it will spark fears in countries like Vietnam already suspicious of China. It also could reinforce the idea that despite Beijing's rhetoric of cooperation, when it comes to core interests, China, like any great power, will think of itself first. The Mekong River offers an obvious example. Though China promises to cooperate peacefully with other countries, in the development of the river, China has proven both uncooperative and meddling. It has meddled by refusing to join the multilateral group monitoring the river and by injecting itself into other nations' domestic politics to get politicians to support China's damming of the river.[8]

China could further alienate other nations if it seems to be using multilateral institutions as a cover, without jettisoning Beijing's own more aggressive, even military aims. Despite signing a deal with the Philippines and Vietnam for joint exploration of the disputed South China Sea, Beijing has not retracted its claim to large swaths of the water. Any Chinese decision that appears arrogant or targeted toward Chinese domination of the region will cause a backlash. Even as officials in Vietnam signed the joint exploration deal, they privately warned that they still could not trust their Chinese counterparts enough to share the most important data with Beijing.

Similarly, if China drops its rhetoric of "win-win" relationships and makes more aggressive, unilateral demands, it could provoke a backlash in Asia, which is relying on multilateral institutions to restrain China from regional dominance. Some Chinese officials have begun to act more assertively. In 2003 one former Chinese ambassador to Singapore warned that Beijing would no longer bow to other nations; as she told a business forum, Singaporeans had to lose their "air of superiority" if they wanted to continue dealing with China.[9]

China's trade relations, too, ultimately could limit its soft power. If China builds the kind of trade surpluses with the developing world that it enjoys with the United States, it could stoke local resentment. Eventually, Beijing could wind up looking little different to people in Asia or Africa or Latin America than the old colonial powers, who mined and dug up their colonies, doing little to improve the capacity of locals on the ground. Whole regions could become trapped in a cycle of mercantilism, in which they sell natural resources to China and buy higher-value manufactured Chinese goods.

Latin America faces the greatest danger of mercantilism, but other regions could face a mercantilist trap. In Thailand companies now export $3.9 billion in electronics to China and import more than $6 billion worth. In Malaysia one study of local manufacturing found that the country is rapidly losing its ability to compete with China in manufactured goods. "To compensate for the decline," the study concluded, "Malaysia is turning towards resource-based exports [like] oil, petroleum products, liquefied natural gas, and wood-based products [that] are top exports to China."[10]

Beijing also may fail in its efforts to persuade diaspora Chinese to return. After years of Chinese officials traveling across the world wooing ethnic Chinese organizations, many diaspora Chinese are shocked by the welcome they get when they finally travel to the People's Republic. In Malaysia, Indonesia, Thailand, and many other countries, local ethnic Chinese businesspeople constantly complain about China. Many of these diaspora Chinese made investments in China expecting some kind of preferential treatment on the mainland. When their Chinese business partners squeezed them, or mainland Chinese looked down on them because they did not speak Mandarin, some found that being in China just emphasized how little they had in common with people in Beijing or Shanghai. "Ethnic Chinese in Indonesia go back to China and find they don't like China," said Ong Hok Ham, an Indonesian Chinese historian. "They are disappointed in how different they are from the Chinese." Conversely, mainland Chinese do not necessarily see the diaspora Chinese as brothers and sisters. Phillip Overmyer, executive director of the Singapore International Chamber of Commerce, says that the chamber conducted research on issues Singaporean businesspeople face in China. According to Overmyer, "The [mainland] Chinese management said they had trouble dealing with Singaporeans because Singaporeans didn't understand Chinese culture, even if they spoke Mandarin."[11]

Even diaspora Chinese companies with the closest links to China sometimes can feel alienated. Charoen Pokphand, the Thai conglomerate that invested so much time over the years cultivating Chinese leaders, found in the mid-1990s that Beijing had denied it valuable telecommunications concessions. Most famously, in the early 1990s China allowed Singaporean companies to build an enormous industrial park in the eastern Chinese city of Suzhou. Lee Kuan Yew, the founder of modern Singapore, took a personal interest in the industrial park. Despite this high-level support, the Singaporeans still came away angry. They complained that their Chinese partners backed a rival industrial park. They alleged that their partners were piling up wasteful spending, resulting in tens of millions in losses. Finally, the Singaporeans just gave up, selling majority ownership in the park to mainland Chinese developers.[12]

When these countries have concerns about China, the obvious place for them to turn is the United States, the other great power. Asian nations are always "playing the US off of the Chinese—dangling what the Chinese will offer in order to get the US more interested in them," one senior American policy maker told me.[13] Washington should be prepared to simultaneously leverage Beijing's charm on issues of interest to both the United States and China, like preventing disruptions in global energy supplies, while rebuilding America's soft power so that the United States has the ability to confront China on issues where American and Chinese interests diverge. To accomplish this, America first has to understand Chinese soft power.

The United States needs to comprehend exactly how China exerts influence. In part, this can be accomplished through efforts like Congress's U.S.-China Engagement Act, which would create more American missions in China.[14] But Washington also should take a page from its Cold War policy. During the Cold War, Washington had at least one person in each embassy who studied what the Soviets were doing on the ground in that country; today the United States should have one person in each embassy examining that nation's bilateral relations with China—China's aid policies, Chinese investment, China's public diplomacy, Chinese leaders' visits.

As anyone who has worked for a large organization knows, if your boss tells you to do five tasks, you will try to finish all five. But if your boss hires you to do only one job, like studying China's charm offensive, you will be more likely to produce great work, since you have no subsidiary responsibilities. After all, Chinese embassies closely monitor US relations with each nation, even as Chinese diplomats cooperate with their American peers on topics of mutual concern. Surely, the world's greatest power should be able to figure out what China is doing while also dealing with Chinese diplomats on issues both Washington and Beijing care about, such as drugs, HIV, and nuclear weapons proliferation.

With a better understanding of China's soft power, Washington can more systematically set clear limits—for itself, for China, and for other nations—and establish where it believes China's soft power possibly threatens American interests. As we have seen, these US interests include other nations' territorial integrity; support for the United States in case of a conflict in regions like Southeast Asia; control of sea lanes and waterways; access to resources; formal alliances with foreign nations; and, perhaps most important, the promotion of democratization and good governance.

To protect these interests, the United States must focus

on rebuilding its soft power. Otherwise, it will face even more situations where citizens of democratic nations put pressure on their leaders not to cooperate with the United States. Indeed, unlike during the Cold War, as the world has become more democratic, America's core interest—its national security—increasingly relies on wooing foreign publics.

Rebuilding soft power will require a multifaceted initiative. It will require a clear, concrete national public diplomacy strategy. This strategy would begin by defining the role of the US public diplomacy czar. If the president names an internationally famous figure, rather than someone like Karen Hughes—say, a revered figure like Colin Powell or Bill Clinton—the czar could then reach out not only to elites abroad but also to larger segments of foreign populations.

The czar will have to rebuild the public diplomacy apparatus, which still has not recovered from cuts in the 1990s, though there are encouraging signs, like congressional support for increases in cultural exchanges. Congress and the administration will have to reconsider past cuts in core public diplomacy tools like Voice of America, or American Centers offering library facilities and cultural programming in foreign countries. The United States also will have to rethink its visa processing and other new security measures, which have alienated so many foreign travelers. The State Department has taken some steps to address the obstacles to foreign visitors, like trying to expedite visa applications.[15]

Some public diplomacy efforts could be targeted at certain ethnic groups, the way China has tried to woo diaspora Chinese. Why not entice Latin American opinion leaders who already have relatives in the United States? Why not reach out to Lao and Vietnamese and Cambodian businesspeople who already have connections to Lao Americans or Vietnamese Americans, so that businesspeople in these countries have more contact with their American counterparts?

The United States also will have to protect its image of fair reporting by government-funded radio and television outlets like Voice of America. It is unbiased, stellar reporting that has earned the British Broadcasting Corporation trust—trust that reflects back upon the United Kingdom. The United States also could support independent and indigenous media organizations in foreign countries—for example, by helping train local reporters. Such support, to be effective, would have to mean turning the other cheek if those very media groups sometimes criticize America.[16]

Renewed public diplomacy also will require Washington to promote its specific policies, and to listen to locals for advice on what kinds of aid to provide. Department of Defense documents reveal that Pentagon contractors who visited Southeast Asia in 2005 repeatedly found a perception that "US policy and assistance programs are mainly focused on counterterrorism rather than social and economic development"—even though local leaders preferred assistance for economic development. But when the United States does use its aid to address local concerns, it can change minds. One study of public perceptions of America in two important developing nations, Morocco and Indonesia, found that when locals learned about specific, concrete US assistance programs, they were more likely to view America positively. By contrast, promoting broader images of the United States, like a poorly conceived post–September 11 public diplomacy initiative to portray America as a land of tolerance toward Muslims, has little effect.[17]

Changing the nature of aid, so that it is more relevant to

recipient nations, will help the United States win back soft power, too. It will reduce the causes of anger at America—as when students dropping out of Indonesia's impoverished public schools wind up in more radical private Islamic schools. It will address concerns that America cares only about security and counterterrorism. It will reflect American strengths, like the United States' skill in combating disease and in providing food and clean water: in 2004, the United States signed an agreement with Indonesia to provide more than $450 million in aid for nutrition, education in Indonesian public schools, and other necessities. US policy makers also have started to recognize that more American assistance needs to go toward local organizations in countries, rather than US aid groups or businesses.[18] This helps distinguish American assistance from Chinese aid linked to jobs for Chinese firms.

Supporting public diplomacy, the United States will need to rethink its formal diplomacy—how its diplomats operate on the ground, and how its top leaders interact with leaders and populaces abroad. Some of these changes should steal ideas from China. China has pushed its diplomats to return to one country for multiple tours of duty and to learn local languages. Unlike China, the US Foreign Service cannot force its employees to go to any country, but the State Department could more aggressively encourage its Foreign Service Officers to pick one region of the world (or even one country), specialize in that area, and return to it over and over. To do so, the Foreign Service could provide incentives to promote taking time off for language training. Currently, many Foreign Service officers complain that if they take time away for extensive language training, they penalize themselves, since it becomes harder for them to get back on career tracks.

This emphasis on better language skills may allow the United States to avoid what the Council on Foreign Relations scholar Julia Sweig calls the "80/20 problem," in which the United States relies on English-speaking elites—20 percent of the population—to understand foreign countries. If diplomats enjoy a more in-depth understanding of a country, they may interact more with the "other" 80 percent of populations, including more nongovernmental organizations, political activists, advocates for the poor, and religious leaders.[19]

The United States could steal other moves from China. As we have seen, in its formal diplomacy China woos countries by bringing its cabinet-level officials on regular trips to nations. Call this using the whole bench—leveraging even minor cabinet members to boost relations, the way good basketball teams bring in sixth and seventh men to spell the starters. Washington could do the same, making sure everyone from the secretary of agriculture to the trade representative devotes as much face time to Asia, Latin America, and Africa as they currently do to Europe.

The United States could take other lessons in formal diplomacy from China. China seems to sign bilateral agreements on cooperation, trade, and security at a moment's notice. Washington will never be able to make deals without analyzing each agreement. Still, the United States can appear open to moving more quickly, and to being a partner that listens to other nations' concerns. Washington could sign the Association of Southeast Asian Nations' Treaty of Amity and Cooperation (TAC), for example, which would not necessarily bind the United States to any concrete promises but would please many countries in Asia. (US officials suggest that America could sign the TAC in such a way that would allow it to be ratified by the Senate, which is historically suspicious that treaties will cost America sovereignty.) The United States could match China's trade diplomacy by using trade and investment framework agreements, which are means of signaling to other nations that the United States will move toward a free trade agreement with them.[20]

During a visit to Southeast Asia in May 2005, former Deputy Secretary of State Robert Zoellick, an experienced diplomat, showed how it could be done. Rather than arriving at meetings touting his own agenda, Zoellick emphasized that he wanted to listen to other countries' concerns. He touted "consulting with our partners, sharing some ideas, and listening to their thoughts." He brought with him new aid not reliant on counterterrorism cooperation, though behind closed doors he discussed terror issues. He talked up America's desire to engage with regional groups. Even "when he publicly discussed thorny issues such as Burma's upcoming chairmanship of ASEAN and religious freedom in Vietnam, Mr. Zoellick was consciously diplomatic in appearing firm but not overbearing," gushed Evelyn Goh, a Singaporean scholar.[21]

None of this public diplomacy or formal diplomacy will matter, though, if the globe continues to detest American policies. The world's anger will not be easily placated—it is more intense than anti-American sentiment during the Vietnam War. But it can be addressed. It can be addressed, first of all, if Washington reconsiders its opposition to multilateral institutions, an opposition that has fostered perceptions of America as bully. This does not mean supporting a multilateral organization that seriously limits American sovereignty. But the UN cultural treaty, the treaty on land mines, the International

Criminal Court, and other institutions—participating in these could help rehabilitate America's image.

Washington should not only reengage with multilateral organizations but also remind the world that the United States was the driving force behind the modern international system—the World Trade Organization, the United Nations, the World Bank, the International Monetary Fund. By creating and participating in these institutions after the Second World War, Washington demonstrated that America would follow international law. According to Ivo H. Daalder and James M. Lindsay, authors of *America Unbound: The Bush Revolution in Foreign Policy*, "The hallmark of [Harry] Truman's foreign policy . . . was its blend of power and cooperation. Truman was willing to exercise America's great power to remake world affairs, both to serve American interests and to advance American values. However, he and his advisers calculated that U.S. power could more easily be sustained, with less chance of engendering resentment, if it were embedded in multilateral institutions."[22]

Developing countries today do not want America to go away; they want America involved in the world, if the United States plays the Truman-era role of an arbiter of fairness and a defender of freedom. "The US should stand up for free trade. Washington should resist new protectionist measures . . . and curb the frequent abuses of trade measures," notes Tommy Koh, ambassador at large in the Singapore Ministry of Foreign Affairs. Indeed, citizens of developing countries still see the United States as a symbol of economic freedom and a country committed to global economic prosperity. In a poll of Thai citizens by the US embassy in Bangkok, 75 percent of respondents believed that Thailand and America were working together to boost economic prosperity in Asia.[23]

America's core values can still resonate, too. As we have seen, many average people around the world desire a free, rights-oriented political system. When they perceive the United States as helping them achieve that type of system, America's appeal booms: as Julia Sweig writes, during the 1990s the United States often "set forth a positive agenda" in Latin America by backing civil societies recovering from years of war and by promoting democracy. Though by the end of the decade many Latin American nations had become alienated by the failure of the free-market "Washington consensus" to boost economic growth, the US commitment to democracy did resonate with many average Latin Americans. "Latin America welcomed the new approach. . . . The message from the North was largely positive, inclusive, and respectful," Sweig notes.[24]

When foreigners perceive the United States as ignoring those core values, America's appeal plummets. To avoid this, America will have to live up to these values in its own actions. This means showing the world that, even when the United States makes mistakes, it remains an open society capable of criticizing itself—for example, by conducting well-publicized investigations of allegations of abuse at places like secret prisons to which the United States allegedly sends terrorism suspects. It means rallying the world to pay attention when real catastrophes threaten, like the genocide in Darfur. It means reinvigorating America's commitment to the post–World War II institutions it created, whether by helping countries enter the WTO so that poor nations benefit from trade, or by resisting American companies' own protectionist impulses, or by taking the lead in revamping the United Nations, rather than giving up when UN reforms falter.

Washington also can subtly push other countries to embrace these democratic values, while minimizing fears that the

United States' promotion of democratization means that it will be going around the world dominating other countries' internal affairs. Indonesia provides an example. As the world's largest Muslim nation has solidified its young democracy, the United States has assisted by promoting visits of Indonesian parliamentarians to Washington and supporting elite Indonesian universities germinating the next generation of Indonesian leaders.[25] Yet the White House has largely ceased lecturing Indonesia on how it should manage its democratization, and it has pushed to eliminate previous sanctions on the country, signaling that it approves of changes in Indonesia. Building on these efforts, the United States could create an informal community of democracies in regions like Africa or Asia. In Asia that community might include Indonesia, Australia, Thailand, South Korea, Japan, and Singapore. Washington would consult closely with the democracies on important regional issues—suggesting that there are clear rewards for countries that pursue a democratic path.

If the United States regains this appeal in the world, it can then deal with a more powerful China from a position of greater strength, and can more easily cooperate with Beijing and tolerate Beijing's becoming a greater power in regions like Southeast Asia. As we have seen, Washington and Beijing have many overlapping interests: both are major energy consumers and desire global stability in order to access resources like oil and gas; neither has any desire to see a nuclear North Korea or a nuclear standoff in South Asia; both want to combat HIV, avian flu, and other transnational disease threats; both are committed to counterterrorism and counternarcotics; both desire continued reductions in barriers to free trade; both want to prevent failed states in the developing world. In fact, in the long run the United States, which has asked China to become a "responsible stakeholder" in the world, may push Beijing to take a larger international role on aid, trade, and many other issues.

Working together on these issues will require Beijing to use its charm and, potentially, to amass more soft power in parts of the world—changes that could cause alarm in the United States if America remains weak and unpopular abroad. By contrast, if America seems popular and strong, allowing China to assume more responsibility for the globe will become easier for America to accept.

During a trip to Burma in 2003, I happened to be in Rangoon during Christmas. Although few people in Buddhist Burma actually celebrate Christmas, as in other parts of Asia the holiday provides a welcome opportunity to throw parties and buy presents for friends.

From my hotel in Rangoon, I called my old friend Khin Maung Thwin, who once worked with me at the newswire Agence France Presse; he would send his stories from Rangoon to Bangkok, where I would edit them and ship them out to the world. A tall Burmese man with smooth, almost babyish skin, Khin Maung Thwin, whom everyone called Eddie, had been working at the wire for more than three decades, after previously having developed the best sources in the military government as a tennis instructor at one of Rangoon's top clubs.

Though aging, Eddie remained one of the few reporters able to produce a relatively independent story in his closed, autocratic country. Perhaps his old military tennis buddies provided him some protection. Perhaps his advanced age saved him from the worst abuses by his government.

When I reached Eddie on a crackling phone line, he invited me to the annual Christmas party at the Rangoon sailing club, on the shores of Rangoon's Inya Lake. Sailing was a bit of an overstatement—it was more like a floating club. Though the club had been around since the 1920s, then the lair of sodden British colonials, its boats, like the Burmese economy, had fallen into disrepair. Today the club's collection of "yachts" consisted of wooden dinghies that looked like they might sink at any moment; though the club attracted Rangoon elites, they apparently did not have enough money to repair the boats properly.

I met Eddie and his wife in the club at nightfall. Rangoon elites dressed in crisp sarongs sat on the lawn sipping tiny glasses of Johnnie Walker and munching on nuts and samosas. Near the water, a band of Burmese rockers in spiked hair played tinny pop songs for teenagers. Eddie and I chatted about working for Agence France Presse, recalling how I used to scream into the phone in Bangkok so that he could hear me through Burma's antiquated phone lines.

A middle-aged Burmese businessman double-fisting glasses of Johnnie Walker cornered me when Eddie strolled off to get his wife a drink. The man, whom I will call Zaw, introduced himself—I seemed to be the only foreigner at the party—and took my arm to guide me into the clubhouse. Inside, plaques honored past skippers and captains of the year, dating back to the British colonial era. "My father used to bring me here," Zaw said with a smile, revealing stubby teeth stained red by years of chewing betel nut, the mild narcotic popular in Burma. He tossed back one drink and got a quick refill from the bartender. "It was great then, but now . . ." His voice trailed off.

We walked back outside. "The economy is just getting worse," he told me. "Foreign companies are pulling out, and I have to switch jobs all the time to keep making money." He passed me his business card, which listed his numerous occupations—antiques dealer, export-import manager, and other titles. "I need to get out here," Zaw said. "Nothing works." He pointed around at the other guests, many of whom seemed to be drinking themselves to sleep.

As the evening wore on, our conversation turned to Iraq; in March, US forces had invaded the country, and by December, before the Iraqi insurgency gained strength, the invasion still seemed a success. I did not want to discuss the Iraq War, but Zaw kept bringing it up. He seemed to have faith that the invasion ultimately would bring benefits to Iraqis, telling me that he envied people in Baghdad, even though security had already begun to deteriorate in the Iraqi capital.

Zaw's eyes were turning red, and he held my arm more firmly. "I'll do anything to leave," he told me. "Or maybe Bush will invade Burma?" I smiled weakly and said that I did not think Rangoon was high on the list of US military targets. Zaw sighed and let go of my arm and almost fell onto the ground. He righted himself and grinned, but it was a grin that concealed fear and anger. "Only the US can save us," he said. He started to walk away, and I saw him collapse in the back seat of a car. I turned back to the party and watched as the rock band attempted mangled versions of Christmas carols.

Notes

Preface

For comparisons of US and Chinese military spending, see Esther Pan, "The Scope of China's Military Threat," *Council on Foreign Relations,* online publication available at http://www.cfr.org/publication/10824/, accessed June 2006, and Adam Segal, *Chinese Military Power: Independent Task Force Report* (New York: Council on Foreign Relations Press, 2003).

Chapter 1: Courting the World

1. "Bush Hecklers Ordered Out," *CNN.com,* 23 Oct. 2003, online publication available at http://www.cnn.com/2003/WORLD/asiapcf/southeast/10/23/apec.special.bush.heckle/index.html, accessed June 2006.

2. Adam Harvey, "Mister Untouchable," *Sunday Sydney Telegraph,* 26 Oct. 2003; "Bush Hecklers Ordered Out."

3. Louise Perry, "Hu a Lesser Evil Among Activists," *The Australian,* 25 Oct. 2003; Nick Squires, "The Chorus of Dissent Is Muted as Protestors Change Their Tactics," *South China Morning Post,* 25 Oct. 2003.

4. Nick Squires, "China's Growth Benefits Region, Says Downer," *South China Morning Post,* 30 Oct. 2003.

5. Ivan Cook, *Australians Speak, 2005: Public Opinion and Foreign Policy* (Sydney: Lowy Institute, 2005).

6. Joseph S. Nye Jr., *Soft Power: The Means to Success in World Politics* (New York: Public Affairs, 2004), 5–6.

7. Ibid., 6.

8. USIA helped oversee the US-Soviet Exchange Initiative, for example, which promoted exchanges of scholars. See "VOA History," http://www.voanews.com/english/About/post-wwii-era.cfm, accessed Nov. 2006.

9. Nye, *Soft Power,* 17.

10. Melinda Liu, "Divide and Conquer," *Newsweek,* 7 Mar. 2005, 14; see also "Interview with Thaksin Shinawatra: Thailand Aims to Further Enhance Thailand-China Strategic Partnership," *People's Daily,* 28 June 2005. Philip P. Pan, "China's Improving Image Challenges U.S. in Asia," *Washington Post,* 15 Nov. 2003.

11. Though Australia historically was not included in Southeast Asia, I will include it, since Southeast Asia is the region of Asia closest to Australia.

12. "Wen Calls for More Help for Africa," *China Daily,* 15 Dec. 2003; BBC/PIPA poll, 15 Nov. 2004–5 Jan. 2005.

13. Andrew Moravcsik, "Dream on, America," *Newsweek,* 31 Jan. 2005, 22.

14. For more on the idea of a Chinese Monroe Doctrine, see Marvin C. Ott, "China's Strategic Reach into Southeast Asia," Presentation to US-China Economic and Security Review Commission, 22 July 2005.

Chapter 2: Changes on the Home Front

1. See, for example, Mao Tse-tung, Opening Address at the Eighth National Congress of the Communist Party of China, 1956.

2. For an insightful analysis of the Great Leap Forward and its consequences, see Jasper Becker, *Hungry Ghosts: Mao's Secret Famine* (New York: Free Press, 1996).

3. On "righteous struggles" see, for example, Mao, Opening Address. On Burma see, for example, Bertil Lintner, *The Rise and Fall of the Communist Party of Burma* (Ithaca: Cornell University, 1990). On the size and scope of Chinese assistance to the Khmer Rouge, see, for example, Ben Kiernan, *The Pol Pot Regime: Race, Power, and Genocide Under the Khmer Rouge, 1975–1979* (New Haven: Yale University Press, 1996). See also Tom Fawthrop, "Middle Kingdom Puts the Squeeze on Little Kingdom," *Phnom Penh Post,* 25 May 2001. On Chinese influence in Africa and the Middle East, see, for example, Stephen A. Cheney, "The Insurgency in Oman, 1962–1976," http://www.globalsecurity.org/military/library/report/1984/CSA.htm, accessed Nov. 2006; and Drew Thompson, "China's Soft Power in Africa: From the 'Beijing

Consensus' to Health Diplomacy," *China Brief,* Jamestown Foundation, 13 Oct. 2005.

4. On the history of the Association of Southeast Asian Nations and its relationship with communism, see Brantly Womack, "China and Southeast Asia: Asymmetry, Leadership, and Normalcy," *Pacific Affairs* 76 (2003–2004): 529–548; and Carlyle Thayer, "Re-inventing Asean: From Constructive Engagement to Flexible Intervention," *Harvard Asia Pacific Review* 3 (1999): 67–70. On the Indonesian response to Chinese intervention, see, for example, Jemma Purdey, *Anti-Chinese Violence in Indonesia, 1996–1999* (Honolulu: University of Hawaii Press, 2006). On the Sino-Vietnamese War see, for example, Gerald Segal, *Defending China* (New York: Oxford University Press, 1985).

5. Interview with Western diplomat, Washington, Sept. 2005. On Deng see, for example, Richard Evans, *Deng Xiaoping and the Making of Modern China* (New York: Penguin, 1997).

6. Willy Lam, "Beijing's New 'Balanced' Foreign Policy: An Assessment," *China Brief,* Jamestown Foundation, 20 Feb. 2004.

7. On modernization see H. Lyman Miller and Liu Xiaohong, "The Foreign Policy Outlook of China's Third Generation Elite," in *The Making of Chinese Foreign and Security Policy in the Age of Reform, 1978–2000,* ed. David Lampton, 123–151 (Stanford: Stanford University Press, 2001). On Deng's reforms see Todd Crowell and Thomas Hon Wing Polin, "Asian of the Century," *Asiaweek,* 10 Dec. 1999, 1.

8. Lampton, *The Making of Chinese Policy.* "Enhance Sino-Singaporean Ties," *China Daily,* 19 Nov. 2003. Interviews with Western diplomats, Sept.–Dec. 2005.

9. See, for example, Roderick MacFarquhar and Michael Schoenhals, *Mao's Last Revolution* (Cambridge, Mass.: Belknap Press, 2006), and Thomas G. Moore and Dixia Yang, "Empowered and Restrained: Chinese Foreign Policy in the Age of Economic Interdependence" in Lampton, *The Making of Chinese Policy,* 191–230.

10. Horizon Group Research, 1995. Joseph Fewsmith and Stanley Rosen, "The Domestic Context of Chinese Foreign Policy: Does 'Public Opinion' Matter?" in Lampton, *The Making of Chinese Policy,* 151–190.

11. Minxin Pei, *China's Trapped Transition: The Limits of Developmental Autocracy* (Cambridge: Harvard University Press, 2006), 51.

12. Ibid., 55.

13. Tsao Tsing-yuan, "The Birth of the Goddess of Democracy," in *Popular Protest and Political Culture in Modern China,* ed. Jeffrey N. Wasserstrom and Elizabeth J. Perry, 140–147 (Boulder: Westview, 1994). The most

authoritative account of the internal decision making leading up to the crackdown is contained in Zhang Liang, *The Tiananmen Papers* (New York: Public Affairs, 2002).

14. Horizon Group Research, 2003.

15. Charles W. McMillon, "US-China Trade Data and Analyses: Purchasing Power Parity," paper prepared for US-China Economic and Security Review Commission, 2005. "China Sees Trade Surplus Triple," *British Broadcasting Corporation,* http://news.bbc.co.uk/2/hi/business/4602126.stm, accessed Jan. 2006. On currency reserves see "China Currency Reserves Top Japan's," *China Business News,* 28 Mar. 2006. On China's reduction of poverty, see the United Nations' annual reports on Human Development in China, available at http://www.undp.org.cn/modules.php?op=modload&name=News&file=article&topic=40&sid=228, accessed Nov. 2006. On foreign investment see *World Investment Report,* United Nations Conference on Trade and Development (Geneva: Unctad, 2006).

16. Interviews with entrepreneurs in Zhejiang Province, 2002.

17. Interviews in Kashgar, 2002.

18. "One Strategy, Multiple Agendas," *China Development Brief,* http://www.chinadevelopmentbrief.com/node/210, accessed Aug 2006; interviews in Kashgar, 2004.

19. Gal Luft, "Fueling the Dragon: China's Race into the Oil Market," *IAGS Spotlight,* http://www.iags.org/china.htm, accessed Feb 2006; "Premier Stresses Exploitation of Oil, Gas," *China Daily,* 26 June 2004. For more on foreign companies' China strategies, see Joe Studwell, *The China Dream: The Quest for the Last Great Untapped Market on Earth* (New York: Grove, 2003). Google's specific issues are chronicled in Clive Thompson, "Google's China Problem (and China's Google Problem)," *New York Times Magazine,* 23 Apr. 2006, 64.

20. Peter Hays Gries, *China's New Nationalism: Pride, Politics, and Diplomacy* (Berkeley: University of California Press, 2005).

21. "Outward Bound," *Economist,* 22 June 2006, 74; Fewsmith and Rosen, "The Domestic Context," 156; "15 Nation Pew Global Attitudes Study," Pew Project on Global Attitudes, 13 June 2006.

22. Jasper Becker, "Mussolini Redux," *New Republic,* 23 June 2003, 16.

23. Fewsmith and Rosen, "The Domestic Context," 152–158; Ben Elgin and Bruce Einhorn, "The Great Firewall of China," *BusinessWeek,* 12 Jan. 2006, 32.

24. Pei, *China's Trapped Transition,* 89–103.

25. Jonathan Unger, "China's Conservative Middle Class," *Far Eastern Economic Review,* Apr. 2006, 27; "Prosperity Brings Satisfaction and Hope: China's Optimism," 2005 Pew Global Attitudes Survey, 16 Nov. 2005.

26. Author observation of Strong Nation forum, *People's Daily* Web site; Ying Ma, "China's America Problem," *Policy Review* 111 (2002): 43–57.

27. "Protestors Attack US Embassy in Beijing," *CNN.com*, http://www.cnn.com/WORLD/asiapcf/9905/08/china.bombing.protests.02/, accessed Nov. 2005. In years of conversations with average Chinese since the 1999 bombing, I have yet to meet anyone convinced that it was an accident.

28. See, for example, "Who Caused the Crash?" British Broadcasting Corporation, http://news.bbc.co.uk/1/hi/world/asia-pacific/1260290.stm, accessed Nov. 2005.

29. *Dong-A Ilbo* Opinion Poll, 25 Apr. 2005.

30. Chen Shengluo, "The Events of September 11 and Chinese College Students' Images of the United States," in *Chinese Images of the United States*, ed. Carola McGiffert (Washington, D.C.: CSIS Press, 2005).

31. Interview with Chinese academic, Shanghai, Aug. 2005.

32. Miller and Liu, "Foreign Policy Outlook"; interviews with Chinese diplomats, Washington and Beijing, Aug.–Dec. 2005.

33. Fewsmith and Rosen, "The Domestic Context," 152–158.

34. Evan S. Medeiros and M. Taylor Fravel, "China's New Diplomacy," *Foreign Affairs* 6 (2003): 22.

35. Joshua Cooper Ramo, *The Beijing Consensus* (London: Foreign Policy Center, 2004), 19–20.

36. Susan L. Shirk, "China's Multilateral Diplomacy in the Asia-Pacific," testimony before the US-China Economic and Security Review Commission, 12–13 Feb. 2004; interview with former US diplomat based in China, Shanghai, 2004.

37. Biwu Zhang, "Chinese Perceptions of American Power, 1991–2004," *Asian Survey* 5 (2005): 667–686; Sangwon Suh and David Hsieh, "From Suspicion to Trust," *Asiaweek*, http://www.asiaweek.com/asiaweek/96/0726/index.html, accessed July 2005.

38. "China Popularizes HIV/AIDS Knowledge Among Officials," Xinhua, 1 Dec. 2004.

39. "Afghans to Learn China's Development Experience, Says Afghan Vice President," Xinhua, 18 Apr. 2005; Zhang, "Chinese Perceptions," 677.

40. "Former Thai Millionaire Reinvents Himself," *CNN Asia Tonight*, 29 Mar. 2001, transcript. For foreign exploitation of the crisis, see, for example, George Wehfritz and Paul Handley, "Beyond Sex and Golf," *Newsweek*, 12 July 1999, 34.

41. Interview with US diplomat formerly posted in Thailand, Washington, Oct. 2005.

42. Interview with former NSC staffers, Washington, Oct. 2005.

43. See, for example, Ministry of Foreign Affairs of the People's Re-

public of China, "Proactive Policies by China in Response to the Asian Financial Crisis," 17 Nov. 2000.

44. Ambassador Chan Heng Chee, "China and Asean: A Growing Relationship," Speech to the Asia Society Texas Annual Ambassadors' Forum and Corporate Conference, 3 Feb. 2006; Michael Richardson, "Japan's Lack of Leadership Pushes ASEAN Towards Cooperation with China," *International Herald Tribune,* 17 Apr. 1998; Robert G. Lees, "If Japan Won't Help Rescue Asia China Might," *International Herald Tribune,* 21 Feb. 1998; interview with Thai diplomat, Bangkok, Sept. 2005.

45. See, for example, Ye Zicheng, "Zhongguo shixing daguo waijiao zhanlue shi zai bixing (China Should Adopt Great Power Diplomacy)," *World Economy and Politics,* no. 1, 2000.

Chapter 3:
A Charm Strategy

1. Ministry of Foreign Affairs of the People's Republic of China, "China's Africa Policy," white paper released Jan. 2006.

2. Esther Pan, "The Promise and Pitfalls of China's 'Peaceful Rise,'" *Council on Foreign Relations,* 14 Apr. 2006, http://www.cfr.org/publication/10446/promise_and_pitfalls_of_chinas_peaceful_rise.html, accessed Nov. 2006.

3. David Shambaugh, *Power Shift* (Berkeley: University of California Press, 2005), 28; Terry McCarthy, "Reef Wars," *Time Asia,* 8 Mar. 1999, 18; Denny Roy, *China's Foreign Relations* (Lanham, Md.: Rowman and Littlefield, 1999).

4. Yang Qing, "Zhongguo Heping Jeuqi yu Zhongguo Deongmeng Zhijian de Guanxi," *Journal of the CCP's Central Party School,* Feb. 2004; David Shambaugh, "China Engages Asia: Reshaping the Regional Order," *International Security* 3 (2004): 64; Robert G. Sutter, *China's Rise in Asia: Promises and Perils* (Lanham, Md.: Rowman and Littlefield, 2005), 12–16.

5. "President Calls for Further Propaganda Work to Enhance China's Image Abroad," Xinhua, 28 Feb. 1999; "China Aims to Be a Giant in Science and Technology Around 2049," *People's Daily,* 26 Nov. 2004.

6. David M. Lampton, "Paradigm Lost," *National Interest* 3 (2005): 73–81.

7. Hu Jintao, "Speech Marking the 60th Anniversary of the Victory of the Chinese People's War of Resistance Against Japanese Aggression and the World Anti-Fascist War," 3 Sept. 2005.

8. "China Encourages Mass Urban Migration," *People's Daily,* 28 Nov. 2003. On Chinese commodity demands, see, for example, "China Effect

Convulses Commodity Markets," *Financial Times*, 15 Nov. 2003, and Energy Information Administration, "China Country Brief," Aug. 2006. See also Andy Rothman, "China Eats the World," CLSA Asia Pacific Investment Strategy, Spring 2005. Tom Holland, "Water Wastage Will Soon Leave China High and Dry," *South China Morning Post*, 8 Mar. 2006; Minnie Chan, "Wen Lays Down Law on Saving Energy," *South China Morning Post*, 5 July 2005; "China to Set up Energy Task Force," Agence France-Presse, 6 Mar. 2005.

9. Interview with Erica Downs, Feb. 2006; Peter S. Goodman, "Big Shift in China's Oil Policy," *Washington Post*, 13 July 2005.

10. Naazneen Barma and Ely Ratner, "Chinese Illiberalism," *Democracy* 2 (2006): 56–68.

11. Lin teh-Cheng, "Beijing's Foreign Aid Policy in the 1990s: Continuity and Change," *Issues and Studies* 1 (1996): 32–56. Alejandro Reyes, "Money for Influence?" *Asiaweek*, http://www.asiaweek.com/asiaweek/98/0116/cs6.html, accessed July 2005.

12. Medeiros and Fravel, "China's New Diplomacy." Xia Liping, "China: A Responsible Great Power," *New Generation, New Voices: Debating China's International Future*, papers for a conference, 13–14 Aug. 1999.

13. "Speech by Hu Jintao at the APEC CEO Summit," Ministry of Foreign Affairs of the People's Republic of China release, 19 Nov. 2005; Antoaneta Bezlova, "China's Soft Power Diplomacy in Africa," *Asia Times*, 23 June 2006. See also Joshua Cooper Ramo, *The Beijing Consensus* (London: Foreign Policy Center, 2004), 53.

14. Information Office of the State Council of the People's Republic of China, "White Paper on China's Peaceful Development Road," 12 Dec. 2005; Wen Jiabao, "Speech to Boao Forum on Asia," 2 Nov. 2003.

15. "Premier Wen Defends African Oil Deals," *South China Morning Post*, 19 June 2006. On the expanding use of US sanctions in the 1990s, see, for example, Jeffrey J. Schott, "US Economic Sanctions: Good Intentions, Bad Execution," testimony to the House Committee on International Relations, 3 June 1998.

16. Interview with Alejandro Melchor, undersecretary of defense of the Philippines, Manila, Mar. 2006; Amnesty International, "People's Republic of China: Sustaining Conflict and Human Rights Abuses," 11 June 2006.

17. Interview with Keo Remy, Phnom Penh, Jan. 2006.

18. Yong Deng and Thomas G. Moore, "China Views Globalization: Toward a New Great Power Politics?" *Washington Quarterly* 3 (2004): 117–136. On Chinese involvement in multilateral initiatives, see, for example, Carlyle Thayer, "China Consolidates Its Long Term Bilateral Relations with Southeast Asia," *Comparative Connections*, http://www.csis.org/media/csis/

pubs/0002q.pdf, accessed Mar. 2005. Interview with Vietnamese policy makers, Nha Trang, Oct. 2005. Philip Saunders, *China's Global Activism: Strategy, Drivers, and Tools* (Washington, D.C.: National Defense University Press, 2006). See also "Thailand Aims to Further Enhance Strategic Partnership," *China Daily,* 28 June 2005.

19. "China, Mexico Sign Seven Cooperation Agreements," *People's Daily,* 25 Jan. 2005; Foreign Ministry of the People's Republic of China, "Great Achievements Obtained in Zeng Qinghong's Visit to Venezuela," 30 Jan. 2005. See also "Forum on China-Africa Cooperation," http://www.fmprc.gov.cn/zflt/eng/, accessed Nov. 2006. Ian Taylor, "Beijing's Arms and Oil Interests in Africa," *China Brief,* Jamestown Foundation, 13 Oct. 2005.

20. Interview with Southeast Asian diplomat, Singapore, Sept. 2005; interview with congressional staffer focusing on Asia issues, July 2005.

21. "Statement by Ambassador Shen Guofang, Deputy Permanent Representative of China, at the 56th Session of the General Assembly, on Item 46," Permanent Mission of the People's Republic of China to the UN, 2001.

22. Interview with former Indonesian activists, Jakarta, Mar. 2006; Dane Schiller, "Justice Doesn't Always Translate Across Border," *San Antonio Express-News,* 27 Apr. 2004. On China's response to Mexico, interviews with Chinese diplomats, Washington, Oct. 2005.

23. Robin Ramcharan, "Asean and Noninterference: A Principle Maintained," *Contemporary Southeast Asia* 1 (2000): 60–88.

24. Susan Shirk, "China's Multilateral Diplomacy in the Asia Pacific," Testimony before the US-China Economic and Security Review Commission, 12–13 Feb. 2004; interviews with Chinese scholars, Nha Trang, Oct. 2005.

25. Andean Community, http://www.comunidadandina.org/ingles/Exterior/asia.htm, accessed May 2006; Ministry of Foreign Affairs of the People's Republic of China, "International and Regional Issues," http://www.fmprc.gov.cn/eng/gjhdq/dqzzywt/2633/default.htm, accessed May 2006; Shirk, "China's Multilateral Diplomacy"; "Sino-Asean Relations Upgraded by New Agreements," Xinhua, 30 Nov. 2004; interview with Southeast Asian diplomats, Singapore, Jan 2006.

26. On how American strategy changed after September 11, see, for example, "The National Security Strategy of the United States of America," Sept. 2002, http://www.whitehouse.gov/nsc/nss.pdf, accessed Nov. 2006. On changing Chinese priorities, see Presentation by Ruan Zongze, Asia Foundation trilateral dialogue on US-Chinese-Vietnamese relations, Nha Trang, Oct 2005. "Jiang Zemin's Report at 16th Party Congress," Xinhua, 17 Nov. 2002, http://www.china.org.cn/english/features/49007.htm, accessed Sept. 2005.

27. William Ratliff, "China Goes South of the Border," *Hoover Digest* 1 (2005); also, Foreign Ministry of the People's Republic of China, "Hu Jintao Holds Talks with the Leaders of India, Brazil, South Africa, and Mexico," 7 July 2005. Cheng Siwei, "Bright Prospects for China-Latin American and the Caribbean Cooperation," speech to Organization of American States, 6 Dec. 2005; Chang Siwei, speech to conference of Latin American business executives, name of event withheld by request.

28. Interview with Federico Macaranas, Manila, Mar. 2006.

29. Jonathan Watts, "Chávez says China Deal 'Great Wall' Against US," *Guardian*, 25 Aug. 2006. See also Ben Schiller, "The Axis of Oil: China and Venezuela," *OpenDemocracy*, http://www.opendemocracy.net/globalization-china/china_venezuela_3319.jsp, accessed Aug. 2006, and William Ratliff, "Pragmatism over Ideology: China's Relations with Venezuela," *China Brief*, Jamestown Foundation, 15 Mar. 2006.

30. "Treaty Signed with Uzbekistan," Xinhua, 26 May 2005; also, Stephen Blank, "Islam Karimov and the Heirs of Tiananmen," *China Brief*, Jamestown Foundation, 14 June 2005. David Blair, "Oil Hungry China Takes Sudan Under Its Wing," *Daily Telegraph*, 23 Apr. 2004.

31. Tim Johnson, "Ahmadinejad Vows to Consider Plan to Limit Iran's Nuclear Program," Knight Ridder News, 16 June 2006; also, Iran News Agency, "Headlines in Major Iranian Newspapers," 17 June 2006. John Calabrese, "China and Iran: Mismatched Partners," Jamestown Foundation occasional paper, Aug. 2006.

32. "China, Ecuador Vow to Further Military Ties," *People's Daily*, 2 Dec. 2004; interviews with South Korean politicians, Seoul, Aug. 2005. See also Jae Ho Chung, "How America Views China-South Korea Bilateralism," CNAPS Working Paper, July 2003.

33. Interview with senior Filipino defense official, Manila, Mar. 2006.

34. Ramo, *Beijing Consensus;* Minxin Pei, *China's Trapped Transition: The Limits of Developmental Autocracy* (Cambridge: Harvard University Press, 2006), 30–32.

35. Zhang Xiaojing, "Tanshuo jinrong quanqiu shidai de fazhan daolu: qianxicong Huasheng gongshi dao 'Beijing gongshi,'" *Xueshi Shibao*, 16 Aug. 2004; Barma and Ratner, "Chinese Illiberalism."

36. Drew Thompson, "China's Soft Power in Africa: From the 'Beijing Consensus' to Health Diplomacy," *China Brief*, Jamestown Foundation, 13 Oct. 2005.

37. "Survey of Economic and Social Conditions in Africa 2004–2005," United Nations Economic Commission for Africa, Apr. 2005.

38. Interview with Dan Erikson, Nov. 2005.

39. Interview with Lao officials, Vientiane, Aug. 2005.

40. "Visiting Chinese President Meets Premier," Xinhua, 14 Nov. 2000; "Lao, Chinese Presidents Reach 'Complete Consensus' in Vientiane Talks," Xinhua, 12 Nov. 2000.

Chapter 4: The Tools of Culture

1. Rumi Aoyama, "Chinese Public Diplomacy in the Multimedia Age: Public Diplomacy and Civil Diplomacy," Waseda University papers, Dec. 2004. For one standard definition of public diplomacy, see "What Is Public Diplomacy?" http://www.publicdiplomacy.org/1.htm, accessed Nov. 2006.

2. "Oceanic Odyssey Remains a Treasure," *China Daily*, 8 July 2004; see also Forum on China-Africa Cooperation, "Addis Ababa Action Plan," 3 Feb. 2004. Telephone interview with Geoff Wade, expert on Zheng He's voyages, National University of Singapore, Aug. 2005.

3. Interview with Kasetsart professor, Aug. 2005; "Chinese Volunteers to Offer Services in Myanmar," *People's Daily*, 11 Jan. 2006. See also "China to Send Overseas More Field Service Volunteers," Xinhua, 30 Oct. 2002.

4. Vivien Cui, "CCTV Tries to Shed its Mouthpiece Image," *South China Morning Post*, 6 Apr. 2004; "People's Daily Overseas Edition Issued in ROK," *People's Daily*, 1 July 2004. See also Aoyama, "Chinese Public Diplomacy." "China Launches Satellite TV Service in Asian Region," Xinhua, 1 Feb. 2005. Also, Eanna O'Brogain, "China's Troubled TV Star," *South China Morning Post*, 15 Mar. 2006.

5. "Xinhua: The World's Biggest Propaganda Agency," Reporters Without Borders, 2005; Joseph Kahn, "China Gives Zhao's Death Scant Notice," *New York Times*, 18 Jan. 2005; Interviews with Chinese journalists, Manila, Bangkok, Kuala Lumpur, Jan.–Mar. 2006.

6. "Report of the Asean-China Eminent Persons Group," http://www.aseansec.org/ASEAN-China-EPG.pdf#search=%22asean%20china%20eminent%20persons%20group%22 and Boao Forum for Asia, http://www.boaoforum.org/Html/, both accessed Nov. 2006, and "China, Arab States Set up Cooperation Forum," *People's Daily*, 30 Jan. 2004. See also "Gu Xiulian Addresses Beijing Reception on Founding of China-Asean Association," Xinhua, 3 Aug. 2004, and Hong Liu, "New Migrants and the Revival of Overseas Chinese Nationalism," *Journal of Contemporary China* 14 (2005): 291–316.

7. Interviews with Chinese diplomats in Bangkok, Washington, Manila, Aug.–Dec. 2005; "Li Zhaoxing Praises Young Diplomats," Xinhua, 27 June 2005; interview with Chinese scholars, Chinese Academy of Social Sci-

ences, Aug. 2005; Jorge Dominguez, "China's Relations with Latin America: Shared Gains, Asymmetric Hopes," Inter-American Dialogue publications, May 2006.

8. Interviews with Chinese diplomats, Washington, Aug.–Dec. 2005; interview with American diplomat, Bangkok, Jan. 2006; interview with Singaporean diplomat, Singapore, Jan. 2006; *The United States and Southeast Asia: A Policy Agenda for the New Administration* (New York: Council on Foreign Relations Press, 2001), 48.

9. Philip Saunders, *China's Global Activism: Strategy, Drivers, and Tools* (Washington: National Defense University Press, 2006); interview with Singaporean diplomat, Jan. 2006; interview with American ambassador, name and location withheld. See also "Chinese, Thai FMs Meet on Tsunami Issues," *People's Daily,* 29 Jan. 2005.

10. The comparison was made by compiling English- and Chinese-language newswire reports of visits by American and Chinese cabinet-level officials. Ralph Cossa, "Rice's Unfortunate Choice," *Asia Times,* 28 July 2005; Glenn Kessler, "In Asia, Rice Is Criticized for Plan to Skip Summit," *Washington Post,* 12 July 2005; interview with White House official, Washington, Mar. 2006.

11. Xing Zhigang, "NPC Deputy Calls for Promoting Chinese," *China Daily,* 10 Mar. 2006.

12. "China Takes Five Measures to Boost Chinese Teaching Overseas," Xinhua, 22 July 2005. See also "Chinese Language School Opens in Seoul," *China Daily,* 23 Nov. 2004, and "Introduction to the 'Confucius Institute' Project," http://english.hanban.edu.cn/market/HanBanE/412360.htm, accessed July 2006. Paul Marks, "China's Cambodia Strategy," *Parameters* 3 (2000): 92–108; see also "20 Chinese School Teacher Representatives to Guangzhou for Training," *Cambodia Sin Chew Daily,* 13 May 2005, and "Dispatching Professional Teachers to Cambodia," *Cambodia Sin Chew Daily,* 30 Nov. 2002. Sirikul Bunnag, "Ministry Pushes Chinese Language," *Bangkok Post,* 16 Jan. 2006. On Mao and Confucianism, see, for example, A. James Gregor and Maria Hsia Chang, "Anti-Confucianism: Mao's Last Campaign," *Asian Survey* 11 (1979): 1073–1092.

13. Bunnag, "Ministry Pushes Chinese Language"; assorted articles from *Cambodia Sin Chew Daily,* the major Chinese-language newspaper in Cambodia, 2003–2005; interviews with Cambodian teachers and education specialists, Phnom Penh, Jan. 2006. See also Marks, "China's Cambodia Strategy."

14. Hong Liu, "New Migrants." See also Cao Cong, "China's Efforts at Turning a 'Brain Drain' into a 'Brain Gain,'" Background Brief, East Asian Institute, National University of Singapore, 1 Nov. 2004; Sam Dillon, "US Slips

in Attracting the World's Best Students," *New York Times,* 21 Dec. 2004; "Foreign Students in China on the Rise," *People's Daily,* 15 Apr. 2003; and Howard French, "China Luring Foreign Scholars to Make its Universities Great," *New York Times,* 28 Oct. 2005. Also, interviews with Chinese education specialists, Shanghai, 2004. David Zweig, "Is China a Magnet for Global Talent?" Paper presented at the conference Immigration and Canada's Place in a Changing World, Vancouver, 24 Mar. 2006.

15. "International Students Find Beijing 'Home,'" *China Daily,* 24 May 2005; interviews with Lao and Cambodian ministers, Vientiane and Phnom Penh, Aug. 2005 and Jan. 2006; Zweig, "Is China a Magnet?" "Global MBA Rankings 2006," *Financial Times,* http://rankings.ft.com/rankings/mba/rankings.html, accessed Nov. 2006.

16. Interview with Joanne Chang, Taipei Economic and Cultural Representative Office former deputy representative in Washington, Feb. 2006; interviews with Lee Poh Ping, Voon Phin Keong, Rita Sim, and several other leaders of Malaysian Chinese community, Kuala Lumpur, Jan. 2006.

17. Carolyn Lochhead, "Drop in US Student Visas by Foreigners," *San Francisco Chronicle,* 5 Apr. 2005. See also Eric Lichtblau and Jonathan Peterson, "US Will Step up Oversight of Student Visa Program," *Los Angeles Times,* 10 May 2002, and Enhanced Border Security and Visa Entry Reform Act of 2002, US Public Law 107-173, 14 May 2002. "Fact Sheet: Changes to National Security Entry/Exit Registration System," Department of Homeland Security, 1 Dec. 2003; Catharin Dalpino, "China's Emergence in Asia and Implications for US Relations with Southeast Asia," Statement to US Senate Foreign Relations Committee, 7 June 2005.

18. World Bank Group, "Philippines Millennium Development Goals," http://ddp-ext.worldbank.org/ext/ddpreports/ViewSharedReport?REPORT_ID=1664&REQUEST_TYPE=VIEWADVANCED, accessed Nov. 2006; "Death Toll in Manila Stampede Rises to 79," *The Age,* Feb. 2006.

19. Lynn Pan, ed., *The Encyclopedia of the Chinese Overseas* (Cambridge: Harvard University Press, 1999), 187–192.

20. Ibid., 98–100.

21. Ibid., 151–167.

22. Ibid., 223–228.

23. Ibid., 113; "Families under Fire," *Time Asia,* http://www.time.com/time/asia/covers/501040223/story.html, accessed May 2005.

24. Pan, *Encyclopedia,* 113. See also Paul Handley, "De-Mythologizing Charoen Pokphand: An Interpretive Picture of the CP Group's Growth and Diversification," in *Ethnic Business: Chinese Capitalism in Southeast Asia,* ed. Jomo K. S. and Brian C. Folk, 153–181 (London: Taylor and Francis, 2001); and "Rise of the Compradore," *China Economic Review,* http://www.chinaeconomicreview.com/subscriber/articledetail/653.html, accessed Jan. 2005.

25. "The Overseas Chinese: A Driving Force," *Economist*, 18 July 1992; see also Keith B Richburg, "Ethnic Chinese Waiting to Die in Indonesia," *Washington Post*, 21 Mar. 1999. For more on the tycoons, see Forbes's rankings of the world's richest people, available at http://www.forbes.com/billionaires/, accessed Nov. 2006. For more on Thaksin's background, see Pasuk Phongpaichit and Chris Baker, *Thaksin: The Business of Politics in Thailand* (Chiang Mai: Silkworm, 2005).

26. Vanessa Hua, "Playing the Panama Card: The China-Taiwan Connection," *San Francisco Chronicle*, 23 June 2002; interviews with East Timorese merchants, Dili, Mar. 2006; Pan, *Encyclopedia*, 254.

27. Handley, "De-Mythologizing Charoen Pokphand"; Hong Liu, "New Migrants," 308; Zhuang Guoto, "The Factor of Chinese Ethnicity in China-Asean Relations as Mirrored in Investments from Southeast Asia in Fujian," paper presented to Conference on Southeast Asian Studies in China: Challenges and Prospects," Singapore, 12–14 Jan. 2006.

28. Zhuang Guoto, "The Factor of Chinese Ethnicity"; William A. Callahan, "Diaspora, Cosmopolitanism, and Nationalism: Overseas Chinese and Neo-Nationalism in China and Thailand," City University of Hong Kong Southeast Asia Research Center Working Paper, Oct. 2002.

29. Interview with Chinese diplomats, Washington and Beijing, Aug.–Oct. 2005.

30. Hong Liu, "New Migrants"; interview with visa officials at Chinese embassy, Bangkok, Aug. 2005; "Cambodian Chinese Organization Documents China's Push to Promote Chinese Learning Abroad," *Cambodia Sin Chew Daily*, 13 May 2005; Callahan, "Diaspora, Cosmopolitanism, and Nationalism."

31. Interviews with Filipino-Chinese business leaders, Manila, Mar. 2006.

32. Vanessa Hua, "Playing the Panama Card: The China-Taiwan Connection," *San Francisco Chronicle*, 23 June 2002.

33. Interview with Amorn Apithanakoon, Bangkok, Jan. 2006.

34. "Overseas Chinese Speak with One Voice Against 'Taidu,'" *People's Daily*, 4 Mar. 2004.

Chapter 5: The Tools of Business

1. Interview with Harry Roque, Manila, Mar. 2006.

2. Joel C. Atencio and Rizal S. Obanil, "Police Conduct Raid on Daily Tribune," *Manila Bulletin*, 26 Feb. 2006; "Arroyo Declares State of Emergency," *Philippine Daily Inquirer*, 24 Feb. 2006; "Seven More in Media Watched," *Philippine Daily Inquirer*, 5 Mar. 2006; "Lift State of National

Emergency Now, Lawmakers Urge Malacanang," *BusinessWorld*, 3 Mar. 2006; Tarra V. Quismundo, "Arrest Warrant Out for Gringo," *Philippine Daily Inquirer*, 2 Mar. 2006; Michael Lim Ubac and Armand Nocum, "Congress Unites Behind Five Solons Linked to Coup Plot," *Philippine Daily Inquirer*, 1 Mar. 2006.

3. Kristine L. Alave, "Framework for RP-China Bilateral Agreements Inked," *BusinessWorld*, 6 June 2006; Angelo Samonte, "China Vows to Invest in RP Industries," *Manila Times*, 6 June 2006; interview with Harry Roque, Manila, Mar. 2006. Also, interviews with a former Philippine senator, and current Philippine officials, Manila, Mar. 2006. See also Raissa Robles, "Railway Project Under Fire After Philippine Contractors Are Sidelined," *South China Morning Post*, 1 Sept. 2004.

4. On the depth of corruption in Philippine politics, see Sheila S. Coronel, *Betrayals of the Public Trust: Investigative Reports on Corruption* (Manila: Philippine Center for Investigative Journalism, 2000), as well as frequent updates on pcij.org about Philippine corruption issues.

5. Interview with Harry Roque, Manila, Mar. 2006.

6. See Henry Yep, "China's Foreign Aid to Asia: Promoting a 'Win-Win' Environment," master's thesis, National Defense University, 2006.

7. Joe Studwell, *The China Dream: The Quest for the Last Great Untapped Market on Earth* (New York: Grove, 2003).

8. For annual reports on investment flows, see the annual *World Investment Report* released by the United Nations Conference on Trade and Development. Jiang Jingjing, "Wal-Mart's China Inventory to Hit US $18 Billion This Year," *China Business Weekly*, 29 Nov. 2004. World Bank Group, "Bolivia Country Data Profile," http://devdata.worldbank.org/external/CPProfile.asp?SelectedCountry=BOL&CCODE=BOL&CNAME=Bolivia&PTYPE=CP, accessed Nov. 2006. For a history of China's annual growth rates, see World Bank Group, "China at a Glance," http://devdata.worldbank.org/AAG/chn_aag.pdf; also see Economist Intelligence Unit, "Foresight 2020," 2006. On Chinese trade surpluses, see, for example, "China Trade Surplus Hits Another Record in July," Agence France-Presse, 8 Aug. 2006. Geoff Dyer, "Figures Show China as Net Vehicle Exporter," *Financial Times*, 11 Feb. 2006; Geoff Dyer and James Mackintosh, "Bought the T-Shirt and TV? Next for the West are Cars 'Made in China,'" *Financial Times*, 1 June 2005. "The Frugal Giant," *Economist*, 24 Sept. 2005; "US Savings Rate Hits Lowest Level Since 1933," Associated Press, 30 Jan. 2006.

9. Philip Saunders, *China's Global Activism: Strategy, Drivers, and Tools* (Washington, D.C.: National Defense University Press, 2006).

10. *Foreign Equity Investment in Singapore 2004* (Singapore: Singapore Department of Statistics, 2006); Philip Saunders, *China's Global Activism:*

Strategy, Drivers, and Tools (Washington, D.C.: National Defense University Press, 2006). See also "China Makes Direct Investments of $50 Billion Overseas in Past Five Years," *People's Daily*, 27 Feb. 2006.

11. "Sino-Cambodian Economic Relations," Cable from US Embassy, Phnom Penh, 14 May 2004.

12. Hu Jintao, "Speech at the Brazilian Parliament," 13 Nov. 2004; Chris Kraul, "China to Invest $5 Billion in Venezuela Oil Projects," *Los Angeles Times*, 29 Aug. 2006. Economic Commission for Latin America and the Caribbean, *Foreign Investment in Latin America and the Caribbean 2005* (Santiago, Chile: United Nations, 2006), 7–8; also see Kerry Dumbaugh and Mark P. Sullivan, "China's Growing Interest in Latin America," Congressional Research Service report, 20 Apr. 2005. "China's Africa Expansion," United Press International, 17 Jan. 2006. "China Agrees to $200 Million in Loans: Jusuf," *Jakarta Post*, 29 June 2005; Genalyn D. Kabaling, "RP, China Sign $1.6 Billion Accords; Hu Cites 'Golden Age' of Ties at Congress Joint Session," *Manila Bulletin*, 28 Apr. 2005.

13. Michael E. Arruda and Ka-Yin Li, "China's Energy Sector: Development, Structure, and Future," *China Law and Practice* 9 (2003): 12–17; Saunders, *China's Global Activism*. For more on the Go Out campaign, see Friedrich Wu, "China Inc International," *International Economy* 3 (2005): 26–31. Zhang Jin, "Wu Yi: China to go Further than WTO Promises," *China Daily*, 9 Sept. 2004.

14. "China Spreads Its Wings: Chinese Companies Go Global," Accenture report 2005.

15. Ibid.

16. Interviews with Chinese diplomats, Bangkok, Vientiane, Washington, Aug. 2005–Apr. 2006. See also Foreign Ministry of the People's Republic of China, "Program for China-Africa Cooperation in Economic and Social Development," Forum on China-Africa Cooperation; Dai Yan, "China Eyeing Regional Investment," *China Daily*, 9 Feb. 2004; and Stephen Frost, "Chinese Outward Direct Investment in Southeast Asia: How Much and What Are the Regional Implications?" Southeast Asia Research Center working paper, City University of Hong Kong, July 2004.

17. Interview with Singaporean diplomats, Singapore, Jan. 2006; on business delegations, see also Dumbaugh and Sullivan, "China's Growing Interest." Interview with Vikrom Kromadit, Bangkok, Sept. 2005.

18. Andy Rothman, "China Eats the World," CLSA Asia Pacific Markets investment strategy report, Spring 2005, 49–51; see also Paula Dittrick, "Chinese NOCs Go Shopping," *Oil and Gas Journal*, 23 Jan. 2006, 15. Erica Downs, "China's Foreign Investments: Comprehensively Planned or 'Muddled Through'?" Presentation for the National Bureau of Asian Research and

the Pacific Northwest Center for Global Security, Washington D.C., 27–28 Sept. 2005.

19. "The Dragon Tucks In," *Economist*, 30 June 2005, 71. Andrew Yeh, "China Backs Chavez's Bid for UN Seat After Oil Deal," *Financial Times*, 25 Aug. 2006; see also William Ratliff, "China and Venezuela: Pragmatism and Ideology," statement to the US-China Economic and Security Review Commission, 3 Aug. 2006. R. Evan Ellis, "US National Security Implications of Chinese Involvement in Latin America," Strategic Studies Institute, US Army War College, June 2005. Carolyn Bartholomew, testimony before the US-China Economic and Security Review Commission Hearing on China's Influence in Africa, 28 July 2005. David Barboza, "Chinese Oil Firm to Invest Billions in Nigerian Field," *New York Times*, 9 Jan. 2006. Jephraim P. Gundzik, "The Ties That Bind China, Russia, and Iran," *Asia Times*, 4 June 2005. "CNPC Set to Buy PetroKazakhstan After Concessions," *Energy Compass*, 21 Oct. 2005. "Indonesia Country Analysis Brief," Energy Information Administration, July 2004; David Fullbrook, "Resource-Hungry China to Devour More of Burma's Gas and Oil Industry," *Irrawaddy*, http://www.irrawaddy.org/aviewer.asp?a=5427&z=155, accessed Mar. 2006.

20. Arruda and Li, "China's Energy Sector"; Saunders, *China's Global Activism;* see also "Dongnanya: Zhongguo qiye 'zouchuqu de zhongdian diqu" (Southeast Asia: Area for Chinese Companies), Ministry of Commerce International Projects, no. 10, 2005. Interviews with Chinese, US, European, Thai, and Cambodian diplomats, Beijing, Washington, Bangkok, Vientiane, Phnom Penh, Nha Trang, Aug. 2005, Oct. 2005, Jan. 2006, Mar. 2006; see also Erik Wasson, "With $80.4 Million, China Top Investor in Cambodia in 2004," *Cambodia Daily*, 18 Feb. 2005. "China to Remove Cap on Investment Abroad by Domestic Firms," *Wall Street Journal*, 9 June 2006. "China Top Investor in Cambodia in 2004," unclassified cable, US Embassy, Phnom Penh, 2 Mar. 2005.

21. Interview with Walter Lohman, Washington, Aug. 2005; interview with Lin Che Wei, Jakarta, Mar. 2006.

22. "Friend or Forager?" *Financial Times*, 23 Feb. 2006.

23. Enzio Von Pfeil, "China: The Third World Superpower," *China Brief*, Jamestown Foundation, 19 Mar. 2004.

24. "Asia Outgrows Japanese Economy," Reuters, 29 Dec. 2005; Eric Teo Chu Cheow, "China as the Center of Asian Economic Integration," *China Brief*, Jamestown Foundation, 22 July 2004.

25. James Brooke, "China 'Looming Large' in South Korea as Biggest Player, Replacing the US," *New York Times*, 3 Jan. 2003.

26. Ian Taylor, "Beijing's Arms and Oil Interests in Africa," *China Brief*, Jamestown Foundation, 13 Oct. 2005. Dumbaugh and Sullivan, "China's

Growing Interest," 2; also see "US-Latin Trade Boom," *Latin Business Chronicle*, Mar. 2006. Richard Lapper, "A New Challenge for America in Its Own Backyard," *Financial Times*, 22 May 2004; see also Richard Lapper, "Run for Investment Bulls as China Shops," *Financial Times*, 13 Apr. 2005. John Calabrese, "China and Iran: Mismatched Partners," Jamestown Foundation occasional paper, Aug. 2006. Matthew Oresman, "Repaving the Silk Road: China's Emergence in Central Asia," in *China and the Developing World: Beijing's Strategy for the Twenty-First Century*, ed. Joshua Eisenman, Eric Heginbotham, and Derek Mitchell (Armonk, N.Y.: Sharpe, forthcoming, 2007). I am indebted to Barry Sautman for the point about Africans' preference for cheaper Chinese goods.

27. Interview with Singaporean diplomats, Singapore, Jan 2006. Joseph Yu-shek Cheng, "The Asean-China Free Trade Area: Genesis and Implications," *Australian Journal of International Affairs* 2 (2004): 257–277; see also John Wong and Sarah Chan, "China-Asean Free Trade Agreement: Shaping Future Economic Relations," *Asian Survey* 3 (2003): 507–526, and Asean-China Expert Group on Economic Cooperation, "Forging Closer Asean-China Economic Relations in the 21st Century," Oct. 2001. 63. Siow Yue Chia and Chalongphob Sussangkarn, "The Economic Rise of China: Challenges and Opportunities for Asean," *Asian Economic Policy Review* 1 (2006): 102–128; see also Jane Perlez, "China Promises More Investment in Southeast Asia," *New York Times*, 8 Oct. 2003.

28. Gary Clyde Hufbauer and Yee Wong, "Prospects for Regional Free Trade in Asia," Institute for International Economics working paper, Oct. 2005. "China Winning Resources and Loyalties of Africa," *Financial Times*, 28 Feb. 2006; see also Government of Pakistan Ministry of Commerce, "Pakistan-China Early Harvest Programme," http://www.commerce.gov.pk/PCEHP.asp, accessed Nov. 2006. Ministry of Foreign Affairs of the People's Republic of China, "China's African Policy," 12 Jan. 2006.

29. Tran Dinh Thanh Lam, "US 'Catfish War' Defeat Stings Vietnam," *Asia Times*, 31 July 2003; US Department of Agriculture Foreign Agricultural Service, "International Trade Report: U.S. Seafood Imports Continue to Soar," 8 July 2005; Alan Sipress, "US-Vietnam Ties Raise Hopes, Hackles," *Washington Post*, 6 Mar. 2004. See also US Department of Commerce, "Notice of Antidumping Duty Order: Certain Frozen Fish Fillets from the Socialist Republic of Vietnam," *Federal Register*, 12 Aug. 2003, 47909–47910.

30. Interviews with Carol Lancaster, Georgetown University, Patrick Cronin, International Institute for Strategic Studies, and other participants in conferences on foreign aid held in Beijing, Aug. and Nov. 2005. See also Michael A. Glosny, "Meeting the Development Challenge in the Twenty-first Century: American and Chinese Perspectives on Foreign Aid," National

Committee on United States–China Relations China Policy series report, Aug 2006.

31. Interview with Thai officials, Ministry of Foreign Affairs of the Kingdom of Thailand, Bangkok, Aug. 2005.

32. Interviews with Filipino, Thai, and Cambodian diplomats, Manila, Bangkok, and Phnom Penh, Jan. 2006 and Aug. 2005; Export-Import Bank of China, annual report, 2002. See also Todd Moss and Sarah Rose, "China Exim Bank and Africa: New Lending, New Challenges," Center for Global Development Note, Nov. 2006.

33. Yep, "China's Foreign Aid to Asia"; Joshua Eisenman and Joshua Kurlantzick, "China's Africa Strategy," *Current History* 5 (2006): 219–224; "China Offers New Aid to Pacific Island Countries," Agence France-Presse, 5 Apr. 2006.

34. Interviews with officials at Philippines Department of Trade and Industry, Manila, Mar. 2006, and Cambodia Ministry of Commerce, Phnom Penh, Jan. 2006; Yep, "China's Foreign Aid to Asia"; *Sin Chew Daily* digests, 2003–2005.

35. Yep, "China's Foreign Aid to Asia." "United States Agency for International Development Tsunami Reconstruction Update," Aug. 2006, http://www.usaid.gov/locations/asia_near_east/tsunami/, accessed Nov. 2006; see also "China Increases Tsunami Aid to $63 Million," Xinhua, 31 Dec. 2004, and Shen Guofang, "Address to the United Nations Meeting on Humanitarian Assistance to Tsunami Affected Countries," 12 Jan. 2005. Sino-Cambodian Economic Relations," cable from US Embassy, Phnom Penh, 14 May 2004.

36. Loro Horta and Ian Storey, "China's Portuguese Connection," *Yale Global Online*, http://yaleglobal.yale.edu/display.article?id=7634, accessed Aug. 2006.

37. "Sino-African Economic, Trade Relations to be Promoted: Official," *People's Daily*, 24 Jan. 2004; "China to Train 3,000 Professionals for Developing Countries," Xinhua, 14 June 2004.

38. Yep, "China's Foreign Aid to Asia"; interview with China specialist in Ministry of Foreign Affairs of the Kingdom of Thailand, Aug. 2005; Hisane Misaki, "China and Japan in Mekong Tug-of-War," *Straits Times* (Singapore), 24 Nov. 2005; Siriluk Masviriyakul, "Sino-Thai Strategic Economic Development in the Greater Mekong Subregion, 1992–2003," *Contemporary Southeast Asia* 2 (2004): 302–320.

39. Peter Bosshard, "China Exim Bank and China Development Bank Case Studies," Report prepared for International Rivers Network, 2004; Jason Kindopp, "China's Energy Security and NOCs," Presentation for the National Bureau of Asian Research and the Pacific Northwest Center for Global Security, Washington D.C., 27–28 Sept. 2005.

40. Interview with Kraisak Choonhaven, Thai senator, Bangkok, Aug. 2005; interviews with Vietnamese officials, Nha Trang, Oct. 2005; see also William Ratliff, *China's "Lessons" for Cuba's Transition?* (Miami: University of Miami Press, 2004). Sheng Lijun and Jiang Shuxian, "The Communist Party of China and Political Parties of Southeast Asia," *Trends in Southeast Asia* 14 (2005). Interviews with Cambodian politicians from ruling party and opposition, Phnom Penh, Jan. 2006.

41. Interview with Kraisak Choonhaven, Thai senator, Bangkok, Aug. 2005.

42. Interviews with Lao diplomats, foreign ministry officials, Vientiane, Aug. 2005.

43. "Lai No Longer on First Name Terms with Solomon Islands," *People's Daily,* 26 Apr. 2006. "China Winning Resources and Loyalties of Africa," *Financial Times,* 28 Feb. 2006; see also China International Contractors Association, "2004 Report on Overseas Chinese Labor." Barry Sautman, "Friends and Interests: China's Distinctive Links with Africa," Working Paper no. 12, Center on China's Transnational Relations, Hong Kong University of Science and Technology, 2006.

44. David Fullbrook, "Chinese Migrants and the Power of Guanxi," *Asia Times,* 30 July 2004; interview with Cambodian diplomats, Washington, Aug. 2005.

45. Interview with Antonella Diana, specialist on Laotian-Chinese border relations, Australian National University, Feb. 2006; for more background on changes in northern Laos, see Chris Lyttleton, Paul Cohen, Houmphanh Rattanavong, Bouakham Thongkhamkhane, and Souriyanh Sisaengrat, "Watermelons, Bars, and Trucks: Dangerous Intersections in Northwest Lao PDR," Institute for Cultural Research of Laos and Macquarie University, 2004. Interview with Western diplomat, Vientiane, Aug. 2005; "China's Growing Presence in Northern Laos," cable from US Embassy, Vientiane, obtained through the Freedom of Information Act, 20 July 2005.

46. Michael Vatikiotis and Bertil Linter, "The Renminbi Zone," *Far Eastern Economic Review,* 29 May 2003, 24.

47. CLSA Asia Pacific Markets, "Chinese Tourists: Coming, Ready or Not!" special report, Sept. 2005; see also World Tourism Organization, *Tourism 2020 Vision* (New York: World Tourism Organization Publications, 2000). "Tourism Gaining Momentum in China-ASEAN Economic Cooperation: Expert," *People's Daily,* 3 Nov. 2006. Ben Blanchard, "Anxious Laos Gears up for Chinese Tourists," Reuters, 10 Aug. 2005; Phusadee Arunmas, "Tripling of Tourists on Agenda," *Bangkok Post,* 14 Sept. 2005; Data compiled by the Pacific Asia Travel Association, provided by Ken Scott, PATA Bangkok.

48. Many group tours do little to improve the image of China abroad.

In Pattaya, a seedy Thai beach resort, the typical Chinese group tour generally looks like this: Twenty or thirty people from one city in China each pay an astonishingly small amount—sometimes less than $400—for a three- or four-day trip; the price includes a flight from China to Pattaya, all meals, and ratty accommodations. Arriving in Pattaya, a megaphone-wielding female guide herds the Chinese group from "attraction" to "attraction"—attractions being overpriced shops that pay commissions back to the travel agent (which makes possible the low price for the trip), beaches covered in sewage and hypodermic needles, and strips of bars packed with blond Russian prostitutes wearing long fake mink coats in the tropical heat. At dinnertime, megaphone girl herds the group into a hotel restaurant or cheap Chinese buffet, where everyone can pig out before going to bed or heading out again to Pattaya's red-light district to get sloshed. CLSA Asia Pacific Markets, "Chinese Tourists." "Chinese Travelers Step out of Boundaries," *China Today*, 7 July 2004.

Chapter 6: Mr. Popular

1. For more on the referendum, see "Situation of Human Rights in East Timor: Note by the Secretary General," United Nations General Assembly Fifty-Fourth Session, 10 Dec. 1999. For more background on the economic devastation, see "World Bank Country Brief: East Timor," http://web.worldbank.org/WBSITE/EXTERNAL/COUNTRIES/EASTASIAPACIFICEXT/TIMORLESTEEXTN/0,,menuPK:294027~pagePK:141159~piPK:141110~theSitePK:294022,00.html, accessed Nov. 2006.

2. For more on the history of the Timorese resistance, see Constâncio Pinto and Matthew Jardine, *East Timor's Unfinished Struggle: Inside the Timorese Resistance* (Cambridge, Mass.: South End, 1996), and Joseph Nevins, *A Not-So-Distant Horror: Mass Violence in East Timor* (Ithaca: Cornell University Press, 2005).

3. Interview with João de Câmara, Dili, Mar. 2006.

4. Interviews with Timorese and American diplomats, Dili, Mar. 2006; Ian Storey, "China and East Timor," *China Brief*, Jamestown Foundation, 15 Aug. 2006.

5. Interview with Elisabeth Huybens, World Bank East Timor, Dili, Mar 2006; interview with Constâncio Pinto, minister-counselor, Embassy of Timor Leste, Washington, Feb. 2006; interviews with Timorese businesspeople, Dili, Mar. 2006.

6. Interviews with Timorese, Chinese, and US diplomats, Washington and Dili, Mar. 2006.

7. Jill Jolliffe, "East Timor Says China Is Its Closest Ally," *Sydney Morning Herald*, 11 July 2002; Michael Richardson, "East Timor Edges Toward Oil Deal with Australia," *New Zealand Herald*, 17 June 2005. See also Timor Sea Office, http://www.timorseaoffice.gov.tp/, accessed Nov. 2006.

8. Department of State, Office of Research, "U.S. Image Positive in Urban Thailand, Bolstered by a Sense of Shared Security Interests: But Public Sees U.S. Becoming Less Important as an Economic Partner in 5–10 Years," obtained from U.S. Embassy, Bangkok, Aug. 2005.

9. Program on International Policy Attitudes, "22 Nation Poll Shows China Viewed Positively by Most Countries Including its Asian Neighbors," http://www.worldpublicopinion.org/pipa/articles/views_on_countriesregions_bt/116.php?nid=&id=&pnt=116&lb=btvoc, accessed Nov. 2005; Program on International Policy Attitudes, "33 Nation Poll on Views of Countries," Feb. 2006; Jorge Domínguez, "China's Relations with Latin America: Shared Gains, Asymmetric Hopes," Inter-American Dialogue publications, May 2006.

10. Interview with Indonesian businessman, Jakarta, Mar. 2006.

11. Gail Dutton, "Grassroots Diplomacy," *Across the Board*, May–June 2005, 1–4; Josef Joffe, *Überpower: The Imperial Temptation of America* (New York: Norton, 2006), 99.

12. Bruce Kligner, "China Shock for South Korea," *Asia Times*, 11 Sept. 2004.

13. Sophie Diamant Richardson, "China, Cambodia, and the Five Principles of Peaceful Coexistence: Principles and Foreign Policy," Ph.D. diss., University of Virginia, 2005.

14. "Hun Sen Cancels Trip to UNGA," cable from US Embassy, Phnom Penh, 7 Sept. 2004; interviews with Cambodian ministers, politicians, journalists, Phnom Penh, Jan. 2006.

15. Vinod Sreeharsha, "East Meets West, with an Argentine Twist," *Christian Science Monitor*, 30 Sept. 2005; Sin Chew Media Corporation, Prospectus, 2004; Chye Wen Fei, "Sin Chew Media Corporation BHD," *SBB Securities Report*, 24 Sept. 2004; Interviews with Lin Zhen Chao, president of Vientiane Chinese Association, Vientiane, Aug. 2005. See also Marks, "China's Cambodia Strategy"; "Chinese Teachers Spread the World to Pass Heritage," *China Daily*, 2 Jan. 2005; and Jean Lin, "Ministry Will Fund Students to Teach Mandarin Abroad," *Taipei Times*, 8 June 2006.

16. Austin Ramzy, "Get Ahead, Learn Mandarin," *Time Asia*, 19 June 2006, 16; see also James Brooke, "China Looming Large in South Korea as Biggest Player, Replacing the US," *New York Times*, 3 Jan. 2003. Jae Ho Chung,

"Korea Between Eagle and Dragon: Perceptual Ambivalence and Strategic Dilemma," *Asian Survey* 5 (2001): 777–796.

17. Ministry of Foreign Affairs of the People's Republic of China, *Zhongguo Waijaaio* (China's Diplomacy) (Beijing: World Affairs Press, 2005); also, Paul Marks, "Impressions of Chinese Government Involvement in Investment in Vietnam," unpublished paper, Mar. 2006; Kurlantzick and Eisenman, "China's Africa Strategy." Jane Perlez, "Chinese Move to Eclipse U.S. Appeal in Southeast Asia," *New York Times,* 18 Nov. 2004.

18. "Number of Foreign Students in China Rises 20 Percent Annually," Xinhua, 19 Jan. 2006; "China Expects Influx of Foreign Students," *China Daily,* 29 Sept. 2004 interview with Eric Teo Chu Cheow, Singapore, Jan. 2006; Ministry of Commerce of the People's Republic of China, *China Commerce Yearbook 2004.*

19. "Constantly Increasing Common Ground: Hu's Speech to the Australian Parliament," 24 Oct. 2003, australianpolitics.com/news/2003/10/03-10-24b.shtml, accessed Nov. 2006; James Hookaway, "Many Asians Flaunt Roots to China as Nation Gains Cachet," *Wall Street Journal,* 16 Mar. 2004; interview with N. C. Siew, Sin Chew Media, Kuala Lumpur, Jan. 2006.

20. Interviews with art professors in Kuala Lumpur, Bangkok, Jakarta, Aug. 2005 and Mar. 2006; Pallavi Aiyar, "The Great Chinese Art Bazaar," *Hindu,* 30 Apr. 2006; Martin Baily, "China Is the World's Second Largest Exporter of Art," *Art Newspaper,* 7 Feb. 2006; Carol Vogel, "Sotheby's Bets on a Windfall for Today's Chinese Art," *New York Times,* 29 Mar. 2006. Carol Vogel, "China: The New Contemporary Art Frontier," *New York Times,* 1 Apr. 2006. Carol Vogel, "Christie's Going, Going to China to Hold Auctions," *New York Times,* 20 Oct. 2005.

21. Interviews with Vietnamese officials, Nha Trang, Oct. 2005. "Chinese Film Festival 2005 Held in Metro Manila," Bulletin of the Chinese Embassy in the Philippines, 13 June 2005; David Barboza, "Hollywood Studios See the Chinese Film Market as Their Next Rising Star," *New York Times,* 4 July 2005. Alexandra Seno, "China's Starring Role in the Philippines," *International Herald Tribune,* 2 Feb. 2006. Luca Bruno, "Chinese Movie Wins Top Prize in Venice," *Associated Press,* 11 Sept. 2006. Interviews with South Korean arts figures and journalists, Seoul, Aug. 2005.

22. Analysis was completed by studying samples of leading Thai and Indonesian newspapers in 1995 and 2005 and comparing analysis of China, columns about China, and news coverage of China. See also "Devastating Blows: Religious Repression of Uighurs in Xinjiang," Human Rights Watch report, Apr. 2005.

23. Interview with Lee Poh Ping, Kuala Lumpur, Jan. 2006; Foreign

Ministry of the People's Republic of China, "President Hu Jintao Meets Thai King," 18 Oct. 2006; Larry Rohter, "China Widens Economic Role in Latin America," *New York Times,* 20 Nov. 2004.

24. For a history of the Indonesian crisis, see Adrian Vickers, *A History of Modern Indonesia* (Cambridge: Cambridge University Press, 2005).

25. For a history of the Chinese in Indonesia, see Leo Suryadinata, *Pribumi Indonesians, the Chinese Minority, and China: A Study of Perceptions and Policies* (Singapore: Eastern University Press, 2005); Jemma Purdey, *Anti-Chinese Violence in Indonesia, 1996–1999* (Singapore: Singapore University Press, 2006).

26. Purdey, *Anti-Chinese Violence;* Leo Suryadinata, "Chinese Politics in Post-Suharto's Indonesia," *Asian Survey* 3 (2001): 502–524.

27. Suryadinata, *Pribumi Indonesians,* 123–125, 210–215; "China Voices Concern for Chinese Indonesians," *Straits Times,* 16 July 1998.

28. Interview with A. B. Susanto, Jakarta, Mar. 2006.

29. Ibid.

30. "The Happy Chinese," *Economist,* 4 Feb. 2006; interview with Christine Susanna Tjhin, specialist in Chinese Indonesian politics, Jakarta, Mar. 2006. Jay Solomon, "Indonesia's Chinese Embrace New Role," *Wall Street Journal,* 9 Feb. 2005; Christine Susanna Tjhin, "More Chinese-Indonesians Become Actively Involved in Politics," *Jakarta Post,* 29 Mar. 2004.

31. "Thai PM Seeks Out Roots in Meizhou," *China Daily,* 4 July 2005; "Thai PM Concludes China Tour," Xinhua, 3 July 2005.

32. Khien Theeravit, "Thaksin Lays Out Regional Vision," *Nation* (Thailand), 20 Apr. 2002. Perlez, "Chinese Move to Eclipse U.S. Appeal"; see also Phusadee Arunmas, "Thai-Chinese Car Venture to Challenge Japanese Firms," *Bangkok Post,* 23 Dec. 2005, and Phusadee Arunmas, "Pact with China Signed to Boost Bilateral Trade to $50 Billion by 2010," *Bangkok Post,* 23 Sept. 2005. Interview with Kraisak Choonhaven, Bangkok, Aug. 2005.

33. Subhatra Bhumiprabhas, "FTA Watch: Movement 'Is Gaining Strength,'" *Nation* (Thailand), 15 Jan. 2006; interviews with US trade negotiators, Washington, Oct. 2005. Interviews with Thai and American trade negotiators, Washington and Bangkok, Jan. and Mar. 2006. See also "Bigots Against FTA," http://sanpaworn.vissaventure.com/log/251/bigots-against-fta, accessed Nov. 2006.

34. Interviews with senior CP executives, Bangkok, Aug. 2005; Paul Handley, "De-Mythologizing Charoen Pokphand: An Interpretive Picture of the CP Group's Growth and Diversification," in *Ethnic Business: Chinese Capitalism in Southeast Asia,* ed. Jomo K. S. and Brian C. Folk, 153–181 (London: Taylor and Francis, 2001).

Chapter 7: Goal Oriented

1. M. Taylor Fravel, "Regime Insecurity and International Cooperation: Explaining China's Compromises in Territorial Disputes," *International Security* 2 (2005): 46–83.

2. Vincent Wei-Cheng Wang, "The Logic of China-ASEAN FTA: Economic Statecraft of "Peaceful Ascendancy," in *China and Southeast Asia: Global Changes and Regional Challenges,* ed. Ho Khai Leong and Samuel C. Y. Ku, 17–41 (Singapore: Institute of Southeast Asian Studies, 2005).

3. Robert Sutter, "China's Rise and U.S. Influence in Asia: A Report from the Region," Atlantic Council of the United States Issue Brief, July 2006.

4. Interviews with Alejandro Melchor, Philippine Department of Defense, Ambassador José V. Romero, and Leticia Ramos Shahani, former Philippine senator, Manila, Mar. 2006; National Defense University, "China's Growing Influence in Southeast Asia: March 2005 Trip to Philippines and Indonesia," *INSS Staff Report,* 4 May 2005; "Workshop on Asean Relations with China and the United States: Event Report," National Bureau of Asian Research, 3 Nov. 2005; David Shambaugh, "China Engages Asia: Reshaping the Regional Order," *International Security* 3 (2004): 64–99.

5. Interviews with Thai diplomats and politicians, Bangkok, Aug. 2005 and Jan. 2006.

6. Robert G. Sutter, *China's Rise in Asia: Promises and Perils* (Lanham, Md.: Rowman and Littlefield, 2005), 166–167.

7. Interviews with Vincent Lim, political secretary to the prime minister of Malaysia, and Jawhar Hassan, director general, ISIS Malaysia, Kuala Lumpur, Jan. 2006.

8. Philip Pan, "China's Improving Image Challenges U.S. in Asia," *Washington Post,* 15 Nov. 2003; Tom Fawthrop, "Middle Kingdom Puts Squeeze on Little Kingdom," *Phnom Penh Post,* 25 May 2001; "Cambodia-China Relations: Steady Improvement, Growing PRC Influence," Cable from US Embassy, Phnom Penh, 1 June 2004; Philip P. Pan, "China's Improving Image Challenges US in Asia," *Washington Post,* 15 Nov. 2003.

9. Interviews with Vietnamese officials and diplomats, Nha Trang, Oct. 2005; see also Eric Teo Chu Cheow, "China Lights Vietnam's Path," *Japan Times,* 12 Jan. 2004. Interview with Bounnheuang Songnavong, deputy director, Ministry of Foreign Affairs, Lao PDR, Aug. 2005.

10. Afshin Molavi, "Fine China," *New Republic,* 8 Sept. 2003, 14.

11. James Mahon, "Goodbye to the Washington Consensus?" *Current History* 2 (2003): 58–64; Michael Shifter, "The US and Latin America Through the Lens of Empire," *Current History* 2 (2004): 61–67.

12. Barry Sautman, "Friends and Interests: China's Distinctive Links with Africa," Working Paper no. 12, Center on China's Transnational Relations, Hong Kong University of Science and Technology, 2006.

13. Interview with I Wibowo, Jakarta, Mar. 2006; interview with Dewi Fortuna Anwar, Jakarta, Mar. 2006; interview with Gavin Khoo, Kuala Lumpur, Jan. 2006.

14. Frank Ching, "China Woos Influence with Softer Style," *Japan Times*, 10 June 2004.

15. Francisco Guerrera, "China Is in Danger of Sinking," *Financial Times*, 6 May 2006; Conn Hallinan, "China: A Troubled Dragon," *Foreign Policy in Focus Commentary*, http://www.fpif.org/pdf/gac/0605dragon.pdf, accessed Sept. 2006; Edward Cody, "China Grows More Wary over Rash of Protests," *Washington Post*, 10 Aug. 2005; Kristin Jones, "China's Hidden Unrest," Committee to Protect Journalists, special report, May 2006.

16. Interviews with Burmese monks, tour guides, laborers, Mandalay and Chiang Mai, Mar. 2006; interviews with Uighur and Kazakh traders, Kashgar, Aug. 2004; phone interview with Antonella Diana, Jan. 2006.

17. Lai Hongyi, "China's Regional Oil Diplomacy" and "China's Oil Diplomacy Going Global," *Background Briefs*, East Asian Institute, National University of Singapore, 2005.

18. Mamoun Fandy, "China vs. US: A View from the Arab World," paper prepared for Energy Security: Implications for US–China–Middle East Relations conference, Rice University, 18 July 2005.

19. "China, Saudi Arabia Ink Oil Cooperation Deal," Associated Press, 23 Jan. 2006; see also "China, Saudi Arabia Forge Closer Relationship," *China Daily*, 24 Jan. 2006. Samuel Blatteis, "Dueling for Economic Dominance: The Quiet Fight for the Persian Gulf," *San Francisco Chronicle*, 30 Apr. 2006; David A. Andelman, "The Sino-Saudi Connection," *Forbes*, 17 Apr. 2006, 18.

20. See, for example, Peter Maass, "The Breaking Point," *New York Times Magazine*, 21 Aug. 2005, 30.

21. Interview with Singaporean diplomats, Singapore, Jan. 2006.

22. John Reed, "Beijing Flexes Its Muscles in Zambian Election," *Financial Times*, 5 Sept. 2006.

23. Sam Rith, "China Revives Dreams of Kampot Mega-Dam," *Phnom Penh Post*, 4 Nov. 2005. Interviews with Masao Imamura, Unit for Social and Economic Research, Chiang Mai, Aug. 2005, and Muanpong Juntamas, Mekong River Commission, Vientiane, Aug. 2005; see also Charlotte McDonald-Gibson, "No Regard for the Neighbors: Blasting the River in China's Backyard," *Phnom Penh Post*, 13 Jan. 2003; and John Vidal, "Dammed and Dying: The Mekong and Its Communities Face a Bleak Future," *Guardian*, 25 Mar. 2004. Interview with Cambodian environmental specialist, Phnom Penh, Jan. 2006.

24. Interview with Cambodian environmental specialist, Phnom Penh, Jan. 2006.

25. Interviews with Singaporean diplomats, Singapore, Jan. 2006; interview with James Wong, Kuala Lumpur, Mar. 2006.

26. Melody Chen, "Grenada, Beijing Re-Establish Links," *Taipei Times*, 21 Jan. 2005; "China, Commonwealth of Dominica Establish Diplomatic Ties," Xinhua, 29 Mar. 2004; "Trying to Win Over Taiwan's Allies," *Latin America Special Reports*, 2 May 2006. Kerry Dumbaugh and Mark P. Sullivan, "China's Growing Interest in Latin America," Congressional Research Service report, 20 Apr. 2005.

27. "Changes in Republic of China and Panama's Diplomatic Relationship?" *United Daily News*, 22 Apr. 2004; Melody Chen, "Taiwan Foreign Ministry Closely Monitoring PRC Official's Tour to Panama," *Taipei Times*, 18 June 2004. Interview with Daniel Erikson, Inter-American Dialogue, Washington, Aug. 2005.

28. Department of Foreign Affairs of the Republic of South Africa, "China, History of Relations," http://www.dfa.gov.za/foreign/bilateral/china.html, accessed Nov. 2006; see also Ministry of Foreign Affairs of the People's Republic of China, "China and Central Africa White Paper," 12 Oct. 2002. "China, Liberia Resume Diplomatic Ties," *People's Daily*, 13 Oct. 2003; "Taiwan: President Defends Africa Tour," Taiwanese Central News Agency, 5 July 2002; "Senegal Picks Taiwan over China," *BBC News*, 26 Oct. 2005. "China, Chad Resume Diplomatic Ties," *People's Daily*, 7 Aug. 2006. Interview with Joanne Chang, Washington, Feb. 2006.

29. "PM Goh Makes Surprise Taiwan Stopover," Reuters, 28 Nov. 1997. Samuel Ku, "Taiwan's Southward Policy and Its Changing Relations with Southeast Asia, 1990–1997," East Asian Institute Background Brief, National University of Singapore, 18 Nov. 2005; Samuel Ku, "Taiwan's Relations with Southeast Asia post-1997," East Asian Institute Background Brief, National University of Singapore, 18 Nov. 2005 Ian Storey, "China's Tightening Relationship with Cambodia," *China Brief*, Jamestown Foundation, 26 Apr. 2006. Lin Chieh-yu and Monique Chu, "Lu Pans China for Restricting her Trip," *Taipei Times*, 16 Aug. 2002; see also "Annette Lu not Allowed to Enter Jakarta: Spokesman," *People's Daily*, 15 Aug. 2002. Monique Chu, "Foreign Ministry Seeking to Improve Ties with Southeast Asia," *Taipei Times*, 21 Aug. 2002. "Malaysia Bars Ministers from Making Visits to Taiwan," *People's Daily*, 24 July 2004.

30. "Taiwan Has Invested $40 Billion in China," Central News Agency, 20 Jan. 2005.

31. Interview with Leticia Ramos Shahani, former Philippine senator, Manila, Mar. 2006.

32. Interviews with DPP officials, Washington, Aug. 2005 and Nov. 2005.

33. "Overseas Chinese Speak with One Voice Against 'Taidu,'" *People's Daily*, 3 Mar. 2004; "Overseas Chinese in Panama Do Not Welcome Chen Shui-Bian's Visit," Xinhua, 17 May 2001; interview with Ellen Palanca, Manila, Mar. 2006; interview with Francis Chua, president of the Federation of Filipino-Chinese Chambers of Commerce, Manila, Mar. 2006.

34. "World Buddhism Summit," *The Times of London*, 10 Aug. 2002; Mickey Spiegel, "Rejection of Visa for Dalai Lama," *Korea Times*, 19 June 2006. For more on China's treatment of Falun Gong, see Human Rights Watch, "Dangerous Meditation: China's Campaign Against Falun Gong," Jan. 2002, and Thomas Lum, "China and Falun Gong," Congressional Research Service report, 25 May 2006. Gregg Jones, "China Is Working Hard to Enhance Its Image in Asia," *Dallas Morning News*, 23 Mar. 2001. "Indonesian Court Jails Falun Gong Activists for Chinese Embassy Protest," Xinhua, 9 May 2005; "Court Convicts 12 Falun Gong Supporters over Protest," *Jakarta Post*, 28 Apr. 2005; Committee to Protect Journalists, "Asia Cases 2005," in *Attacks on the Press in 2005*, ed. Paul E. Steiger and Ann Cooper (New York: Committee to Protect Journalists, 2006).

35. Joshua Eisenman, untitled chapter, in *China and the Developing World: Beijing's Strategy for the Twenty-First Century*, ed. Joshua Eisenman, Eric Heginbotham, and Derck Mitchell (Armonk, N.Y.: Sharpe, forthcoming, 2007).

Chapter 8: Wielding the Charm

1. Interview with Songpol Kaoputumptip, *Bangkok Post* reporter who has frequently visited Mong La, Bangkok, Aug. 2005.

2. Ibid. See also Xia Hailong, "Casino Town Loses Out," *Asia Times*, 25 Nov. 2003.

3. Interview with Songpol Kaoputumptip. See also Andrew Marshall and Anthony Davis, "Soldiers of Fortune," *Time Asia*, 9 Dec. 2002, 16.

4. Clive Parker, "The Rise and Fall of Burma's Casino Capital," *Irrawaddy*, Feb. 2006; interview with Songpol Kaoputumtip. See also Joan Williams, "Mong La: Burma's City of Lights," *Irrawaddy*, Jan.–Feb. 2003.

5. Parker, "Rise and Fall"; "Burma," CIA World Factbook, https://www.cia.gov/cia/publications/factbook/geos/bm.html, accessed Nov. 2006.

6. Freedom House, *Freedom in the World: The Annual Survey of Political Rights and Civil Liberties* (Lanham, Md.: Rowman and Littlefield, 2005). On Burma's health spending, see United Nations Development Program,

Human Development Report 2005 (New York: Oxford University Press, 2005). On its military spending, see Gerhard Will, "Case Study: Burma," paper presented to Third Europe–Southeast Asia Forum, Berlin, 13–15 Dec. 2004.

7. Andrew Marshall, "Soldiers of Fortune," *Time Asia,* 16 Dec. 2002. See Interpol statistics on global opium and heroin production at http://www.interpol.int/Public/Drugs/heroin/default.asp, accessed Nov. 2006. James East, "Up to Two Million Thai Students into Drugs," *Straits Times,* 27 Dec. 1999; see also Aung Zaw, "Drugs, Generals, and Neighbors," *Irrawaddy,* June 2001. Kyaw Zwa Moe, "Yunnan's Sin City," *Irrawaddy,* Jan. 2005; see also "Anatomy of an Epidemic," *Economist,* 28 July 2005; Naw Seng, "Drug Trade Booms on China-Myanmar Border," *Asia Times,* 31 Mar. 2004; and "Drugs-Wa Link to Triads Confirmed," *Bangkok Post,* 22 Dec. 2000.

8. Interviews with Chinese diplomats, Bangkok and Washington, Aug. 2005 and Mar. 2006; interview with Curtis Lambrecht, specialist on the Burmese military, Hua Hin, Jan. 2006. See also Michael Schuman, "Going Nowhere," *Time Asia,* 30 Jan. 2006, 26; and Thomas Carroll, "China's Penetration into Burma," M.S. thesis, Georgetown University, 2001.

9. Parker, "Rise and Fall"; Naw Seng, "Chinese Troops on Burma's Border," *Irrawaddy,* http://www.irrawaddy.org/aviewer.asp?a=801&z=23, accessed Jan. 2005. "Chips Are Down for Cadres," *South China Morning Post,* 31 Dec. 2004; see also Edward Cody, "China Targets Corrupt Officials in a Battle Against Temptation," *Washington Post,* 20 Feb. 2005. "103 Foreign Casinos Compelled to Close," *People's Daily,* 25 Mar. 2005. Interview with Chinese officials, Beijing, Aug. 2005. See also "China Presses Myanmar to Crack Down on Drug Trafficking," Deutsche Press-Agentur, 14 Feb. 2006.

10. "China Watch," *Jane's Intelligence Review,* Jan. 2004; see also Elizabeth Economy, "China's Rise in Southeast Asia: Implications for Japan and the United States," *Japan Focus,* 6 Oct. 2005. Michael Black and Roland Fields, "Virtual Gambling in Myanmar's Drug Country," *Asia Times,* 26 Aug. 2006. Parker, "Rise and Fall."

11. Global Witness, "A Choice for China: Ending the Destruction of Burma's Frontier Forests," Global Witness publications, Oct. 2005.

12. Ibid.

13. "Chinese Environmentalist Goes on Trial Over State Secrets," Agence France Presse, 15 May 2006; E-mail interviews with Chinese scholars, Kunming, Aug. 2005; interview with Thai monk based in Burmese border areas, Chiang Mai, Aug. 2005. See also Kyaw Zwa Moe, "The 'Made in China' Syndrome," *Irrawaddy,* Nov. 2004, and Graeme Lang and Cathy Hui Wan Chan, "The Impact of China on Southeast Asian Forests," Southeast Asia Research Center Working Paper Series, City University of Hong Kong, June 2005.

14. Global Witness, "A Choice for China."

15. Ibid.; "China and the Global Market for Forest Products: Transforming Trade to Benefit Forests and Livelihoods," Forest Trends report, http://www.forest-trends.org/documents/publications/China%20and%20the%20Global%20Forest%20Market-Forest%20Trends.pdf, accessed Apr. 2006.

16. National Intelligence Council, "NIC 2020 Project: NIC-Sponsored Seminar on Asian Responses to the United States," 24 Nov. 2003; Robert Zoellick, "Whither China? From Membership to Responsibility," Remarks to the National Committee on U.S.-China Relations, 21 Sept. 2005.

17. State Council Information Office, "China's Peaceful Development Road," white paper, 22 Dec. 2005; Fu Ying, "China and Asia in a New Era," *China: An International Journal* 2 (2003): 304–312; interview with Chinese diplomat, Washington, Sept. 2005.

18. "Frequent Blasts Make Coal Mining Most Dangerous Job in China," *People's Daily,* 14 Nov. 2004. See also Li Qiang, "The World's Most Dangerous Job?" *South China Morning Post,* 22 Feb. 2005, and Zijun Li, "The Cost of China's Energy Boom: Miners' Lives," Worldwatch Institute report, 10 Nov. 2005.

19. "Chinese Peacekeepers Sent to Liberia," *China Daily,* 27 Nov. 2003; Michael Fullilove, "Angel or Dragon?" *National Interest,* Sept.–Oct 2006, 67–71.

20. Richard Paddock, "Rumor of Thai Actress' Words Salted a Wound," *Los Angeles Times,* 3 Feb. 2003. See also Andrew Perrin and Matt McKinney, "Blast from the Past," *Time Asia,* 2 Feb. 2003, 42.

21. Paddock, "Rumor"; see also "Khmers Raze Embassy," *Nation* (Thailand), 30 Jan. 2003. Howard Altman, "The King of Bling Bling," *American Journalism Review,* Sept. 2002, 54-59.

22. Perrin and McKinney, "Blast from the Past"; Kimina Lyall, "Thais Flee Cambodia as Mobs Riot," *The Australian,* 31 Jan. 2003.

23. Interviews with Cambodian diplomats, Phnom Penh, Jan. 2006; see also "China Hopes Thailand, Cambodia Settle Unrest Calmly," Xinhua, 30 Jan. 2003. Seth Mydans, "Thailand: Apology from Cambodia Accepted," *New York Times,* 5 Feb. 2003. "Cambodian Border: Checkpoints Reopen," *Nation* (Thailand), 22 Mar. 2003.

24. Johanna McGeary, "Look Who's Got the Bomb," *Time Asia,* 21 Oct. 2002. 38; Leon V. Sigal, "Negotiating with the North," *The Bulletin of the Atomic Scientists* 6 (2003): 19–25.

25. "China and North Korea: Comrades Forever?" International Crisis Group report, Feb. 2006. Robert Marquand, "US Looks to China to Influence North Korea," *Christian Science Monitor,* 10 July 2006; see also Mark E.

Manyin, "U.S. Assistance to North Korea: Fact Sheet," Congressional Research Service Report, 31 Jan. 2006. Craig S. Smith, "North Korean Leader Kicks the Tires in Shanghai," *New York Times*, 18 Jan. 2001. "With Unusual Praise for Shanghai's Great Changes, North may Pursue Chinese-Style Opening," *Chosun Ilbo*, 21 Jan. 2001.

26. "China and North Korea: Comrades Forever?"

27. State Council Information Office, "China's Peaceful Development Road"; "A Regional Discussion of the Six-Party Process," transcript, Brookings Institution, 11 Mar. 2005.

28. Interviews with former South Korean officials, Seoul, Aug. 2005.

29. "China," International Narcotics Control Strategy Report 2002, US Department of State, released Mar. 2003; Economy, "China's Rise"; Zhang Yan, "Speech to the 47th Session of the Commission on Narcotics Drugs," Vienna, 15 Mar. 2004.

30. Interview with Heather Peters, Bangkok, Aug. 2005; "China, Vietnam Launch Joint Campaign to Combat Trafficking in Border Area," Xinhua, 3 June 2004.

31. For a comprehensive account of the SARS crisis, see Karl Taro Greenfield, *China Syndrome: The True Story of the 21st Century's First Great Epidemic* (New York: HarperCollins, 2006). Wen Jiabao, "Speech to Ministerial Meeting of the International Pledging Conference on Avian and Human Pandemic Influenza," 18 Jan. 2006; Margie Mason, "Donors Pledge $1.9 Billion to Fight Bird Flu," Associated Press, 18 Jan. 2006.

32. Centro de Investigación y Docencia Económicas, "Mexico y el Mundo: Global Views 2004," Mexican Public Topline report, Sept. 2004; "Trade, Investment, and Economic Cooperation Between China and Southeast Asia: The Case of Malaysia," JETRO report, Nov. 2003–Feb. 2004; "Prime Minister: China Not a Threat to Economy," *Star* (Malaysia), 25 Feb. 2004.

33. Chia Siow Yue, "Asean-China Free Trade Area," Paper for presentation at the AEP Conference Hong Kong, 12–13 Apr. 2004; interview with Bounnheuang Songnavong, deputy director, Ministry of Foreign Affairs, Lao PDR, Aug. 2005; interview with Takao Tsuneishi, JETRO Bangkok, Aug. 2005; see also Robert Devlin, Antoni Estevadeordal, and Andrés Rodríguez-Clare, *The Emergence of China: Opportunities and Challenges for Latin America and the Caribbean* (Washington: Inter-American Development Bank, 2006), 11–15, and *Key Indicators 2005: Labor Markets in Asia* (Manila: Asian Development Bank, 2006), 275–276. Jorge Domínguez, "China's Relations with Latin America: Shared Gains, Asymmetric Hopes," Inter-American Dialogue working paper, June 2006, 37–40. Petchanet Pratruangkrai, "Service Sector Can Profit from Asean-China FTA: Thanong," *Nation* (Thailand), 28 June 2005.

34. James Allen, "Lula Admits He Made Political Decision," *O Estado*

de São Paulo, 13 Nov. 2004; Devlin, Estevadeordal, and Rodríguez-Clare, *The Emergence of China,* 146.

35. Jonathan Wheatley, "China Dashes Brazil Trade Hopes," *Financial Times,* 3 Oct. 2005; Matt Moffett and Geraldo Samor, "Brazil Regrets its China Affair," *Wall Street Journal,* 10 Oct. 2005; Mark O'Neill, "Record Trade Surplus Raises Ire of Foreign Partners," *South China Morning Post,* 10 Oct. 2005; Devlin, Estevadeordal, and Rodríguez-Clare, *The Emergence of China,* 189; Joel Millman and Peter Wonacott, "For China, a Cautionary Tale," *Wall Street Journal,* 11 Jan. 2005; Greg Hitt, "Latin Trade Deal Has Chinese Flavor," *Wall Street Journal,* 26 Jan. 2005.

36. Busakorn Chantasasawat, "Burgeoning Sino-Thai Relations: Heightening Cooperation, Strengthening Economic Security," *China: An International Journal* 1 (2006): 86–112; interviews with representatives of manufacturers, electronics companies, textile associations, Phnom Penh, Kuala Lumpur, Jakarta, Jan. 2006 and Mar. 2006.

37. "Chinese Are Oil Thieves," *Business in Africa,* 4 May 2006; Laurie Goering, "China's Investment, Clout in Africa Cause Concern," *Chicago Tribune,* 19 Feb. 2006; Joseph J. Schatz, "Zambian Hopeful Takes a Swing at China," *Washington Post,* 25 Sept. 2006; David Blair, "Ignored by the Mob," *Daily Telegraph* blog, 2 Oct. 2006, http://blogs.telegraph.co.uk/foreign/davidblair/oct06/mob1.htm, accessed Nov. 2006.

38. See Elizabeth C. Economy, *The River Runs Black: The Environmental Challenge to China's Future* (Ithaca: Cornell University Press, 2005).

39. Ben Schiller, "The China Model of Development," Open Democracy, 20 Dec. 2005, http://www.opendemocracy.net/content/articles/PDF/3136.pdf, accessed Nov. 2006; interview with Tod Ragsdale, environmental impact consultant, Washington, Aug. 2005. On Chinese dams see also Michael Richardson, "Damming up the Flow of Information," *South China Morning Post,* 5 May 2006.

40. Interviews with Cambodian, Lao, and Singaporean diplomats, Aug. 2005. Southeast Asian Rivers Network, "Downstream Impacts of Hydropower and Development of an International River: A Case Study of Lancang-Mekong," paper prepared for the UN Symposium on Hydropower and Sustainable Development, Beijing, 27–29 Oct. 2004; see also "Trying to Save a Catfish as Big as a Bear," Associated Press, 1 Dec. 2003, and Seth Mydans, "Mission on the Mekong: Save the Giant Catfish," *New York Times,* 18 Dec. 2002. Milton Osborne, "River at Risk: Mekong and the Water Politics of Southeast Asia," Lowy Institute paper, 24 Aug. 2004; see also Peter Goodman, "Manipulating the Mekong," *Washington Post,* 30 Dec. 2004, and Milton Osborne, "The Strategic Significance of the Mekong," *Contemporary Southeast Asia* 3 (2000): 429–444.

41. Kuch Naren, "Villagers Say Officials Gave Land to the Chinese," *Cambodia Daily*, 3 July 2005; see also Cambodia Business Press digest, no. 59, 3 July 2005. "UN Asks Cambodia Cancel Land Grant to China Firm," Reuters, 5 July 2005. "UN Official Calls on Cambodia to Cancel Concession on Indigenous Land," UN News Service, 6 July 2005.

42. "Human Rights in Cambodia: The Façade of Stability," Licadho Report, http://www.licadho.org/reports/files/8682LICADHOFacadeDemocracyReport2005-06.pdf, accessed June 2006; Cambodia Business Press digest, no. 59, 3 July 2005.

43. Paul Magnusson, "A Milestone for Human Rights," *BusinessWeek*, 24 Jan. 2005, 63.

44. Minxin Pei, "The Dark Side of China's Rise," *Foreign Policy*, Mar.–Apr. 2006, 32–40; Minxin Pei, *China's Trapped Transition: The Limits of Developmental Autocracy* (Cambridge: Harvard University Press, 2006), 155.

45. "Bank of China Facing Another Scandal," Agence France-Presse, 8 Mar. 2006.

46. Interview with oil executive, Jakarta, Mar. 2006.

47. Robin Emmott, "Peru Miners Feel Oppressed by China's Shougang," Reuters, 21 July 2005.

48. Ibid.

49. Joel Millman and Peter Wonacott, "For China, a Cautionary Tale: Insularity, Unfamiliar Ways Strain Investments," *Wall Street Journal*, 11 Jan. 2005; Stephen Frost, "Chinese Investments Abroad; Shougang and Labor Protests in Peru," *CSR Asia Weekly* 1, week 33. Emmott, "Peru Miners Feel Oppressed."

50. Millman and Wonacott, "For China, a Cautionary Tale"; Frost, "Chinese Investments Abroad."

51. Millman and Wonacott, "For China, a Cautionary Tale"; Frost, "Chinese Investments Abroad."

52. Simon Zadek, "China's Route to Business Responsibility," Open Democracy, 30 Nov. 2005, http://www.opendemocracy.net/content/articles/PDF/3076.pdf, accessed Nov. 2006.

53. Rory Carroll, "China's Goldmine," *Guardian*, 28 Mar. 2006; Goering, "China's Investment, Clout."

54. Goering, "China's Investment, Clout."

55. Interview with Filipino mining activists, Manila, Mar. 2006; Ben Schiller, "The Axis of Oil: China and Venezuela," Open Democracy, 3 Feb. 2006, http://www.opendemocracy.net/debates/article.jsp?id=6&debateId=83&articleId=3319, accessed Nov. 2006.

56. "Overview: Millennium Challenge Corporation," http://www.mca.gov/about/index.php, accessed Mar. 2006; Donald Greenless, "At World

Bank, a Pledge to Focus on Corruption," *International Herald Tribune,* 31 May 2006.

57. "Cambodia to Lose Much of Foreign Aid over Poor Governance," Kyodo News Service, 6 Dec. 2004; "Statement by Peter Leuprecht," 61st Session of the United Nations Commission on Human Rights, 19 Apr. 2005.

58. Interview with Sokhem Pech, Phnom Penh, Jan. 2006; "China Pledges $600 Million in Grants, Loans for Cambodia," Kyodo News Service, 10 Apr. 2006; interviews with French, Canadian diplomats, Phnom Penh, Jan. 2006; interviews with World Bank, Asian Development Bank officials, Washington and Vientiane, Aug. 2005.

59. "Country Reports on Human Rights 2003: Central African Republic," US Department of State, released 25 Feb. 2004; Louisa Lombard, "Africa's China Card," *Foreign Policy,* http://www.foreignpolicy.com/story/cms.php?story_id=3419, accessed Oct. 2006.

60. "All the President's Men," Global Witness report, http://www.globalwitness.org/reports/show.php/en.00002.html, accessed Jan. 2005; John Reed, "A Peace Dividend," *Financial Times,* 14 Nov. 2005.

61. Schiller, "The China Model of Development."

62. Ibid.; see also John Reed, "A Patchy Performance," *Financial Times,* 1 Mar. 2006.

63. "Election Budget: Angola," *Africa Confidential,* 31 Mar. 2006.

64. Reed, "A Patchy Performance."

65. John Donnelly, "China Scooping Up Deals in Africa as US Firms Hesitate," *Boston Globe,* 24 Dec. 2005.

Chapter 9: America's Soft Power Goes Soft

1. Program on International Policy Attitudes, "23 Nation Poll: Who Will Lead the World?" 15 Nov. 2004–5 Jan. 2005; Program on International Policy Attitudes, "33 Nation Poll on Views of Countries," Feb. 2006; Richard Holbrooke, "Get the Message Out," *Washington Post,* 28 Oct. 2001.

2. "Tumultuous Crowd Welcomes Clinton to Hanoi," *Cnn.com,* 17 Nov. 2000, http://archives.cnn.com/2000/ASIANOW/southeast/11/16/clinton.vietnam.02/, accessed Nov. 2006.

3. Kishore Mahbubani, speech to Carnegie Council, 2 Mar. 2005.

4. Foreign Affairs Council, "Secretary Colin Powell's State Department: An Independent Assessment," Mar. 2003; "America's Overseas Presence in the 21st Century," Report of the Overseas Presence Advisory Council, Department of State, Nov. 1999.

5. US Department of State, "Program Alumni—International Visitor Leadership Program," http://exchanges.state.gov/education/ivp/alumni.htm, accessed Nov. 2006; Martha Bayles, "Goodwill Hunting," *Wilson Quarterly* 3 (2005): 46–55; US Department of State, Bureau of Educational and Cultural Affairs budgets, 1993–2002; Juliet Antunes Sablosky, "Recent Trends in Department of State Support for Public Diplomacy, 1993–2002," Center for Arts and Culture, 2003.

6. Andrew Kohut and Bruce Stokes, *America Against the World* (New York: Times Books, 2006), 73; Program on International Policy Attitudes, "Americans on UN Peacekeeping: A Study of US Public Attitudes," Center for the Study of Policy Attitudes, 28 May 1995.

7. Cynthia Watson, "Testimony to the Western Hemisphere Subcommittee of the US House of Representatives Committee on Foreign Affairs," 6 Apr. 2005.

8. Carol Matlack and Pallavi Gogoi, "What's This? The French Love McDonald's?" *BusinessWeek,* 13 Jan. 2003, 50.

9. Interviews with business leaders in Bangkok, Jakarta, Singapore, Seoul, Aug. 2005–Mar. 2006.

10. Craig Charney and Nicole Yakatan, *A New Beginning: Strategies for a More Fruitful Dialogue with the Muslim World* (New York: Council on Foreign Relations Press, 2005), 49.

11. Thom J. Rose, "US Visas: Applications Down, Prices Up," United Press International, 15 Apr. 2004; see also Government Accountability Office, "Improvements Needed to Reduce Time Taken to Adjudicate Visas for Science Students and Scholars," Feb. 2004. Steve Clemons, "United States Visa Application Rejection Rates," www.steveclemons.com/visafees.htm, accessed Nov 2006.

12. Sanford J. Ungar, "Pitch Imperfect," *Foreign Affairs* 3 (2005): 7–13; see also Art Levine, "Voice Over America," *American Prospect,* Sept. 2005, 11–12. Glenn Kessler, "The Role of Radio Sawa in Middle East Questioned," *Washington Post,* 13 Oct. 2004.

13. Interviews with State Department consular service officials, July and Aug. 2005; interview with Allan Gyngell, Washington, Dec. 2005.

14. Government Accountability Office, "State Department Efforts to Engage Muslim Audiences Lack Certain Communication Elements and Face Significant Challenges," *GAO Reports,* May 2006.

15. Karen Hughes, "Remarks with Turkish Foreign Ministry Under Secretary Ambassador Ali Tuygan," http://www.state.gov/r/us/2005/54077.htm, accessed Jan. 2006.

16. Interviews with Millennium Challenge Corporation officials and

former officials, Oct. 2005; Farah Stockman, "US to Shift Envoys to Developing Countries," *Boston Globe,* 19 Jan. 2006. For information on the Millennium Challenge Corporation, see mcc.gov.

17. Jane Perlez, "Letter from Asia: China Is Romping with the Neighbors (US Is Distracted)," *New York Times,* 3 Dec. 2003.

18. "Does Paul O'Neill Have Argentina Issues?" *Financial Times,* 21 Aug. 2001.

19. Interview with Mean Sophea, Phnom Penh, Jan. 2006.

20. Cambodia Bilateral Textile Agreement, http://phnompenh.usembassy.gov/uploads/images/M9rzdrzMKGi6AjfoSIuJRA/uskh_texttile.pdf#search=%22us%20cambodian%20bilateral%20textile%20agreement%22, accessed Nov. 2006; interviews with United States Trade Representative officials, Washington, Sept. 2005; "U.S.-Cambodian Textile Agreement Links Increasing Trade with Improving Workers' Rights," Office of the United States Trade Representative, 7 Jan. 2002.

21. Sheridan Prasso, "Trading Up," *The New Republic,* 16 Aug 2004, 11–12; Tom Fawthrop, "The Price of Free Trade, Part II," Yale Global Online, http://yaleglobal.yale.edu/display.article?id=4627, accessed Feb. 2005; interview with Mean Sophea, Phnom Penh, Jan. 2006.

22. Peter S. Goodman, "Pinning Hope on Fair Labor Standards," *Washington Post,* 17 Nov. 2004.

23. Phann Ana and Kevin Doyle, "Radicals Try to Strengthen Ties in Cambodia," *Cambodia Daily,* 13 Sept. 2003; US Department of State, "Country Reports on Terrorism: East Asia and the Pacific," released 28 Apr. 2006; Tariff Relief Assistance for Developing Economies Act of 2005, http://www.theorator.com/bills109/hr886.html, accessed Nov. 2006.

24. Interview with Mean Sophea, Phnom Penh, Jan. 2006.

25. Stanley Foundation, "US Human Rights Policy in Southeast Asia: New Issues for a New Era," Stanley Foundation report, 10 May 2004, 3.

26. "US Human Rights Record in 2000," Information Office of State Council, released Feb. 2001; "Human Rights Record of the US in 2004," Information Office of State Council, released Mar. 2005.

27. Frances Williams, "US Stands Alone over Cultural Diversity Treaty," *Financial Times,* 20 Oct. 2005; Nicholas Kristof, "Schoolyard Bully Diplomacy," *New York Times,* 16 Oct. 2005; Anholt Nation Brands Index, 2005, 1 Aug. 2005; see nationbrandindex.com.

28. Charney and Yakatan, *A New Beginning,* 32.

29. Park Song-wu, "48% of Youth Would Side with North Korea in Case of US Attack," *Korea Times,* 22 Feb. 2006.

30. Council on Graduate Schools, International Graduate Admissions

Survey 2004, 2005; United Nations High Commissioner for Refugees, "Asylum Seekers and Trends in Industrialized Countries, 2005," report released 17 Mar. 2006.

31. Kohut and Stokes, *America Against the World*, 24.

32. Joseph Nye, *Soft Power: The Means to Success in World Politics* (New York: Public Affairs, 2004); Pew Global Attitudes Survey, released 23 June 2005.

33. Kohut and Stokes, *America Against the World*, 34; Anholt Nation Brands Index 2005.

34. Joseph Nye, "Grand Strategy and Global Public Goods," *New Perspectives Quarterly*, http://www.digitalnpq.org/archive/2002_spring/nye.html, accessed Jan. 2005.

35. Interview with US policy makers responsible for US-Indonesian relations, Washington, Aug. and Sept. 2005.

36. Anthony Shadid and Steve Fainaru, "Militias on the Rise Across Iraq," *Washington Post*, 21 Aug. 2005.

37. Interview with US policy makers responsible for US-Indonesian relations, Washington, Aug. and Sept. 2005; Ellen Nakashima and Alan Sipress, "Southeast Asia's New Corps of Suicide Bombers, *Washington Post*, 16 Aug. 2003.

38. Glenn Kessler and Robin Wright, "Report: U.S. Image in Bad Shape," *Washington Post*, 24 Sept. 2005.

Chapter 10: What's Next?

1. Ministry of Foreign Affairs of the People's Republic of China, "Shanghai Cooperation Organization," brief released 7 Jan. 2004. The SCO's genesis was in an international grouping founded in 1996 called the "Shanghai Five."

2. Interview with senior State Department planning officials, Washington, Oct. 2005; Greg Austin, "European Union Policy Responses to the Shanghai Cooperation Organization," European Institute of Asian Studies publications, European Institute of Asian Studies, Dec. 2002; "Country Brief: Kazakhstan," Energy Information Agency, US Department of Energy.

3. Gao Fuqiu, "The Real Purpose of the American March into Central Asia," *Outlook* (*Liaowang*), 10 May 2002.

4. "Chinese Delegation Visits Confucius Institute in Tashkent," Uzbekistan National News Agency, 1 Nov. 2005; Jeremy Bransten, "Central Asia: China's Mounting Influence," *Eurasia Insight*, 23 Nov. 2004.

5. "China's Growing Influence in Central Asia," Radio Free Asia, 19 Nov. 2004; Andrew Kohut, "American Public Diplomacy in the Islamic World," Remarks to the Senate Foreign Relations Committee, 27 Feb. 2003.

6. Interviews with Chinese, US diplomats, Washington and Beijing, June and Aug. 2005; Stephen Blank, "Islam Karimov and the Heirs of Tiananmen," *Eurasia Daily Monitor,* Jamestown Foundation, 14 June 2005.

7. "Central Asian Security Group Demands Deadlines for Western Bases to Pull Out," *AFX News,* 5 July 2005; Josh White, "Uzbekistan Senate Says U.S. Troops Must Leave," *Washington Post,* 27 Aug. 2005; Ann Scott Tyson, "Russia and China Bullying Central Asia, US Says," *Washington Post,* 15 July 2005; Bates Gill and Matthew Oresman, *China's New Journey to the West: China's Emergence in Central Asia and Its Implications for US Interests* (Washington, D.C.: CSIS, 2003), 1–10.

8. Sam Knight, "China to Send 1,000 Peacekeepers to Lebanon," *Times* (London), 18 Sept. 2006; "China Ratifies UN Safety Convention," Xinhua, 28 Aug. 2004.

9. Anthony Lake, Christine Todd Whitman, Princeton N. Lyman, and J. Stephen Morrison, eds., *More Than Humanitarianism: A Strategic U.S. Approach Toward Africa* (New York: Council on Foreign Relations Press, 2005), 48; interview with Elizabeth Huybens, World Bank East Timor, Dili, Mar. 2006; interview with Western diplomats, Phnom Penh, Jan. 2006; interview with Carol Lancaster, Georgetown University aid specialist, Washington, Aug. 2005; interview with Chinese officials, Washington and Beijing, July 2005 and Aug. 2005.

10. Elizabeth Economy, "China's Rise in Southeast Asia: Implications for Japan and the United States," *Japan Focus,* 10 Oct. 2005; interview with Burma activists, Washington, Bangkok, Jan. 2006; "Premier Wen Jiabao Holds Talks with Prime Minister of Myanmar Soe Win," Foreign Ministry of the People's Republic of China statement, 14 Feb. 2006; Larry Jagan, "Burma, China Strengthen Bilateral Ties," *Bangkok Post,* 15 Feb. 2006; "UN Votes to put Burma on Agenda," BBC news, 16 Sept. 2006.

11. Interview with Dom LaVigne, American Chamber of Commerce Malaysia, Kuala Lumpur, Jan. 2006.

12. Web Japan, "Major Recipient Countries of Japan's Bilateral ODA," http://web-japan.org/stat/stats/23ODA31.html, accessed Nov. 2006; Citizenship and Immigration Canada, "Immigrants in Canada: Census 2001 Highlights," http://www.cic.gc.ca/english/monitor/issue02/06-feature.html, accessed Dec. 2004.

13. Interview with Japanese diplomat, Washington, Oct. 2005.

14. Michael Green, "Is Japan a Responsible Stakeholder?" *CSIS Commentary,* 2 June 2006.

15. Satoshi Nakagawa, "ODA Reform Essential to Regain Public Trust," *Yomiuri Shimbun,* 25 Dec. 2004; personal visit to Yasukuni Shrine, Aug. 2006.

16. Robert Marquand, "Gulf Widens Between Japan, China," *Christian Science Monitor,* 11 Apr. 2006.

17. Interview with State Department official, Washington, Nov. 2005; interviews with Japanese diplomats, Washington and Tokyo, Aug. 2005; Mayumi Negishi and Kanako Takahara, "Japan Settles for 'Low Risk, Low Return' FTA Goals," *Japan Times,* 22 Apr. 2005.

18. Interview with Ajit Singh, Kuala Lumpur, Jan. 2006; interview with State Department official, Washington, Nov. 2005.

19. Energy Information Administration, *Annual Energy Outlook, 2005,* available at http://www.eia.doe.gov/oiaf/aeo/; John Vidal, "The End of Oil Is Closer than You Think," *Guardian,* 21 Apr. 2005.

20. Erica Downs, "The Chinese Energy Security Debate," *China Quarterly,* Mar. 2004, 21–41; Mikkal Herberg, "Asia's Energy Insecurity, China, and India," Testimony Before the Senate Committee on Foreign Relations, 26 July 2005; R. Evan Ellis, *US National Security Implications of Chinese Involvement in Latin America* (Carlisle, Pa.: Strategic Studies Institute, 2005), 5.

21. Danna Harman, "Chávez Seeks Influence with Oil Diplomacy," *Christian Science Monitor,* 25 Aug. 2005.

22. William Ratliff, "Pragmatism Over Ideology: China's Relations with Venezuela," *China Brief,* Jamestown Foundation, 15 Mar. 2006; Ellis, *US National Security Implications,* 8.

23. Michelle Billig, "The Venezuelan Oil Crisis," *Foreign Affairs* 5 (2004): 2.

24. "China's National Defense in 2004," State Council Information Office release, 27 Dec. 2004.

25. Downs, "The Chinese Energy Security Debate"; Gal Luft and Anne Korin, "The Sino-Saudi Connection," *Commentary,* Mar. 2004, 26–29.

26. Ilan Greenberg and Andrew E. Kramer, "Cheney, Visiting Kazakhstan, Wades into Energy Battle," *New York Times,* 6 May 2006; Peter Baker, "US Warns Russia to Act More Like a Democracy," *Washington Post,* 5 May 2006; Peter Baker, "With Kazakh's Visit, Bush's Priorities Clash," *Washington Post,* 29 Aug. 2006.

27. Peter Maass, "A Touch of Crude," *Mother Jones,* Jan/Feb 2005, 48–56.

28. Dennis Blair, "Address to Carnegie International Non-Proliferation Conference," 16 Mar. 2000; interviews with Singaporean and Thai diplomats, Singapore and Bangkok, Jan. 2006.

29. Interview with Philippine defense planners, Manila, Mar. 2006.

30. John Wong, Zheng Yongnian, and Tok Sow Keat, "China's Reaction to DPM Lee Hsien Loong's Visit to Taiwan," *East Asian Institute Background Brief,* 25 Aug. 2004; John Burton, "Singapore Warns Taipei on Independence," *Financial Times,* 23 Aug. 2004.

31. "Australians Speak 2005: Public Opinion and Foreign Policy," Lowy Institute Poll, 29 Mar. 2005; "BHP Billiton Posts Record Interim Profit," *Australian Broadcasting Corporation,* http://www.abc.net.au/news/newsitems/200602/s1570146.htm accessed Mar 2006.

32. Richard Baker, "US Sent 'Please Explain' to Downer over China Comments," *The Age,* 17 May 2006.

33. John Kerin, "Beijing's ANZUS Warning," *The Australian,* 8 Mar. 2005.

34. Freedom House, *Freedom in the World 2005* (Lanham, Md.: Rowman and Littlefield), 2005.

35. Human Rights Watch, "Human Rights Overview: China," http://hrw.org/english/docs/2006/01/18/china12270.htm, accessed Nov. 2006; United States Department of State, "Country Reports on Human Rights Practices, 2005: China," http://www.state.gov/g/drl/rls/hrrpt/2005/61605.htm, accessed Nov. 2006.

36. "The National Security Strategy of the United States of America," Sept. 2002, http://www.whitehouse.gov/nsc/nss.pdf, accessed Nov. 2006, 3–4; Paul Starobin, "John Kerry: Leader of the Free World," *National Journal,* Sept. 2004, 2792–2799.

37. Alberto Abadie, "Poverty, Political Freedom, and the Roots of Terrorism," *National Bureau of Economic Research,* Oct. 2004, working paper, available at http://ksghome.harvard.edu/~aabadie/povterr.pdf; Alan B. Krueger and Jitka Maleckova, "Education, Poverty, and Terrorism: Is There a Causal Connection?" *Journal of Economic Perspectives* 4 (2003): 119–144.

38. "Zimbabwe," in *Amnesty International Report 2006: The State of the World's Human Rights* (New York: Amnesty International, 2006); Andrew Meldrum, "Gloating Mugabe Vows to Rule Until He Is 100," *Guardian,* 4 Apr. 2005; Michael Wines, "Opposition in Zimbabwe Sees Fraud in Vote Data," *New York Times,* 7 Apr. 2005.

39. Human Rights Watch, "Zimbabwe: Mass Evictions Lead to Massive Abuses," *Human Rights Watch Report,* 11 Sept. 2005.

40. Abraham McLaughlin, "A Rising China Counters US Clout in Africa," *Christian Science Monitor,* 30 Mar. 2005; Hu Jintao, "Consolidate Traditional Sino-African Friendship, Deepen Sino-African All-round Cooperation," Address to the National Assembly of Gabon, 2 Feb. 2004.

41. "Zimbabwe Press Review," *BBC Monitoring*, 30 Jan. 2006; "Zim Varsity Students Will be Forced to Learn Chinese," *Africa News*, 26 Jan. 2006; interview with Chinese diplomats, Washington, July 2005; Carolyn Bartholomew, Testimony Before the House of Representative Committee on International Relations Subcommittee on Africa, 28 July 2005.

42. Robert Mugabe, Interview with SkyNews (UK), 24 May 2004; Andrew Meldrum, "Mugabe Turns Back on West and Looks East," *Guardian*, 19 Apr. 2005.

43. Nazila Fathi, "Wipe Israel Off the Map, Iranian Says," *New York Times*, 27 Oct. 2005; Ramita Navai and Richard Beeston, "Iran Sacks Diplomats in Purge of Reformers," *Times* (London), 2 Nov. 2005; "Iran Cracks Down on Bloggers," Associated Press, 28 Mar. 2006. "Iran Nuclear Plan 'Irreversible,'" BBC.com, 29 Apr. 2006, http://news.bbc.co.uk/2/hi/middle_east/4957282.stm, accessed Nov. 2006. Robert Tait and Ewen MacAskill, "Iran Declares: We Are in the Nuclear Club," *Guardian*, 12 Apr. 2006.

44. John Tkacik, "Confront China's Support for Iran's Nuclear Weapons," Heritage Foundation Web memo, http://www.heritage.org/Research/AsiaandthePacific/wm1042.cfm, accessed June 2006; John Calabrese, "China and Iran: Mismatched Partners," Jamestown Foundation occasional paper, Aug. 2006.

45. For extended background on the crisis in Darfur, see http://sudanreeves.org/, accessed Nov. 2006.

46. Eric Reeves, "Next Casualty," *New Republic*, 15 May 2006, 18–19; Glenn Kessler and Colum Lynch, "U.S. Calls Killings in Sudan Genocide," *Washington Post*, 10 Sept. 2004.

47. Peter S. Goodman, "China Invests Heavily in Sudan's Oil Industry," *Washington Post*, 23 Dec. 2004; Yitzhak Shichor, "Sudan: China's Outpost in Africa," *China Brief*, 13 Oct. 2005; Stephanie Giry, "Out of Beijing," *New Republic*, 15 Nov. 2004, 19–21; Howard W. French, "China in Africa: All Trade, with No Political Baggage," *New York Times*, 8 Aug. 2004.

48. For all Human Rights Watch documents on Darfur, see http://www.hrw.org/doc?t=africa&c=darfur, accessed Nov. 2006.

49. Peta Thornycroft, "Mugabe Rejects Call for Dialogue; Looks to China for Help," *Voice of America News*, http://voanews.com/english/archive/2005-08/2005-08-08-voa32.cfm?CFID=57801953&CFTOKEN=10423582 accessed Dec 2005.

50. Interview with Burma activist, Bangkok, Aug. 2005.

51. Lyall Breckon, "A Lull—and Some Complaints," *Comparative Connections*, 1st Quarter 2004, http://www.csis.org/media/csis/pubs/0401q.pdf, 69–76.

Chapter 11: Responding to the Charm Offensive

1. Joseph Nye, "Can America Regain Its Soft Power After Abu Ghraib?" Yale Global Online, http://yaleglobal.yale.edu/display.article?id=4302, accessed Nov. 2006.

2. Tom McCawley, "US Tsunami Aid Still Reaps Goodwill," *Christian Science Monitor,* 28 Feb. 2006; "Taliban: 'No Jihad Unless US Attacks,'" *Guardian,* 18 Sept. 2001; Susilo Bambang Yudhoyono, "Keynote Address," USINDO Dinner, Washington, 25 May 2005.

3. Office of Research and Opinion Analysis, "US Image Positive in Urban Thailand, Bolstered by a Sense of Shared Security Interests," Department of State, 31 Oct. 2005; interview with Vietnamese official, Nha Trang, Oct. 2005.

4. *What the World Thinks in 2002,* Pew Global Attitudes Project (Washington, D.C.: Pew Publications, 2002).

5. "Academic Ranking of World Universities 2006," Shanghai Jiao Tong University, http://ed.sjtu.edu.cn/ranking.htm, accessed Nov. 2006.

6. To-Chol Sin and Jason Wells, "Is Democracy the Only Game in Town?" *Journal of Democracy* 2 (2005): 88–101; Simon S. C. Tay, "Asia and the United States After 9/11: Primacy and Partnership in the Pacific," *Fletcher Forum of World Affairs* 1 (2004): 113–132.

7. Andrew Kohut and Bruce Stokes, *America Against the World* (New York: Times Books, 2006), 130.

8. Interviews with Cambodian politicians, Phnom Penh, Jan. 2006.

9. Zheng Yonginan and Tok Sow Keat, "How China Views Singapore," *Background Brief,* East Asian Institute publications, 10 June 2004.

10. Woranuj Maneergungsee, "China Likely to Profit Most from Asean Free Trade Deal," *Bangkok Post,* 10 Sept. 2005; "Trade, Investment, and Economic Cooperation Between China and Southeast Asia: The Case of Malaysia," Institute of Developing Economies—Japan External Trade Organization, Nov. 2003–Feb. 2004.

11. Interview with Dwi Hartanto, Jakarta, Mar. 2006; interview with Ong Hok Ham, Jakarta, Mar. 2006; interview with Phil Overmyer, Singapore, Jan. 2006.

12. Paul Handley, "De-Mythologizing Charoen Pokphand: An Interpretive Picture of the CP Group's Growth and Diversification," in *Ethnic Business: Chinese Capitalism in Southeast Asia,* ed. Jomo K. S. and Brian C. Folk, 153–181 (London: Taylor and Francis, 2001); Ben Dolven, "Suzhou Project: Wounded Pride," *Far Eastern Economic Review,* 8 July 1999, 71.

13. Interview with senior US official, Washington, Oct. 2005.

14. "U.S.-China Engagement Act of 2006," introduced 26 Apr. 2006, http://www.govtrack.us/congress/bill.xpd?bill=h109-5199, accessed Nov. 2006.

15. Joseph Nye, "Europe's Soft Power," *Globalist,* http://www.theglobalist.com/DBWeb/printStoryId.aspx?StoryId= 3886, accessed Dec 2005; Stephen Johnson, "Voice of America's Death by a Thousand Cuts," Heritage Foundation Web memo, http://www.heritage.org/Research/NationalSecurity/wm1019.cfm, accessed June 2006; see also Tri Evers, "Successes of and Challenges Facing U.S. Public Diplomacy: Statement Before the House Committee on Government Reform Subcommittee on National Security, Emerging Threats and International Relations," 23 Aug. 2004. Iam Limbach, "Wooing Back Foreign Travelers," *Financial Times Special Report: Global Traveler,* 15 May 2006; see also Condoleezza Rice, "Secure Borders and Open Doors in the Information Age," speech at Dean Acheson Auditorium, Washington, 17 Jan. 2006.

16. Phone interview with Jamie Metzl, former senior adviser to the undersecretary for public diplomacy and public affairs, Nov. 2005.

17. National Defense University, "China's Growing Influence in Southeast Asia: March 2005 Trip to Philippines and Indonesia," *INSS Staff Report,* 4 May 2005; Craig Charney and Nicole Yakatan, *A New Beginning: Strategies for a More Fruitful Dialogue with the Muslim World* (New York: Council on Foreign Relations Press, 2005), 6; Documents on March 2005 visit to Southeast Asia, obtained from Department of Defense through Freedom of Information Act request.

18. Kohut and Stokes, *America Against the World,* 26; "Aid for Indonesia," *Advertiser,* 31 Aug. 2004; interview with congressional staff for Senator Sam Brownback, Washington, June 2005.

19. See Julia E. Sweig, *Friendly Fire: Losing Friends and Making Enemies in the Anti-American Century* (New York: PublicAffairs, 2006).

20. Richard P. Cronin, "A New U.S.-Asean Trade Track," *Wall Street Journal,* 9 Feb. 2006.

21. Robert Zoellick, "Remarks at a Press Roundtable in Thailand," Bangkok, 4 May 2005; Evelyn Goh, "Renewed American Diplomacy: Keeping Southeast Asia on US Radar Screen," *IDSS Commentaries,* 24 May 2005.

22. Ivo H. Daalder and James M. Lindsay, *America Unbound: The Bush Revolution in Foreign Policy* (New York: Wiley, 2005), 9.

23. Tommy Koh, "America's Role in Asia," *PacNet* 53, 21 Dec. 2004, http://www.csis.org/media/csis/pubs/pac0453.pdf, accessed Feb. 2005; "U.S Image Positive in Urban Thailand, Bolstered by a Sense of Shared Security Initiatives," State Department Office of Research, 31 Oct. 2005.

24. Sweig, *Friendly Fire,* 150.

25. Alphonse F. La Porta, "Statement for Hearing on Indonesia in Transition," Committee on International Relations Subcommittee on Asia and the Pacific, 10 Mar. 2005.

Index